National and International	
July	Germans capture Sevastopol. Heavy losses in British convoy PQ17 taking supplies to Russia. US Air Force first offensive against enemy in Europe. British resume offensive in Egypt.	First US servicemen arrive. Cambridge Union building bombed. Censorship of letters from areas near ports and aerodromes. Efforts to persuade farmers to use more WLA "land girls".
August	US forces land on Guadalcanal—start of Pacific counter-offensives. Gandhi and Congress leaders arrested. Churchill visits Moscow. Russian offensives on Stalingrad and Moscow fronts. Nine-hour raid on Dieppe.	Servicemen, schoolboys and Italian prisoners help harvest work. Colchester mental hospital bombed: 38 killed. King watches exercises in Stanford battle area. "Holidays at Home" programmes in all main centres.
September	Heavy RAF raids on Saarbrücken, Düsseldorf, Bremen, Flensburg and the Ruhr. Russians bomb Budapest, Vienna, Breslau and Königsberg.	Record harvest completed. First USAAF planes and crews arrive. Widespread cycle thefts. Public controversy over Italian prisoners-of-war behaviour.
October	400 fighter aircraft in daylight sweeps over France. US raid on Lille (biggest daylight operation of war). Japanese offensive on Guadalcanal. British launch offensive in Western Desert.	RAF plane crashes in Somersham, near St Ives; 11 killed. Cambridge University year opens with greatly reduced numbers. London Philharmonic plays to 1,000 children in Norwich cathedral.
November	British break through in Egypt; Axis forces in full retreat. US and British forces land in French North Africa; French forces capitulate. Axis troops enter Vichy France. Heavy Japanese naval losses in Solomons. Russian offensive opens; victory in central Caucasus.	US President's wife Mrs Eleanor Roosevelt visits Cambridge. Red Army delegation attends Cambridge Armistice Day service. No bus services after 9 pm. First published list of East Anglian prisoners of war in Far East. Felixstowe UDC insolvent. Cambridge speaker predicts new and wider role for women after war.
December	Beveridge Report published. Darlan assassinated after assuming leadership French Colonial Empire. US and RAF bombers bomb Naples. Retreating Axis forces in Libya cut off at Wadi Matratin. Advance into Burma by British and Indian troops announced.	Farmers, urged to grow more wheat, seek longer working week for employees. Norfolk children entertained at US bases; thousands of gifts from US. Service of carols and nine lessons in King's College Chapel, Cambridge.

EAST ANGLIA 1942

Overleaf: A special constable, his bicycle leaning nearby, directs traffic past the scene of devastation at St Benedict's Gates, Norwich, after the air raids of April, 1942.
George Swain

EAST ANGLIA 1942

by

R. DOUGLAS BROWN

Published by
TERENCE DALTON LIMITED

ISBN 0 86138 056 8

Text photoset in 10/12pt Times

Printed in Great Britain at
The Lavenham Press Limited, Lavenham, Suffolk

Contents

Publishers' Note

The publishers regret that the reproduction of certain illustrations is below the quality that they would normally demand. The *East Anglian Daily Times* and the *Eastern Daily Press*, who kindly permitted us the use of their files, were unfortunately unable to provide original photographs and, consequently, the pictures shown are reproductions from the printed newspapers. The same applies to those photographs acknowledged to the *Cambridge Evening News* that were so kindly provided by the Cambridge Collection of the Cambridgeshire Libraries. Where applicable, it was considered preferable to show illustrations, even if below our usual standard, rather than no pictures at all. This volume is the fourth of a series which will fully document the events in East Anglia, year by year, and we would welcome any photographs that apply to 1943 or subsequent years. These would be forwarded to the author for his use and duly returned.

Index of Illustrations

Introduction and Acknowledgements

WITH the publication of this volume, I have passed the halfway point in my narration of the East Anglian experience during the war of 1939–45. This seems an appropriate moment at which to restate the objectives of the series. My aim has been to recapture the atmosphere of those years as it was sensed by people *as they lived through them*. With hindsight one often re-assesses the significance of events; memory usually filters out much detail and accentuates what was most dramatic. Reminiscence is unreliable source material nearly half a century after the event. My basic rule, therefore, has been to depend upon the contemporary evidence: what was done, said, written, and felt by the people of East Anglia in the immediate aftermath of the events of 1942.

This has dictated the method of research and presentation. The largest body of primary source material is to be found in the regional newspapers published during the year. Not only did they report, within certain limits imposed by wartime censorship, what actually happened; their editorial comment, the views expressed by their regular columnists, the contents of the speeches of leading personalities in the region, and the debates which took place regularly in the correspondence columns provide a wealth of information about the attitudes, opinions and prejudices of both officialdom and the ordinary man and woman. I must record my indebtedness to the editors and publishers who have permitted me to reproduce much of this material, and also many photographs, from their columns. The pictures, unfortunately, have suffered in reproduction, because none of the original negatives or prints has survived; but they are part of a unique pictorial record of the period.

Impressions of a more personal kind, appropriate to a diary rather than a newspaper, are, fortunately, available in the Mass Observation Archive at Sussex University, and I have quoted extensively from diarists who lived in Norwich, Chelmsford, Bury St Edmunds and Sheringham. I have to express my thanks to the custodians of the Archive for permission to publish, and to its archivist, Ms Dorothy Sheridan, BA, for her help and guidance.

The third important primary source has been found in the archives at the Public Record Office at Kew, the Local Studies Department of the Norfolk County Library at Norwich, the Cambridgeshire Local History Collection at Cambridge Central Library, and the Suffolk Record Office at Bury St Edmunds and Ipswich, and I should like to record my appreciation of the help and co-operation of staff at each location.

A number of individuals have kindly given me information and advice, and this is acknowledged in the detailed "Notes on Sources" later in the book.

I have chosen to quote directly from the primary sources whenever possible, in the belief that this will best recapture the flavour of the time. As the author, my principal task has been to organise this material into a logical pattern and to set it into the complex pattern of national and international events in 1942. This I have done with the assistance of the various official histories of the war and the fourth volume of Sir Winston Churchill's own account, *The Hinge of Fate*. In the few cases where it seemed to me desirable to introduce a fact or a recollection which was unknown or unrecorded at the close of 1942, this has been added as a footnote to the main narrative.

There is no reason to suppose that the behaviour of the people of East Anglia during the war years was significantly different from that of the British people as a whole. A detailed regional study of this kind may shed light on features which remain unremarked on a canvas of wider sweep, when dramatic highlights hold the attention. War is not always exciting, and its participants are not always heroic, although official propaganda at the time and much reminiscence later would have us believe so.

The following pages tell of courage, but also of fear; of determination, but also of doubt; of pride, but also of shame. There were many men and women of valour at the guns, but also a procession through the courts of men and women "on the make", including some looters. There were some moments of public despair, when Winston Churchill was thrust from his pedestal; the first American troops arriving in the Eastern Counties were cold-shouldered; children of twelve were overworked on the farms. These were lesser-known realities of life on the home front in 1942. They do not undermine the overall impression of a nation bearing its sufferings bravely, holding to its chosen course with dogged determination, resolute in defence of the principles it espoused, idealistic in its aspirations.

R. DOUGLAS BROWN
Stoke-by-Clare, Suffolk.
October, 1987.

LETT'S

CHAPTER ONE

A Sombre Mood

BRITAIN had been at war for two years and four months. Now, on 1st January, 1942, the hardships and the sacrifices had brought few results, and there appeared no early prospect of victory. The New Year's Day editorial in the *Eastern Daily Press* did nothing to cheer its Norfolk readers:

> The probability, as Mr Churchill has lost no opportunity of reminding us, is that 1942 will be another year of effort and struggle, of mingled success and failure, to be followed by the year in which we have every hope of being able to strike our decisive blow.

In most of the East Anglian communities there was a brave attempt to greet the New Year with a show of confidence. Cambridge, for example, staged three big New Year's Eve balls; the Guildhall was packed to capacity as "Josephine's Gipsy Orchestra" fiddled enthusiastically, and at the Rex Ballroom, Sammy Ash and his band played to another crowd of five hundred. Cambridge, Norwich and Ipswich all staged the traditional Christmas pantomimes.

This revelry only briefly camouflaged the popular anxiety and the almost universal weariness. William Stock, a young Chelmsford shop assistant, wrote in his diary in February:

> To me time goes at a tremendous pace, yet, looking back on it, the war seems to have lasted an eternity. It seems to have blotted out all previous existence . . .[1]

The early weeks of 1942 proved a harrowing time for the many East Anglian families with men serving in the region's regiments. The 18th Division, which included battalions of the Suffolk, the Royal Norfolk and the Cambridgeshire Regiments, had sailed from Britain at the end of October. They did not know, and still less did their families, where they were bound; but the flow of war news left no doubt that British forces were being sent to meet the new threat in the Far East which had developed rapidly after Japan's bombing of the United States naval base at Pearl Harbour on 7th December and the associated invasion of Malaya, Hong Kong, the Philippines, Burma and Borneo. By the New Year it was clear, despite tight control of news coming from that theatre of war, that things were going badly

The results of the "Blitz" of April, 1942. Looking across the rooftops of Norwich with the remains of the old *Boar's Head* in the foreground and Caley's chocolate factory in the distance—a picture taken some time after the raids, when much of the rubble had been cleared. *George Swain* for the Allies. The front-page headlines of the *Cambridge Daily News* on the first day of the year heightened the fears:

OUR TROOPS WITHDRAW FROM SARAWAK

JAPANESE RAIDS ON SINGAPORE

In the following weeks there came what a distinguished historian has called "the worst succession of defeats in British history"[2]. Their effects on morale were noted in diaries kept by residents in the Eastern Counties.

On 21st January General Erwin Rommel began an advance in North Africa which carried his forces into Benghazi and to the allied airfields which were vital to the protection of Malta. As news of these reverses was released, Mrs Sarah Williams, who lived in Sheringham and worked in Cromer, wrote on 27th January:

> I feel quite frightened, as I have done all day, at the state of mind existing in this place. The place seems on the point of revolution. They are tired of inefficiency and blame it all on "The Old School Tie" (a convenient catchphrase) and if I have heard once I have heard half a dozen times today "Whatever Hitler is, he does at least get things done"[3].

Mrs Williams wrote these words after a deliberate and careful effort to assess local public opinion. She was a regular correspondent of the Mass Observation organization, which gathered diaries, reports and replies to specific questions from a network of such correspondents throughout the country. The government used

Headlines on the front page of the *Eastern Evening News* record the escape of the *Scharnhorst* and *Gneisenau*, an event which caused grave misgivings in Britain.

EASTERN EVENING NEWS, Feb. 13, 1942

Garlands for Spring Fashions

Black-out— 6.39 p.m. to 7.49 a.m.

Eastern Evening News FINAL

No. 18,442—One Penny

Friday, February 13, 1942

54-INCH NOVELTY CHECKS
GREEN, BLUE OR GREY GROUND SUITABLE FOR SKIRTS, COSTUMES, ETC.
PER 8/11 YARD
BONDS, NORWICH

NAZI BATTLESHIPS SAFE IN PORT?

Daring escape via Channel

BERLIN CLAIMS DESTROYER SUNK

THERE CAN BE LITTLE DOUBT THAT UNLESS ANY OF THE THREE GERMAN WARSHIPS WHICH MADE GOOD THEIR ESCAPE FROM BREST WAS SERIOUSLY DAMAGED, THEY ARE NOW BACK IN THEIR HOME PORT IN HELIGOLAND BIGHT.

There has been no further news from the Admiralty since this morning's communiqué, stating that when last sighted the ships (the Gneisenau, the Scharnhorst and the Prinz Eugen) had become separated and were making for port.

... we ... to get full ... of their daring move it ... of the ga...

Two of the girls who, having reached school certificate standard, ar... keenly interested in ... are receiving a three ... ing course at the ...

Japanese throw more planes into Singapore battle

THROWING INCREASED AIR AND ARTILLERY FORCES INTO THE BATTLE, THE JAPANESE HAVE MAINTAINED SEVERE PRESSURE ON THE WESTERN FRONT IN SINGAPORE ISLAND DURING THE PAST TWENTY-FOUR HOURS.

To-day's communiqué, reporting this, says that shelling to-day has been frequent on the forward area and on Singapore town.

... has also carried ...

20th, owing to the continued deterioration of the situation in the Pacific.

In Washington military and naval circles are watching with grave concern the final phases of the battle of Singapore and the serious deterioration in the united nations' position in the Pacific.

There is the keenest anxiety as to whether the Indies will recei... sary reinforcements. ... reinforce...

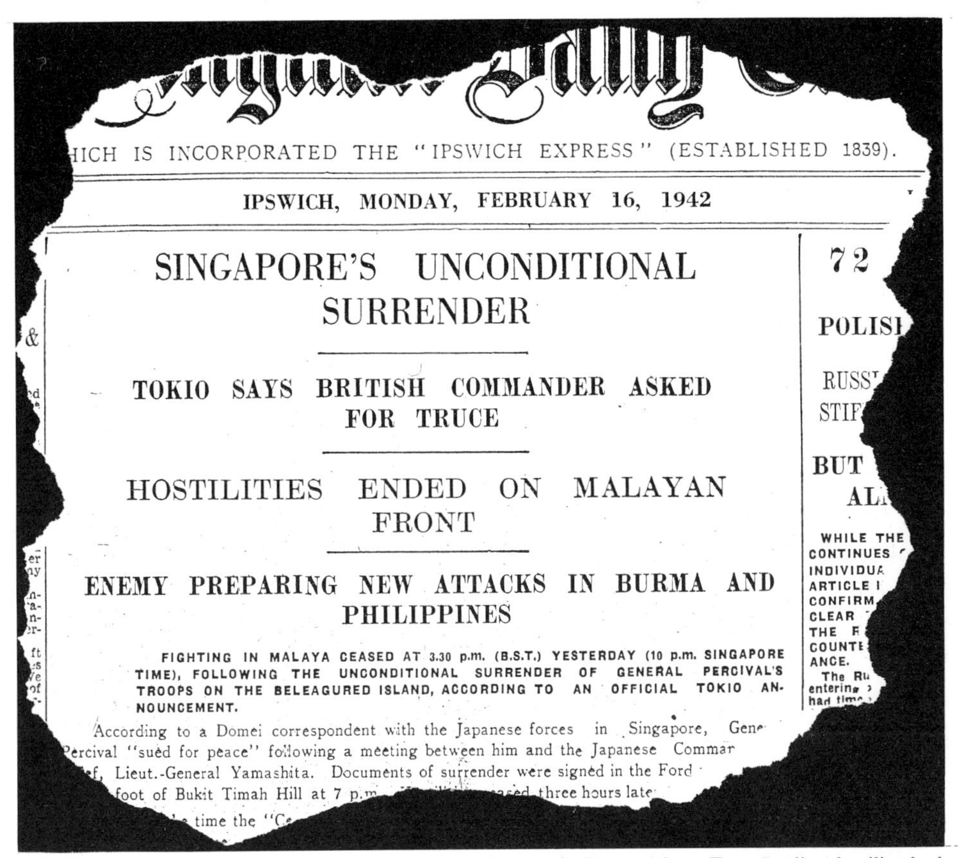
...ICH IS INCORPORATED THE "IPSWICH EXPRESS" (ESTABLISHED 1839).

IPSWICH, MONDAY, FEBRUARY 16, 1942

SINGAPORE'S UNCONDITIONAL SURRENDER

TOKIO SAYS BRITISH COMMANDER ASKED FOR TRUCE

HOSTILITIES ENDED ON MALAYAN FRONT

ENEMY PREPARING NEW ATTACKS IN BURMA AND PHILIPPINES

FIGHTING IN MALAYA CEASED AT 3.30 p.m. (B.S.T.) YESTERDAY (10 p.m. SINGAPORE TIME), FOLLOWING THE UNCONDITIONAL SURRENDER OF GENERAL PERCIVAL'S TROOPS ON THE BELEAGURED ISLAND, ACCORDING TO AN OFFICIAL TOKIO ANNOUNCEMENT.

According to a Domei correspondent with the Japanese forces in Singapore, Gen... Percival "sued for peace" following a meeting between him and the Japanese Commar... ...f, Lieut.-General Yamashita. Documents of surrender were signed in the Ford ... foot of Bukit Timah Hill at 7 p.m. ... three hours late... ... time the "C...

72

POLIS...

RUSS... STIF...

BUT ... AL...

WHILE THE ... CONTINUES ... INDIVIDUA... ARTICLE I... CONFIRM... CLEAR ... THE F... COUNTE... ANCE.

The Ru... entering ... had tim...

More grim news on the front page of the *East Anglian Daily Times*. Many East Anglian families had good reason to read this with dismay.

this information as a reliable guide to the state of popular morale. Mrs Williams was one of the best-qualified correspondents in the Mass Observation ranks: a thirty-year-old graduate and former teacher, who had lived with her husband — now a serving soldier — in both France and Germany before the war, and was doing a temporary job in the Civil Service and living with her mother and a young son. Her diary shows her to have been a well-read, highly cultured, intelligent woman, without strong political prejudices, and her testimony may be evaluated accordingly.

The Allied reverses in North Africa were soon followed by another disaster. For nearly a year the German battleships *Scharnhorst* and *Gneisenau* had been blockaded in the port of Brest. On the night of 11th February they escaped and, accompanied by the cruiser *Prinz Eugen*, sailed through the Straits of Dover and reached their home ports in the Baltic. Mrs Williams wrote in her diary:

> Great indignation continues about the German Fleet sailing through the Straits of Dover. It seems such an insult to most people.

A few days later she noted an even greater catastrophe:

> *15th February:* At tea my younger cousin rushed in to tell us Singapore had surrendered. My mother was very much upset. But Winston Churchill always has a cheering effect upon me, because he is so sensible.

Others with whom she came in contact felt differently, however:

> *20th February*: General campaign today of "We must get rid of Churchill".

Another Mass Observation diarist, young William Stock in Chelmsford, writing at the same moment, confirmed this anti-Churchill sentiment:

> "We never seem to do anything adequately" said my landlady. She told me that a woman had said that her husband in the Army had told her that there would soon be an uproar over Churchill, as he was always drunk. The tone of all the talk I have heard lately shows not only a deep dissatisfaction and lack of confidence, but also alarm. Said my landlady tonight: "I wonder if we shall win this war. Sometimes I feel doubtful."

Soon afterwards, Mrs Williams left her temporary job as a civil servant and returned to teaching, taking a post in Norwich, where she was able to note the feelings of a wider cross-section of the public. In March she wrote:

> Lovely weather. People seem to be becoming apathetic about the war. They don't argue about it, as they used to . . . Later in the staffroom a discussion on the shortage of beer. Mr H. says "If beer disappears, we shall have lost the war", and Mr B says "We've lost it already, so why worry?" Perhaps because it's the end of winter, but the crusading spirit has gone, or seems to have done so.

It was as well that the public did not know what was in the minds of some of the nation's leaders. At about the same time as Mrs Williams made her sombre observations. Sir Alan Brooke, who had just been appointed chairman of the British Chiefs of Staff Committee, wrote in his diary:

> During the last fortnight I have had for the first time since the war started a growing conviction that we are going to lose this war unless we control it very differently and fight it with more determination . . . I wonder if we shall muddle through this time like we have in the past?[4]

Next morning Brooke was more cheerful, as he threw himself with new determination into the efforts which established his reputation as one of Britain's greatest warlords.

Winston Churchill had been called to leadership as the man perceived to be outstandingly the best for the job in hand. As soon as the United States was drawn into the conflict, as a result of the Japanese attack on Pearl Harbour on 7th

December, 1941, Churchill — who had always believed that victory depended upon active American participation in the fighting — went to Washington to confer with President Roosevelt. Even this aroused criticism. The London editor of the *Eastern Daily Press* reported "murmurings . . . about the absence of the Prime Minister from the country", adding: "It is said that Mr Churchill should not take so much power into his own hands and then go abroad at a critical time."

It did not help that, during his absence, the war in the Far East was going very badly. The Japanese were claiming big successes in Malaya, Hong Kong and Burma, and it seemed clear, despite the very scant official information being released, that the vital naval base of Singapore was in danger. Any suggestion that the British war effort was not being conducted with the utmost efficiency touched a raw spot with East Anglian families whose menfolk had left England in October and, it was feared, were now caught up in the Far Eastern battles.

Churchill, however, pursued his plans relentlessly. He secured a public assurance from Roosevelt — embodied in the President's State of the Union message to Congress — that "American land, air and sea forces will take stations in the British Isles . . . which constitute an essential fortress in this world struggle". And when he flew back to England in mid-January (his 3,287-mile flight made headlines because it was the longest non-stop flight which any aircraft had made to that time), he knew that the first American troops would be following him over the Atlantic before the month was out. On 27th January a front-page story in the *Eastern Daily Press* disclosed:

> To the blare of Sousa's "Stars and Stripes", the vanguard of America's Expeditionary Force in Europe landed in the British Isles yesterday morning, just six weeks after Germany's declaration of war against the United States. Several thousands of infantry, with field artillery, disembarked at a Northern Ireland port . . .

Mrs Williams noted in her diary in January:

> Rumour in the town today has it that Americans are coming here in their hundreds, preparatory to going somewhere . . .

In fact, they did not set foot in Cromer, nor anywhere else in East Anglia, until seven months later.

Churchill returned from America to face a restless House of Commons, but he met them boldly. "It is because many things have gone badly, and worse is to come, that I demand a vote of confidence", he told MPs. There were tensions within the Cabinet, too, and some sort of government reconstruction was inevitable. The changes were not made swiftly and smoothly, but were spread over several weeks. First it was announced that Australia, New Zealand, Canada and South Africa would have representatives in the Cabinet. Later changes, in March, had a special interest to East Anglia. Geoffrey Shakespeare, a Norwich MP who had been Under Secretary for Dominions Affairs since May, 1940, was dropped; but another Norwich MP, H. G. Strauss, was made Parliamentary Secretary to the Ministry of

Works and Buildings, with responsibility for planning functions. In the Birthday Honours in June Shakespeare was given a baronetcy.

Finally, and not until 19th April, a new War Cabinet (reduced in number from nine to seven) was announced, with Sir Stafford Cripps, who had been in Moscow as ambassador since June, 1940, brought in as Lord Privy Seal and Leader of the Commons. Lord Beaverbrook, who had been Minister of Production for less than three weeks, left the Cabinet "for health reasons" and went off to the USA on "special duties"; unofficially, it was said that he had "flounced out" of the government as the culmination of a long-running feud with Ernest Bevin. Cripps' first task was to travel to India to negotiate with the Congress Party. Burma was being invaded by the Japanese, and Britain could not afford instability in India. Cripps offered Congress a new British plan for the government of India; Congress rejected it on 11th April.

Family and neighbours greet a Cambridge soldier, Donald W. R. Foister, outside his flag-decorated home at 2a Napier Street in July, when he was repatriated from Italy in an exchange of prisoners arranged three months earlier. He had been captured in September, 1940, in North Africa.
Cambridge Daily News

The news of the loss of Singapore came after a seemingly endless catalogue of retreat. Each day's newspapers heightened the suspense and the apprehension. On 23rd January there was an admission:

MALAYA: "GENERAL WITHDRAWAL"

On 3rd February it was:

JAPS DIVE-BOMB SINGAPORE

By 14th February the official Allied communique reported that "the defenders are disputing every (Japanese) attempt to advance further towards the heart of

Singapore Town." The Japanese, in fact, occupied Singapore the following day — Sunday, 15th February. On the 16th the *Cambridge Daily News* front-page banner read:

SINGAPORE: NO LARGE EVACUATION

But, in the small print down-page, the message was clear:

> No official news has yet arrived from Batavia concerning the circumstances of the surrender of Singapore, but the last message of the Singapore GOC, General Percival, has been received in London.

The *Eastern Daily Press* made no such attempt to "play down" the bitter news. On 16th February its main headline was:

FIGHTING ENDS AT SINGAPORE
UNCONDITIONAL SURRENDER, SAYS TOKIO

Within a day came confirmation of what many East Anglian families had feared: among the troops in Singapore when it fell were those of the 18th Division, which included battalions of the Royal Norfolks and the Suffolk, Cambridgeshire, and Beds and Herts regiments.

During the days that followed every effort was made to switch attention away from Singapore, with such headlines as:

RUSSIANS' RELENTLESS ADVANCES,
BRITISH LINE HOLDS IN BURMA,
and ALLIES BLOW AT JAP FLEET

The "management" of news from the Far East during this period became a matter of controversy. It was not the fault of the *Cambridge Daily News* that its readers were fed short rations; all newspapers were in the same situation, dependent on what the Service censors and the Ministry of Information would release. On 15th January the Cambridge paper gave its readers a broad hint of the difficulties when it prefaced its main story with a paragraph printed in bold black capitals:

> British official silence on the military operations in Malaya — stated in London to be for the purpose of denying information to the enemy — means that most of the "news" of developments in the Far East today has come from enemy sources.

To families anxious about the fate of their menfolk, the Japanese reports were distressing. A reader, signing himself — or herself — "Justice" wrote to the paper at mid-February concentrating complaint on BBC news bulletins:

> While a life and death struggle is in progress . . . the Singapore news was dismissed in a few sentences . . . What is the Ministry of Information doing? BBC news bulletins would tend to convey the impression that it should be named the "Ministry of Non-Information".

The *Cambridge Daily News* columnist "Robin Goodfellow" sought a few days later to meet such complaints, and, in the course of a long argument, made it clear that the absence of firm news was stimulating rumour. He referred to problems of communication over such long distances and asserted:

> The War Office are obviously faced with great difficulties in collecting and distributing accurate information . . . As soon as any official information is received from this or any other theatre of war, we will assist to the best of our ability by passing on that information with the least possible delay, but we have to abide by the rules.

So the agonised East Anglian families went on waiting until, on 17th February, they were at last told that their menfolk *had* been fighting in Malaya. Newspaper stories on that day revealed that the Allied forces had included the 53rd, 54th and 55th Infantry Brigades, which embraced battalions of the Royal Norfolk, Suffolk, Cambridgeshire and Beds and Herts regiments. "Our men put up a magnificent fight, but the odds against them were too great," declared the official communiqué. It then stated that 100,000 men had been involved, none had been evacuated, and the Japanese claimed to have taken 60,000 prisoners. That left an ominous, unexplained gap in the numbers.

During the days that followed there were many rumours. One was that a list of casualties was available at the Guildhall in Cambridge. Many wives and parents went there to inquire, some of them travelling in from villages around, but their hopes were dashed; there was no information. In March the rumours reached Norwich, too. The *Eastern Daily Press* published a letter making clear that no list of Singapore prisoners of war had reached the City Hall.

Countless families were kept in suspense. There was one isolated but firm report of a local man killed in Singapore on 21st February; he was Sergeant Bernard Paul Blowers, RAF, whose home was in Cambridge. From mid-March families began receiving a standard form of communication from the War Office. It confirmed that such-and-such a man had been serving in Malaya, and added that every effort was being made to obtain information about him.

> It is hoped he is safe, although he may be a prisoner-of-war. It will be necessary, however, to post him as "missing" pending receipt of some definite information.

From this time onwards the newspapers carried a regular daily feature: "Missing in Malaya". One of those in the lists published in the *Cambridge Daily News* was Sapper Ronald William Searle, a local lad who had begun work as a cartoonist on that newspaper, and who had begun to make a reputation with his cartoons in magazines such as *Lilliput* and *London Opinion*. On the day he was posted missing an exhibition of his work, which included scenes of army life, came to a conclusion at the Heffer Gallery in Cambridge.

One of the first in East Anglia to receive a direct communication from her husband was Mrs Johnson, of 4 Cambridge Road, Milton: a telegram arrived on 16th March from Lance Corporal Peter Johnson, of the Cambridgeshire Regiment:

"Escaped Singapore. Safe, well. Writing. Love." An air mail card followed:

> I am terribly sorry I haven't written before, but the circumstances simply would not permit, as you probably have gathered. I haven't had a very easy time of it, and naturally I cannot tell you about it here, so that will have to wait until we meet again.

Later letters disclosed that he had reached India. Mrs Johnson was one of a fortunate minority. The parents in Norwich of Lance Corporal Arthur C. Potter received a letter from him in mid-April, posted in India, reporting:

> Rather than be taken a prisoner, we got a lifeboat and got away at dawn, with a lot of luck and hard work. We were twelve days in that boat getting to Sumatra, rowing most of the time and getting very little rest. We had a few rations and some water, but had to rely on the natives and coconuts for most of our food. Anyway, we made it, and are now at rest camp waiting further orders and getting fit again.

A month later in Dereham the wife of Captain Douglas R. Gray, of the Royal Norfolks, received a letter reporting that thirty-four officers and men of his regiment had taken a boat from a burnt-out ship in Singapore and had rowed out of the harbour in full daylight, under the eyes of the Japanese. Taking it in turns, with four oarsmen on each side of the boat, they had rowed as hard as they could for a day and a night. They had landed on a small island, and from there, in stages, they had been towed by native motor launches to Java.

The *East Anglian Daily Times* published an account said to have been received from "a friend of the Suffolk Regiment" who had been at Singapore until the early afternoon of 14th February. By that time, he wrote, many had been ordered to find their way out of Singapore as best they could and to get to Sumatra. "It is known that quite a lot got into Chinese junks and sampans, Malay prahus and any other craft which could be got to move and carry people." This was a generally reassuring report on what conditions were thought likely to be in Singapore and in Sumatra, but there was no indication of the status of the writer.

These messages printed in the local papers gave some encouragement to all East Anglian families with men in the Far East, but could not end their anxieties.

The authorities had clearly decided on a policy of trying to break the bad news piecemeal, and anyone who challenged this policy was in danger of being accused of spreading alarm and despondency, but this challenge was made. A speaker at a meeting of the Cambridgeshire branch of the Royal Empire Society, Mr W. S. Thatcher, Censor of Fitzwilliam House, put it bluntly when, according to a newspaper report, he declared that we had not suffered such an outstanding and colossal disaster in 200 years of our history:

> . . . Had it been given to choose between the blotting out of Cambridge or of Singapore, we could have better afforded the blotting out of Cambridge . . .

Discontent rumbled on, at Westminster and in the country. When there was another debate on the war situation, in May, the critics were still in full cry. Mr

Richard Stokes, the MP for Ipswich and chairman of the engineering firm of Ransomes and Rapier, was one of the most articulate of them. "My constituents in East Anglia, who had sons, husbands and sweethearts in the Forces", he said, "want to know what was the sense of sending 40,000 troops who had no experience of tropical conditions? A great number of them arrived just in time to lay down their arms. Who was responsible? Why were those troops inadequately equipped, as the Prime Minister admits? Surely, if the decision was that Singapore could not be held, then the troops should have been sent to Burma?"

In June the War Minister, Sir James Grigg, reported that there was still no news of those who had been posted missing. The Japanese were being pressed to supply lists of those held in their prisoner-of-war camps. By mid-July families were being advised that they might write to their menfolk who had been posted missing — but without any assurance that the letters would ever be received. Letters had to be addressed to the men by name, c/o Japanese Red Cross, Tokyo. They had to be typewritten, so the Shirehall office of the Cambridgeshire Troops Comfort Fund offered to type them.

East Anglians had been taken prisoner in other theatres of war before 1942, so some families were already familiar with the problems. In several towns clubs had been established where relatives could meet to try to give mutual support. In Cambridge, for example, there were gatherings on the first Wednesday of every month "for Tea and Talk" in the British Legion Hall in Petty Cury. Now, with the need greatly increased, many more such clubs were brought into being. Wisbech, March and Ely were among the first.

The worries of the wives were accentuated by uncertainty about payment of their dependents' allowances. The rule was that after the lapse of a certain time

Association.

Missing in the Far East of the Suffolk Regt.

A MEETING

will be held on

TUES., July 21st, 3 p.m.

At DIOCESAN HALL, 13, TOWER STREET, IPSWICH,

for next-of-kin to exchange information and to hear Mrs. Backhouse, wife of Brigadier Backhouse, of the Regiment. Relatives of others missing in the Far East, Service or Civilian, will be welcome.

This meeting is not connected with Missing or Prisoners-of-War in Germany, Italy and Libya.

The Regimental Band of the NORTHAMPTONSHIRE

A problem shared . . . Many families whose menfolk had been reported missing following the fall of Singapore welcomed the opportunity to get together with others to exchange whatever information they had—but most had none to offer.

East Anglian Daily Times

Workers pouring concrete during the construction of an East Anglian base for the United States Army Air Force. Enormous amounts of concrete were needed for the runways and perimeter tracks of these airfields. *Imperial War Museum*

without news after a man was posted missing, government allowances were reduced. The Soldiers', Sailors' and Airmen's Families Association then stepped in with aid, if it was necessary to alleviate distress. In July the Commons was told that dependents' allowances would be continued for a further three months, and in November this undertaking was renewed to cover the remainder of the year.

Considerable discrepancies in wealth and earnings caused problems more widely than among the wives of prisoners-of-war. Many families, assailed by the exhausting problems of "carrying on" amid so many difficulties with the breadwinner away, found that shortage of cash was the final depressant. The government must have recognized this, for in February it increased the allowance to Servicemen's wives by 3s 6d a week, with a further increase of one shilling a week for each child. Men and women in the forces were, at the same time, allocated sixpence a day as a "postwar credit" — the government said it would provide them with a nest-egg when they were demobilized.

Contrasts still remained. By the early months of 1942 a massive programme of aerodrome construction was well under way in the Eastern Counties, labour was being moved in from other parts of the country, and women and boys were also recruited. Their conditions of employment caused dissatisfaction among farm workers and the families of servicemen, and the Hartismere RDC gave expression to this feeling when it resolved:

> The country's money is being wasted in connection with the construction of public works in the area . . . and the payment of excessive wages to inexperienced and unskilled men and boys is causing great dissatisfaction to genuine agricultural workers and is tending to seriously handicap food production.

DAILY TIMES, MONDAY, APRIL 6,

STRICTER TEA RATIONING

SUPPLIES TO BE TAKEN MONTHLY

GOOD-BYE TO WHITE BREAD

New austerity regulations concerning food which come into operation to-day are:—

Stricter rationing of tea, under which retailers will be required to cut out and retain coupons.

Only national bread will be sold in future.

Condensed milk and cereal breakfast foods included in the points scheme.

The need for closer rationing of tea was emphasised by Warrington (Lancs) Food Office officials, who have disclosed that 19 cwt. of tea more per week than rationing allowed was reaching the public.

MONTHLY TEA PURCHASES

The public will be required to purchase at one time their tea requirements for any four-weekly period. The four coupons for each four-weekly period must be surrendered together. Purchases must not exceed 8ozs. per ration book—four times the weekly ration.

The public may continue to buy tea at any shop. No registration is required.

Existing arrangements as to quantities bought will continue to apply to holders of the weekly seamen's ration book, leave or duty ration cards, and the emergency ration documents. Coupons will be cut, and each coupon can be used by itself.

Catering establishments and institutions must detach tea coupons in the ration books of residents.

OLD-AGE PENSIONERS

Old-age pensioners, on presentation of pension books, may buy each week's ration separately. Residential establishments may buy one week's ration at a time, on the ration books of residents.

Coupons for tea numbered 27 to 36 on page 20 of the General Ration book —R.B.E.—and page 18 of the Child's Ration book—R.B.2—are no longer valid, and should be cut out and destroyed.

CONDENSED MILK AND CEREALS

RATIONED FROM TO-DAY

Condensed milk and cereal breakfast foods will cost points from to-day, when the new rationing period begins. Values:—

Condensed milk, four or eight [illegible] ding to size; skimmed [illegible] eight, 4d. six.

As food supplies became further restricted rationing was tightened—and it was "Good-bye to white bread" as orders were given that only the national loaf should be sold.
East Anglian Daily Times

The budget in April, 1942, brought no joy, but emphasized the need to tighten belts. The price of beer went up to twopence a pint, whisky by 4s 8d a bottle, cigarettes by threepence a packet. And a wide range of what were considered to be luxury articles were subjected to a 66 ⅔ per cent "purchase tax"; they included silk dresses and stockings, fur coats, ornaments, cut glass, leather trunks and bags, musical instruments, and gramophone records.

The breakup of families, the anxieties about the safety of husbands far away, and the acute financial problems were not the only reasons for the poor state of morale in the opening months of 1942. We must look deeper. Even those who suffered less were showing signs of strain. The *East Anglian Daily Times* published a letter from a reader:

> I do not know how things are in the towns, but am convinced that quite a lot of people in the villages only realize when bombs drop near that there is a war on. The farm workers are better off than ever before, and pretty sure in most cases of exemption from military service; so why worry? . . . There is more money for getting into the towns and for pleasure. One wonders if indifference and complacency are not as much in evidence and as dangerous as defeatism . . .

It was a combination of many factors which had taken toll. Firstly, there were the basic problems of food, clothing and shelter. Sarah Williams made these entries in her diary after shopping expeditions in Sheringham in the early weeks of the year:

> *7th January:* There is no meat or fish in the town, just a few fishes' heads, for which the fish shop wanted to charge us 9d, which we didn't pay.
> *9th January:* We bought a tin of something called Fish Kedgeree and it was dreadful stuff. I ate a little and feel half-poisoned, and even the cat refused to eat it.

Throughout East Anglia acute shortage of goods not officially rationed caused queues to form immediately it was rumoured that a shop had something in stock, and this stirred up a good deal of discontent. Often a police officer had to be posted to keep order in the queues. A letter to the editor of the *Cambridge Daily News* signed "Onlooker" declared:

> Surely the time is well overdue for the stopping of queues in Cambridge. It has been remarked more than once by strangers to the town what a surplus of idle people there must be in Cambridge.

In fact, the secretary of the Cambridge Housewives' Association had anticipated this complaint and had proposed that all foods and commodities in short supply should be formally rationed immediately in order to avoid queues. Another correspondent of the local newspaper followed up:

> These queues are becoming impossible. What has come over the women of Cambridge? They are so impatient that it is agony to stand against some of them. Where is the respect for old people these days? Personally, I like to take my turn and not cause trouble.

But some people grumbled about the official rationing, like the woman signing herself "Disgusted", who wrote:

> I would like to point out to the mothers of very young children how lucky they have been. For nearly three years they have been enjoying rations intended for children who cannot possibly eat them. Now that Lord Woolton* has realized that small children cannot drink tea, perhaps he would like to know that babies are born without teeth and cannot by any chance eat their meat, cheese or bacon rations. I hope he will take all these rations off . . . It is time that older children had more. Growing children eat a lot . . .

Typical of a number of indignant replies was this:

> Perhaps "Disgusted" does not know that the health of a breast-fed child depends on the health of its mother, and that the quality of the food it gets from her depends on the quality of the food she eats herself . . .

A happy footnote to this argument was provided by "Another Housewife", who wrote:

> I must say I've never seen such lovely babies about the town as we see this year. A pleasure to all — war or no war.

As for clothing, a time had been reached when there was actually a bureaucrat with the title "Director General of Civilian Clothing". In March he announced that buttons were to be banned from the sleeves of men's jackets, and that double-breasted coats and trouser turnups were to be forbidden. There was to be a reduction in the amount of embroidery and other ornamentation on women's and children's clothing. He added, cheerfully and illogically: "I should imagine skirts will be kept as short as possible, to increase the amount of material available."

Many women still tried hard to look smart, despite the obstacles. Apart from clothes rationing, they were finding it difficult to get their hair styled. An advertisement in the *Eastern Daily Press* in January read:

> Ladies — HURRY FOR YOUR PERMANENT WAVE. Material is rationed, manufacturers have stopped making paper sachets, assistants are being called up.
>
> Be wise. To the wise woman this means your perm will be almost impossible to get.
>
> We can still offer a perfect perm for 17s 6d whole head, no extras, for the next three months. But you must book at once, so that we can reserve necessary material. . .

The comfortably-off middle class fought hard to maintain some of its standards at home. One still saw occasional advertisements in the Norwich and Cambridge papers for cooks-general, housekeepers, domestic maids of all kinds, and gardeners. The "salary" usually offered for a general maid was £1 a week. There was even an advertisement in Cambridge in January for a butler-valet. But most of the advertisements were for staff for the hard-pressed hospitals, schools and

*Minister of Food, 1940–43.

institutions. St Mary's Hospital, Colchester, for example, wanted an Assistant House Matron and offered a salary of £60, rising to £70, a year, "plus residential emoluments".

For everyone, most of the comforts of pre-war life had evaporated. Not even the Cambridge women's colleges escaped the new rigours. In May it was reported that undergraduates at Girton, who had already had to learn to make their own beds, were now being asked to take turns at clearing the tables and washing up, because domestic staff was unobtainable.

Many people felt their homes had been "invaded" by evacuated schoolchildren and mothers. Especially in the western parts of the region, there were still large numbers of such children living with foster parents, and although hostesses and "guests" had arrived at some sort of *modus vivendi*, tensions remained.

In January, when the Ministry of Health offered to meet the cost of a welfare officer to keep an eye on children evacuated to Cambridgeshire, the county council accepted this offer, and then had to beat a retreat when the rural district councils objected. South Cambridgeshire RDC thought such an appointment "absolutely unnecessary and undesirable", and one of its members observed that "she would probably prove more of a nuisance and make more trouble". At the same time the Ministry asked the county council for a list of householders in the county who would be prepared to accommodate unaccompanied children under five years of age if they needed to be evacuated from areas being heavily bombed during the following autumn and winter. The clerk to the council reported that he had circulated a request, but no accommodation had been offered. The council advised the Ministry that the best solution would be the provision of special hostels.

The main waves of evacuees from London had ceased, but occasional parties still arrived in the Eastern Counties, and the problems had still not been ironed out. Chesterton RDC was told in February that its billeting officers had been given only four days' notice of the arrival of a party of ninety children and that twenty of them had been "unbilletable" and had been placed in hostels — fourteen were found to be suffering from scabies. The sanitary inspector at Ely reported to his urban district council that eleven houses in various parts of the city which had been requisitioned to accommodate evacuees were infested with bugs. When seventy children arrived in Newmarket from Walthamstow some had to be sent to hospital for medical attention and several were in desperate need of new boots and shoes.

Clare RDC was one of many local authorities which voiced strong criticism of the government scheme for the evacuation of unaccompanied schoolchildren. The clerk reported that of one party of fifty-two, twenty-four had been evacuated before; for one child it was the eighth evacuation, for another the fifth, for three others the fourth, and for eight others the third. "The first child to whom I spoke at the reception centre replied quite brightly that her mother wished her to have another holiday before the winter set in," the clerk said. Parties of unaccompanied children continued to be sent out of London fortnightly during most of 1942, but eventually the government suspended the scheme. By that time, more children were drifting back to London than were leaving.

Saffron Walden Council learned in April that 139 evacuees had returned to London during the previous month; 579 remained in the town — 206 adults and 373 children. The Mayor, Alderman Ellis Rooke, gave a tea party in the Jubilee Gardens to the hostesses who had received evacuees, and he disclosed that 2,223 evacuees had "passed through" the billeting officer's books since the outbreak of the war, and had been accommodated in more than two hundred different homes.

Some evacuation schemes, however, went very smoothly, as when the Leys School at Cambridge was evacuated to Pitlochry in Scotland in July, 1942.

After the evacuees came another invasion. Cambridge Borough Council was told in June that it must find accommodation in the town for thousands of war workers, and the chairman of its Civil Defence Committee reported that almost all the voluntary billets were full. He thought compulsory billeting would have to be brought in, and he said he was not looking forward to it. It had been suggested that only big houses should be used, but many of the workers preferred not to be put into big houses. Soon afterwards the Cambridge Trades Council and Labour Party discussed the problem and decided to urge the authorities to build hostels for the new arrivals. In fact, no special action was necessary in 1942.

Then there was the blackout, and the resulting difficulties and dangers of getting about. The newspapers regularly reported inquests on the victims of road accidents. Cyclists appeared in droves before local magistrates and were fined for riding their machines without lights, and they were followed into the dock by householders who were fined for letting chinks of light escape through the blacked-out windows of their homes. It was not easy to secure efficient blackout with thick curtains or with screens placed on windows each day at dusk, and from time to time planes were sent up to make surveys. After one such, the assistant solicitor to Norwich Corporation, prosecuting an offender, told the court that the pilot, flying at 3,000 to 4,000 feet, had seen between two and three hundred window lights caused by badly fitting blackout screens and curtains, and had reported: "The blackout is appalling".

Some relaxation was being permitted, however. Rail travellers had difficulty knowing when they had reached their stations, where lights had been completely doused; so in January, 1942, the LNER began to experiment at Ipswich, Peterborough and some other stations with what it called "controlled beam lighting" — directing a minimal amount of light on to small black nameboards bearing station names in white letters. In Norwich, in May, masks were removed from traffic lights during daylight hours and police constables on their beats switched off the lights altogether half an hour before blackout. Later in the year, some of the traffic lights were taken out of commission altogether, to save electricity.

Public transport vehicles were in short supply and always overcrowded. When a bus drew up, there was often a headlong rush, with no holds barred, to get aboard. Inasmuch as they had breath to spare for explanations, struggling would-be passengers excused themselves by telling of the emergencies they were confronting, or the young children or the sick awaiting them, or the urgent national business on which they were engaged. And, very often, these were plain truths. Ipswich seems to have had a special problem with its bus travellers. A letter appeared in the local paper in March:

> Cannot steps be taken to overcome the unseemly scrambles on Ipswich Cornhill for trolley buses? If the passengers were compelled, as in other towns, to form queues, with rails erected for the purpose, elderly people would not be roughly handled by younger people, who have no manners and no respect for their elders, as in the much-derided Victorian days . . . Let the inspectors organize the waiting passengers until the queue habit becomes ingrained in the unruly younger people, if that be possible.

Soon afterwards an advertisement appeared, proclaiming boldly: "You must queue now". The complaints continued — now some individuals were breaking the

"In order to succeed in its aim, the propaganda-poster has three main obstacles to overcome—firstly, a general aversion to reading any notice of any sort; secondly, a general disinclination to believe that any notice, even if read, can possibly be addressed to oneself; thirdly, a general unwillingness, even so, to remember the message long enough to do anything about it."
Those words were written by "Fougasse", who sought through the humour of his cartoons to get the message across to the unseeing and the unwilling.
East Anglian Daily Times

queues. There must have been similar problems elsewhere, for in mid-April the Ministry of Transport issued an Order that whenever there were six or more people waiting at a bus stop they must form a queue. The system worked well.

Many buses were taking on a new shade of "battleship grey" as they fell due for overhaul and repaint, because the red cellulose paint normally used for their livery was no longer available. Additionally it was felt the overall grey made them less visible to enemy airmen who might be tempted to machine-gun a bus trundling along a country road.

Second-hand cars were still advertised for sale, despite the rationing of petrol; in the *Cambridge Daily News* on 1st January a five-year-old Vauxhall 14 saloon was offered at £115 and a 1934 7 hp Jowett saloon for £55. Perhaps more surprisingly, Marshalls were still offering "early delivery of new Austin cars and trucks". Early in the year the Eastern Regional Commissioner, Sir Will Spens, reminded the public that no private cars were allowed in a coastal belt extending from the Wash to the Thames. Soon afterwards, the small "basic" petrol ration was ended, and cars had then to be laid up — unless one was on some sort of official business.

In the East Anglian farming community there was concern, even anger, about the manner in which agricultural land was requisitioned for the construction of airfields.

In these and a whole range of other matters there were, inevitably, a great and

Four young airmen pose in front of a Bristol Blenheim IV on the snow-covered airfield at Wattisham. The aircraft belonged to No 18 (Bomber) Squadron. *Peter Hills*

growing number of restrictions on personal behaviour. But Nature provided some consolations; there were some things that no authority could control. On the first Sunday in April thousands walked through Trinity and King's at Cambridge to see the massed crocuses on the Backs — "a springtime scene of peace and tranquillity", said the local paper. Addenbrooke's nurses collected donations for their hospital. April also saw several letters in the Press reporting the first cuckoo, the first nightingale, the first chiff-chaff. The Vicar of Haughley scored twice, with a chiff-chaff in the Abbey Gardens at Bury St Edmunds on 7th April and a nightingale in his own village on 14th April.

These early months of 1942 witnessed morale in British homes at its lowest-ever ebb. Was the situation of the nation at that time as grim as the mood suggested? The harsh facts were not, of course, revealed to any but those in authority whose responsibility it was to grapple with them. But, had they been, they would have done little to restore confidence.

There was one all-transforming reality, however — the whole resources of the United States had now been thrown into the global battle. Further, the armies of Soviet Russia were fighting with a dogged courage which few in British official circles had anticipated, and were holding down the bulk of Hitler's forces on the eastern front in Europe. A year earlier Britain and its Commonwealth had been fighting alone, its Allies of 1939 all defeated and occupied by Nazi armies. Now Britain was part of a powerful alliance.

The problems, however, remained formidable. In the retreat from the European mainland and in the subsequent Battle of Britain in the air and the Battle of the Atlantic at sea, a large part of Britain's fighting weapons had been lost. The year 1941 had seen a nation which had been battered to its knees slowly beginning to regain its breath and to organize its people and its resources so as to be able to hit back. On 1st January, 1942, a great deal remained to be done.

As an example, most of the RAF airfields in East Anglia lacked concrete runways; they were still grass surfaced and could not handle the size and weight of new bombers just coming forward. The new airfields being built were given 2,000-yard-long main runways which, with subsidiary runways and dispersal areas, required about a million cubic yards of concrete, but the established bases were only just beginning to be converted. It was proving difficult to get sufficient materials and manpower.

The Blenheims, Whitleys and Hampdens which had comprised more than half the bomber force of 1941 were obsolete — they were taken out of service between May and September, 1942 — but the first of the new breed of Lancaster bombers was not ready for operations until March. Stirling bombers had been in service for more than a year, but were only just beginning to come from the factories in significant numbers; from January, 1942, the airfield at Waterbeach was given over to the training of their pilots, who took off, made short circuits of the field and landed repeatedly all day and every day. When Air Chief Marshal Sir Arthur

Harris was appointed C-in-C of Bomber Command in February, however, he was held back in his policies by shortage of planes, as he could not mobilize many more than four hundred bombers for an operation[5].

New fighter planes were also only just coming forward. In January, 1942, Castle Camps near Haverhill was the first airfield to receive the new de Havilland Mosquito fighters, and it was several months before their first operational use; on 27th April they went into action against the German bombers blitzing Norwich. At nearby Duxford the main task in 1942 was to work the Hawker Typhoon into operational service — it first went into action in June.

Training pilots and crews for the new planes seemed a long-drawn-out and costly business when the need was so urgent. Churchill sent a sharp note to the Chief of the Air Staff on the last day of January:

> Please observe that, out of 1,550 serviceable aircraft, Fighter Command has managed to smash up 126, or one aircraft in twelve, during a week in which there has been hardly any fighting . . . Fancy all this wanton waste happening at a time when we have got so few in the kitty . . .[6]

Airfields close to the coast of East Anglia, including Bircham Newton, Ludham, Coltishall, Swanton Morley and Martlesham Heath, provided many of the fighters giving protection to convoys and were also concerned with air–sea rescue operations. The main threat to British shipping was not in the North Sea, however, but in the Atlantic. In the first six months of 1942 the tonnage of merchant shipping sunk in the North Atlantic was nearly a million tons more than in the same period a year earlier. The situation looked desperate. The ships were needed not only to feed the British people but to bring men and equipment from America and to send supplies to British forces in North Africa and the Mediterranean.

The Army had by the beginning of 1942 been built up to 2,250,000 men, with 900,000 more in the Commonwealth forces, and 1,500,000 in the Home Guard. But only half a dozen of the thirty-two divisions or their equivalent in Britain were fully armed and equipped to fight the Germans on the Continent, and only two were held ready to proceed overseas at immediate notice. About one in every three soldiers were in beach-defence units, without motorized transport — many of these were on the East Coast — and at least 500,000 were engaged in AA duties and on the defence of factories, ports and shipping[7].

While these forces cried out for equipment, Britain was obliged to send tanks and aircraft to Russia; this was the only effective help possible at this stage of the war. There were certainly not yet the resources with which to launch the "Second Front" in Europe for which British Communists vigorously campaigned, with the slogan "Victory in 1942".

If the housewife was beset by the problems of shortages at the table and in the wardrobe, those problems were a thousand-fold greater for the leaders obsessed with the shortages of planes and ships and tanks and raw materials of all kinds.

CHAPTER TWO

The New Alliance

THE PRE-WAR education system had provided the average Englishman and woman with a profound conviction that they were "God's chosen people", but most had been offered no standards of comparison. Foreign travel had been experienced by a comparatively small minority; few had been to America and only a handful to the Soviet Union. Most of the newspapers and the radio had offered them a meagre diet of foreign news, so that even their nearest neighbours in Europe were little understood; in most minds the United States was a *pastiche* of Wall Street skyscrapers, Chicago gangsters and Hollywood glamour; a blurred image of Russia presented Tolstoyan peasants and hairy Bolsheviks jostling one another in a Siberian waste. The East Anglian way of life had been insulated to a remarkable degree against outside influences in the pre-war years.

Now these strange foreigners were Britain's desperately-needed allies. Their strengths and virtues would help to determine whether Britain and its Commonwealth could survive as a world power. The quality of the working relationship with them would influence how well the battles went and how quickly victory would be achieved. The Ministry of Information in London faced a gigantic task of public enlightenment.

Press and radio coverage of the fighting in 1940 and 1941 had familiarized most people with towns and rivers and mountains in Europe and in North and East Africa, and now previously little-known areas of the Far East were becoming familiar in headlines. Refugees from European countries overrun by the German forces were frequently seen in the Eastern Counties; Polish and Czech airmen flew with the RAF from local airfields; Free French sailors had had shore leave in some East Coast ports.

Cambridge was a special case. In many ways, but especially in the cultural and intellectual activities which were natural to it as a university town, it had become a principal satellite to the capital. Few of the leaders or official representatives of the Allied nations came to Britain without visiting Cambridge. The information they wished to convey and the propaganda they felt it necessary to use reached a Cambridge audience before any other. The *Cambridge Daily News* columnist "Robin Goodfellow" observed that "Cambridge must be unique in the opportunities afforded to its people of hearing about our Allies and about the various countries suffering under enemy oppression". There was, indeed, an almost non-stop flow of oratory in the town, in the accents of many nations.

China had been occupied by the Japanese. Dr Wellington Koo, the Chinese

Ambassador to London, came to Cambridge and addressed an audience of about a thousand in the Guildhall under the auspices of the Anglo-Chinese Friendship Committee. At the ADC Theatre Chinese war films were shown on three successive evenings. The Cambridge Anglo-Chinese Friendship Committee held a meeting in the Master's Lodge at St John's College and the speaker related that:

> The Chinese family, with a large house containing many relations, was run on lines of Communism. Everything in the house was common property. All money earned by the family was put in a common chest and any expenses were paid out of the chest . . . The new idea of young couples setting up a separate house was not encouraged, as this broke up the old family.

In a single, typical week in Cambridge there were meetings addressed by a vice-premier of Yugoslavia, the Czechoslovak Ambassador to London, and the Polish Minister for Foreign Affairs, plus a lecture on Russia, a Service of Intercession for China, and attendance of high-ranking American officers at Cambridge Rotary Club's weekly gathering.

The Yugoslav royal family was one of several which had taken refuge in England, and the eighteen-year-old King Peter was an undergraduate at Clare College. When Cambridge organized an Anglo-Yugoslav Week, King Peter, in Air Force uniform, addressed a public meeting in the Guildhall and his mother, Queen Marie, opened an exhibition of Yugoslav art at the Fitzwilliam Museum.

King Peter of Yugoslavia with his mother and the Vice-Chancellor of Cambridge University during a visit to his college, Queen's, in March.
Cambridge Daily News

In the case of the Soviet Union there was something like an explosion of public interest. As 1942 opened, the epic armed struggle on the eastern front was making most of the headlines. During 1941 the Russians had been driven back from the regions of Moscow and Leningrad and the Ukraine to the Volga and the Urals and Central Asia. German troops had invested Leningrad (where nearly a third of its three million people had died of starvation), and had made contact with the outer ring of Moscow's last-ditch defences. Losses on both sides had been staggering. Britain and the United States had undertaken to supply equipment and raw materials to their Russian allies, and the Royal Navy was convoying supply ships through icy and dangerous waters to the north Russian ports of Murmansk and Archangel. Everything that was thus added to the Russian strength had, of necessity, to be subtracted from the buildup of forces in the United Kingdom, putting off the day when an attack in the West might be feasible. Meanwhile, very little encouraging news was coming from the battle fronts in the Far East and North Africa.

Against this background, Mr Anthony Eden, after a visit to Moscow, broadcast a carefully measured address to the nation on 4th January in which he said:

> The Soviet Union is determined upon the utter defeat of Germany. So are we. The Soviet Union is determined to do all that is in its power to ensure that Germany cannot launch further wars upon the world. So are we. Out of the untold human suffering of the present war, the Soviet Union wishes to gain a lasting peace for all its peoples. So do we. For these common objects we must work together to win the war and to win the peace. With the experience of our Moscow talks fresh in my mind, I am convinced that we can do both.

Anglo-Soviet Friendship Committees had by this time sprung up in towns and villages all over East Anglia, and they gathered support from every quarter. For example, when Stowmarket opened its Anglo-Russian Friendship Week in January with a service in the parish church, the Salvation Army band headed the procession through the town, with the Boys' Brigade band and more than three hundred representatives of the urban district council, the Home Guard, the Air Training Corps, Civil Defence and youth organizations following behind. All denominations of the clergy took part, and the congregation included the Lord Lieutenant and the Countess of Stradbroke, Mr Edgar Granville, MP, and the chairman of the urban district council. In the evening the Regal Cinema was packed for a film show.

Cambridge displayed its own special enthusiasm. The Master and Fellows of Trinity College readily gave the use of their hallowed hall for events. Three hundred children took part in a programme of Russian dances and folk tales in January. At another event, the *Cambridge Daily News* reported, "The Cambridge People's Choir sang Soviet songs, with some of which, it was clear from their readiness to join in, the audience were already well acquainted". The Soviet composer Khatchaturian had the first performance in England of his *Violin*

Concerto at the Arts Theatre at about the same time. A Russian film, *The Rich Bride*, pulled in a crowd, but had a lukewarm reaction from the *Cambridge Daily News* critic, who wrote of "a somewhat melodramatic plot . . . glorifying the mechanical and making every character fit in with the general scheme of things". The hero was a tractor driver.

Alongside the continuous government campaign to collect scrap and to save money for the British war effort, there now developed vigorous official propaganda to stimulate aid to our Soviet allies. It was announced early in February that Suffolk's total contribution to Mrs Churchill's Red Cross Aid to Russia Fund was £3,400. In that month, a Cambridge committee despatched over 70lb of soap, candles, cigarettes and chocolates, as well as helmets, seaboot stockings and gloves which had been knitted locally. There was no more coupon-free wool available, however, so the public was now asked to concentrate its efforts on raising £1,500 for a mobile X-ray unit for the Russian Red Cross. By the end of April this money had been collected, the last £300 of it at a big demonstration on Parker's Piece, which was preceded by a procession round the town, headed by the band of the 5th Battalion, Cambridgeshire Home Guard, and including Civil Defence workers, members of the Trades Council and the Labour Party, the Communist Party, the Transport and General Workers' Union, the Free German Youth Movement, and the Youth of Austria and Young Czechoslovakia organizations. The organizers set a new target of £3,000, so that they could send a second mobile X-ray unit, and that was soon achieved.

When the time came to mark the second anniversary of the German invasion of Russia, the Ministry of Information and the Anglo-Soviet Friendship Committee joined forces to stage a demonstration of popular support in the Guildhall for the Soviet people and the Red Army. The Mayor of Cambridge, Sir Montagu Butler, took part. In the afternoon there was an exhibition and a film illustrating the scope of the joint Allied war effort; and there were storms of applause when at a public meeting that evening Sir John Russell insisted that after the war it would be important to build "a solid bond of enduring friendship with the Russian people" and when Fire Brigades Union official John Horner called for the opening of a Second Front in Europe.

The British Communist Party found that audiences were receptive to its message as never before; but its newspaper, the *Daily Worker*, had been suppressed by the government a year earlier (before Germany had invaded Russia) for "systematically publishing matter calculated to foment opposition to the war". Now the Communist message was different: "Victory in 1942", and one of the most distinguished propagandists, Professor J. B. S. Haldane, came to Cambridge Guildhall to urge the removal of the ban on the newspaper. Communists and their supporters kept up a steady campaign and a visit to Cambridge on 28th April by Mr Herbert Morrison, the Minister who carried the formal responsibility for the ban, gave them an opportunity to demonstrate. Students formed a large section of his

Anglian Daily Ti

WHICH IS INCORPORATED THE "IPSWICH EXPRESS" (ESTABLISHED 1839).

IPSWICH, FRIDAY, JUNE 12, 1942

TWENTY YEARS' TREATY BETWEEN BRITAIN AND RUSSIA

UNDERSTANDING ON SECOND FRONT IN EUROPE THIS YEAR

M. MOLOTOV'S SECRET VISITS TO LONDON AND WASHINGTON

PACT PROVIDES FOR JOINT ACTION IN WAR AND COLLABORATION IN PEACE

Britain and Russia have signed a twenty years' mutual aid pact confirming their alliance, and have reached "full understanding" on the urgent task of creating a second front in Europe year. No separate peace will be made with Germany without mutual consent.

Eden, Foreign Secret... this dramatic announcement in the House

Anglo-Soviet friendship found political expression in June when the newspapers announced the signing of a mutual aid pact between the two countries. *East Anglian Daily Times*

audience in the Guildhall, and they bombarded him with questions. Reports in the press stated that, judged by volume of applause, the supporters and opponents of the ban on the *Daily Worker* were about equally balanced. But Morrison was a seasoned manipulator of left-wing audiences, and he gave every appearance of enjoying the experience.

Alternative approaches to understanding Russia were on offer. The Communists inquired rhetorically "What makes Russia strong?" and Mr George Matthews, one of the party's leaders, offered a Cambridge Guildhall audience in January an explanation based on "The Life and Work of Lenin". Typical of the innumerable lectures and meetings arranged by the Ministry of Information was one in Ely at which Mr Harold Gibson, who had spent some time in Russia, said of the Russian people that

> they had faults, and very serious ones, but he did not think the present the right time to find fault. The Russians were great lovers of children, which, he felt, was common with the two countries, and it was because of our love of children that we were able to understand Russia. The Russians were all like big children. During the past 25 years we had been told they were great, hairy, blood-thirsty monsters, and believed it. "They are", said the speaker, "not even hairy. They are very, very like the British. You", he informed his listeners, "would pass as Russians in Moscow, while Russians in Britain would pass as British"(1).

Churchmen were prominent in praise of the Russians. The Bishop of Chelmsford, at a meeting organized by the Chelmsford Anglo-Soviet Unity Committee in the Shirehall, declared that a million people in Britain would be able to say that they had their husband or their son safe because a Russian had died on the battlefield.

Behind the new-found enthusiasm for most things Russian, however, old suspicions lingered in the minds of authority. A Mass Observation representative reported that the Communist Party regularly held open-air meetings in Tindal Square, Chelmsford. He observed about one passer-by in ten pausing to listen, and his report added:

> A few policemen in plain clothes hear the speeches "officially" and watch how people behave. At one of the public meetings a few soliders stood on the pavement listening to the speech about Soviet Russia, when an Army officer came and asked the soldiers to move away(2).

This report suggested that the popular interest was not reflected in any big increase in direct support of the British Communist Party:

> I enquired from the secretary of the Communist Party the membership of the party in Chelmsford and was surprised to find that he was supposed not to tell, but could only say that membership of the party had been doubled during the last six months of 1941. That means, roughly, the membership would be about 30.

The new and novel element in 1942 was the attention paid to the Americans. The *East Anglian Daily Times* greeted the New Year with a frank recognition that the behaviour of the United States was going to be decisive in determining the outcome of the war. In its 1st January editorial it declared:

> The productive capacity of the United States is unlimited, Mr. Churchill has evidently been convinced during his stay in Washington that the American effort will be unstinted. There lies the new guarantee for ultimate victory.

A few Americans had been fighting the war before the Japanese attack on Pearl Harbour had led to a full commitment by their country. Enough volunteers had crossed the Atlantic of their own free will to form three Spitfire squadrons — the so-called Eagle Squadrons.

The first American troops posted across the Atlantic after the United States declared war began to arrive in January, 1942. It was announced on the 27th that US Army forces had established a General HQ "somewhere in England", and that the first contingent of troops had been shipped over, without loss, to stations in the United Kingdom.

The preparations had been long under way, months before the Japanese

Young American pilots of an Eagle squadron pose with their mascot at RAF Martlesham Heath in Suffolk. *Gordon Kinsey*

bombing of Pearl Harbour had made the United States an active combatant. Major General James E. Chaney, who was now named as the commander of the US forces in Britain, had actually arrived on 15th May, 1941, as head of a "Special Observer Corps", with a carefully selected staff of seventeen officers. Now it was revealed that they had been making "a detailed study of British military and air technique" and had been planning "quietly for eventual operations in the event that the US should become a belligerent Power".

So — an official American bulletin stated — they had "perfected an organization which enabled immediate action once President Roosevelt and Mr Churchill decided in Washington late last month to have American troops assist in the defence of the British Isles as an essential fortress in this world struggle. . ."

The first evidence of an American in East Anglia seems to have been a wedding picture published in the *Cambridge Daily News* on 26th February, 1942. It showed an American pilot officer, in uniform, Udell Thomson, of St Louis, Missouri, after his wedding at St Paul's Church, Cambridge, to a London bride. Probably he was a volunteer in one of the American "Eagle" squadrons of the RAF, but no clue was provided why the wedding had taken place in the town, nor with which force the man was serving.

A little later the *Cambridge Daily News* reported that American fighting men had arrived in London. "Americans of all three services are frequently seen in Oxford Street — not far from the US Embassy in Grosvenor Square — and it is a common sight to see an American sailor, in his little white cap, giving a very correct salute to British and Allied officers." By the middle of May there were sufficient US servicemen in London to require their own military police, who, like the British "redcaps", patrolled the streets in pairs.

In Washington a special handbook was produced by the US War Department, *A Short Guide to Great Britain*. It claimed to deal with everything from an outline of British politics to the intricacies of darts in public houses. One paragraph read:

> You will find yourself among a kindly, quiet, hard-working people, who have been living under a strain such as few people in the world have ever known. In your dealings with them, let this be your slogan: "It is always impolite to criticize your hosts. It is militarily stupid to criticize your Allies".

Education was seen as a two-way process, and the Ministry of Information sprang into action. When Bernard Newman lectured a large audience in Cambridge Guildhall on life in the United States, enlightenment began gently: he suggested that

> New York, with its dense traffic, and Washington, the seat of the government, were wonderful places . . . He thought that the average American had a higher standard of living than our own people — all had cars and refrigerators.

Anyone who had actually visited America seemed keen to spread knowledge. When the Provost of Kings, Mr J. T. Sheppard, was invited to address Rotary on

"The Wisdom of the Greeks", he contrived an introduction about "the great friendliness and the great intelligence of the Americans", among whom he had spent three or four weeks before the war.

It was as well that the public had no inkling of impressions which had been formed by some who were serving in high places. Sir Alan Brooke, the Chief of the British Imperial General Staff, deeply involved in building the alliance with the Americans, thought that "her leaders and people had no idea of what modern war involved and of how unprepared they were for it . . .". Field Marshal Sir John Dill, head of the British Military Delegation in Washington, sent Brooke a message in January, 1942: "Never have I seen a country so utterly unprepared for war and so soft"(3).

Throughout the first half of the year, East Anglians were given a much more flattering account in newspapers and magazines and books, and at many meetings and lectures. None of them had an opportunity to make acquaintance with an American until Independence Day — 4th July, 1942 — when the first US Army Engineer Battalions arrived.

The great orchestrated symphony of Allied solidarity developed month by month. It reached a climax at Cambridge Guildhall later in the year with a pageant designed as an "International Commemoration of the heroic deeds of the United Nations in their fight for freedom". Twenty-nine nations were represented. There were no speeches. Instead, there were music, hymns, songs, recitals: sonorous passages from the Bible and from Kipling, rousing music by Elgar and Vaughan Williams. A roll of honour was called and as each name was pronounced a representative group in uniform stepped forward from the back of the hall, carrying a banner aloft. Trumpeters of the RAF Symphony Orchestra sounded a fanfare for each group, which then marched forward, the whole length of the hall, mounted the platform, and acknowledged the cheers of the audience.

The British armed forces came first: the Royal Navy, the Women's Royal Naval Service, the Army, women of the Auxiliary Territorial Service, the Royal Air Force, the Women's Auxiliary Air Force. Then came two captains of the Merchant Navy, fresh from convoy duty; then groups representing the Home Guard, the Red Cross and St John Ambulance. The United States representatives followed on: half-a-dozen soldiers headed by a girl carrying the Stars and Stripes. Next, the Soviet Union: three women, the youngest carrying aloft the Red Banner, with its hammer and sickle emblem in white. China came next, represented by six students, including a girl in national costume. Then the British Dominions, soldiers, sailors and airmen. After them, representatives of Belgium, Brazil, Czechoslovakia, Fighting France (just one girl carrying a Tricolour and wearing a Cross of Lorraine at her breast), Greece, Luxembourg, the Netherlands, Poland, Yugoslavia. Finally, parties of British Legion members and of Old Contemptibles. The pageant ended with the singing of *Jerusalem*, led by the King's College Choir. The audience filed out in a state of high emotion.

CHAPTER THREE

Defending the Homeland

FEARS of an invasion of Great Britain had not been eliminated by Germany's swing to the east. The minute written by Prime Minister Mr Churchill on 10th October, 1941, still guided Cabinet decisions throughout 1942:

> A scheme must be prepared for the evacuation of civilians from the coastal areas from the Wash to the Isle of Wight, and also of Nodal Points like Colchester, Ipswich and Canterbury[1].

The "nodal points" were centres which controlled communications in the region and where stocks of food, petrol and other essentials were concentrated.

About 60 per cent of the residents in the coast towns had been persuaded to leave voluntarily during 1940, but many had later returned. Two thousand of the evacuees were back in Lowestoft. They were still flocking back into Southend at the rate of 250 every week. Churchill's minute began a re-examination of the problem.

Detailed plans were prepared for a compulsory evacution, and approved by the Cabinet's Home Defence Committee in February, 1942. They were to be implemented only if and when air reconnaissance suggested that an invasion was imminent — "approximately three weeks before the enemy's preparations for invasion are likely to be completed"; it was estimated that it would take two or three days to complete the evacuation. A list prepared a little later showed that the War Cabinet proposed to order complete evacuation of Great Yarmouth, Lowestoft, Southwold, Aldeburgh, Felixstowe, Harwich, Frinton and Walton, Clacton, Trimley St Mary, Ipswich, Colchester and Southend-on-Sea[2].

Meanwhile, efforts to secure voluntary evacuation were renewed. In February the chairman of the Ipswich Emergency Committee announced that "the conditions which would be likely to prevail in this town in the case of invasion have been very carefully examined from every angle and in considerable detail" and he urged everyone who could leave Ipswich and live further inland to do so immediately.

The Home Defence Committee had the responsibility of constantly updating anti-invasion plans. It reported to the War Cabinet in March, 1942, on the state of preparedness reached[3]. By that date a five-day reserve of non-perishable foodstuffs had been stored in all small towns and villages in the coastal belt, sufficient to provide for a population of about five millions. The arrangements were being extended to cover an additional five million people in the immediate hinterland of the coastal belt.

The committee had also looked at all factories making war equipment and it had found that, in the view of the Ministry of Supply, only two in the proposed evacuation area in East Anglia were engaged on "vital" war production— both in Ipswich. It had decided against moving them to another part of the country; if there was an invasion, these factories would simply close down.

Plans were also drawn up, and presented to the Invasion Staffs Committee in February, to evacuate hospital patients from a large part of East Anglia(4). They were designed to ensure that there would be 170,000 beds available in the Eastern Region for invasion casualties, military and civilian.

A three-phase operation was envisaged. In the first phase, before "Stand-to",

British troops practising house-to-house fighting in a battle school exercise at Frinton. The photograph was taken on 16th October, 1942. *Imperial War Museum*

when the "trend of information indicates that invasion is probable", hospital bed occupancy was to be kept to fifty per cent (in Kent and Sussex, where the invasion danger was considered to be greater, it was to be held down to only twenty-five per cent). In the second phase, at "Stand-to", all patients considered fit enough to travel in special ambulance trains were to be evacuated from the area. In the third phase, during actual invasion conditions, there was to be a general evacuation by road. These rules were to apply to all hospitals within twenty miles of the coast.

A number of others, situated further inland, were subject to a rather less stringent three-phase plan: sixty per cent bed occupancy during phase one and forty per cent during phase two, but in actual invasion conditions all their patients were to be evacuated. These hospitals included Addenbrookes, the County Infirmary and the wartime hospital at Leys School in Cambridge; the West Suffolk General at Bury St Edmunds; Black Notley Hospital, near Braintree; White Lodge at Newmarket; Hartismere House at Eye; St Audry's at Melton; and Attleborough Emergency Hospital.

The Home Defence Committee also prepared an Order in Council which

The men and women who bore the brunt of air attacks on East Anglian towns—the staff of the Curriers Lane first aid post at Ipswich. *Mrs F. Holden, via Gordon Kinsey*

would have empowered the Eastern Regional Commissioner, Sir Will Spens, after consultation with the military authorities, to declare any part of his region an "operational area", within which all labour could be directed to perform whatever duties the military authorities decreed[(5)].

Another part of the detailed plans provided for the handling of enemy soldiers who were taken prisoner. The general idea was that they would be transferred quickly from the fighting area into "command cages" in the Newmarket and Dunstable areas and then moved westward, in stages, into a group of camps around Ludlow and Oswestry, where there would be accommodation for 20,000 to 30,000 of them[(6)].

The military authorities began the year with a new appreciation of the invasion possibilities, in a document submitted to the Invasion Staffs Committee at their meeting on 11th January[(7)]. The greatest danger was believed to be in Kent and Sussex, but the whole coastal area from the Wash round to Weymouth was considered to be vulnerable. The Germans were credited with an ability to land nine armoured divisions (each with 400 tanks) and twenty-three infantry divisions. Thirty thousand airborne troops might arrive in gliders on the first day of an invasion, it was conjectured, and 55,000 more during the following three days. From this assessment, the military authorities made the following deductions:

(a) The front open to the enemy is so great that only a minimum of troops will be held on the coast to deal with a seaborne attack, or inland to deal with an airborne attack. Behind these there must be sufficient reserves capable of staging rapid counter offensives against both enemy infantry and armoured formations.
(b) Outpost lines will be stronger between the Wash and Weymouth.
(c) Special protection is required for Fighter Command.
(d) Ground suitable for the landing of airborne troops will need special watching.

When the essence of this appreciation had been made known to the Regional Commissioner in Cambridge, he circulated on 23rd January guidance to the Parish Invasion Committees which had been set up during the previous year. "Do not persuade yourselves, and do not allow others to persuade you, that invasion is improbable", he declared. "It is very much more probable than not that at some point before the end of the war Hitler will see fit to order invasion. When invasion does take place, it is practically certain that there will be a heavy attack in East Anglia."

The Regional Commissioner reiterated what might happen if the enemy gained a bridgehead: emergency rations would be distributed from special stores when necessary; all drinking water might have to be boiled; because there would be heavy bombing, families should dig themselves (when so advised) slit trenches about 15 feet away from their homes; and everyone should sleep with a gas mask beside the bed.

The Regional Commissioner, however, resisted a proposal to reimpose in February the restrictions on visiting the coastal belt which had been removed in

November, 1941, when winter weather ruled out any possibility of invasion. On 20th January, Sir Will Spens wrote to the Home Office:

> The Regional Commissioner considers it important that the reimposition of the visitors' ban should be postponed so long as the competent military authorities consider that there is no immediate risk of invasion. He is satisfied that real harm would be done to morale by the imposition of restrictions to meet a situation which many are aware is not regarded as probable in the near future[8].

In the event, the ban was not reimposed until 15th April.

The discussions and decisions which occupied so much of the time and attention of civil and military authorities in the early part of 1942 were, of course, highly secret. What was released to the public, mainly in the form of exhortations and warnings, did not always produce the desired response, as is clear from an entry in Mrs Sarah Williams' diary after a night during which she had heard "lots of bangs":

> Lots of Sheringham people got up and went down to the prom. so that they should have a good view of the invasion[9].

In fact, what she had heard was German aircraft bombing a convoy offshore.

What was really expected of the public in the event of an invasion was explained at a meeting of Cambridge Town Council by the chairman of its Civil Defence Committee, Alderman W. L. Briggs. Every family, he said, should have made certain clear decisions:

> Unless they have duties elsewhere, they should have fixed where they will take cover and stop there whilst the cover remains, or until they are told to move. They should advise their warden of their arrangement, and have gas mask and some first aid material with them. Mutual arrangements with another household should have been settled whereby either will accommodate the other family if either family becomes homeless.
> It should be remembered that many lives may be saved from shock — a certain result of bombing — by supplying warmth and hot drinks, with plenty of sugar.

Everyone should know the location of their nearest "rest centre" (there were sixteen in the borough, with twenty-nine "reserve alternatives"), where they would find staff to help and direct them, and supplies of food, clothing, and some bedding. Emergency broadcasts on the radio and local public announcements by loudspeaker vans would be made as necessary, and the statement ended:

> We depend upon each individual to follow instructions issued . . . Attention should be given to authorized persons only and no rumour should be accepted or acted upon until officially confirmed.

Behind this sort of public statement lay a vast amount of detailed planning work by the local authorities. In each of the "nodal point" towns a local Invasion Committee produced early in the year a "combined military and civil defence scheme" dealing with invasion possibilities. The 28-page printed document drawn up in Bury St Edmunds, one of the "nodal points" in East Anglia, was signed by the Mayor, Alderman E. L. D. Lake, and the Senior Military Representative, Lieutenant-Colonel H. R. Gadd. Numbered copies were issued to the key individuals involved. It read, in part:

> ENEMY'S PLAN — The enemy will probably land at various places on the Suffolk coast, and Aldeburgh can be taken as their centre. He will attempt to establish a bridge-head and then push on with all possible speed towards London. As soon as the enemy has aircraft to spare he will carry out extensive bombing of Centres of Communication, of which Bury St Edmunds will be one. Fifth Column and Sabotage activities may also be expected. This part of East Anglia is ideal for airborne attack, but there are so many more important objectives that it is unlikely that Bury St Edmunds will be the object of any airborne attack until the invasion has well advanced.
> Deductions from the enemy plan, therefore, are that Bury St Edmunds may expect a heavy attack on the east face about 48 hours after the invasion has commenced, but that the other faces would only have to deal with infiltration parties until such time as it is necessary for the enemy to capture the town for its communication facilities. This might be expected about the fourth day.
> OUR MILITARY PLAN — The general military plan is that there must be no withdrawal and such enemy forces as penetrate will be counter-attacked. Its success depends on the rapid movement of large forces and it is imperative that roads required for their movement are kept open and clear of refugees.
> MAIN TASKS — The main combined military and civil tasks may, therefore, be (a) to keep open the roads detailed later in this order; (b) to defend the town to the last man and last round . . .

The document then went on to detail the resources available: 700 soldiers in training locally, 400 men of the Home Guard, 50 from the Observer Corps, 400 ARP personnel, 70 from the NFS, 42 regular policemen and 77 "specials", 2,000 firewatchers, 30 Red Cross workers, and 200 voluntary workers at eight rest centres. Thus everyone who already had a specific role in the town was counted into the "last ditch" resistance force. There was also a "Reserve of Able-bodied persons":

> Lists are prepared of both men and women. At present, a reserve of 400 men and 150 women has been earmarked.

The document laid it down that if communications with the outside world were cut, or if hostilities began in the neighbourhood, full control would be assumed by the local military commander, "in accordance with common law". In bold type it then added:

> In the event of attack, it is the duty of the local Military Commander, aided by the civil authorities, to hold the town until relieved, completely regardless of the cost to civil and military life and property.

The Invasion Committee headquarters were at the Borough Offices on Angel Hill, with an alternative held in reserve at the Cricketers' Arms in King's Road. The military commander's headquarters were at Gibraltar Barracks, with a reserve at the Old Barracks in King's Road. An observation post was established on the top of the brewhouse at Greene King's brewery in Westgate Street.

The defence system was based on a series of strongpoints at the entrances to the town. These were connected by a series of posts, lightly held, looking out on the anti-tank ditch which surrounded the whole town. In the inner area, road blocks were erected, intended to deny to the enemy entry to the centre, if he succeeded in penetrating the strongpoints further out.

It was decreed that inhabitants of the borough whose homes were outside the anti-tank ditch would be allowed to come in across it on production of their identity cards, but that refugees from elsewhere would not be allowed in.

The document stated that there would be twenty-five centres for distribution of food, and that stocks held in the town would be sufficient for fourteen days. It detailed the arrangements for water rationing and indicated how milk would be provided:

> Arrangements have been made to bring in herds of cows, which have been earmarked, and public-house yards have been reconnoitred for their accommodation. These number approximately 100 cows in all . . .

All kinds of vehicles were adapted for civil defence purposes. This mobile first aid post at Ipswich was equipped with a former bus. *Gordon Kinsey*

"The main responsibility for reporting night-time fires due to enemy action to the National Fire Service will be transferred to the Fire Guard," says this memorandum issued by the Ministry of Home Security explaining the new Fire Guard scheme.

F. P. Leaflet No. 6

ISSUED BY THE MINISTRY  OF HOME SECURITY

THE FIRE GUARD AND THE NATIONAL FIRE SERVICE: WORKING ARRANGEMENTS.

MEMORANDUM ISSUED BY THE MINISTRY OF HOME SECURITY

for the guidance of local authorities in England and Wales, and appropriate authorities under the Fire Prevention (Business Premises) (No. 2) Order, 1941, and the Fire Prevention (Government Premises) Order, 1942.

1. The Home Secretary and Minister of Home Security has had under review the methods now followed for meeting incendiary attack by the enemy. He has decided that the duties with which the Fire Guard is at present charged, namely:—

(i) the duty of detecting and combating outbreaks of fire caused by hostile attack, and

(ii) the duty of summoning any necessary assistance,

shall be made the basis of a new plan to secure that the most effective use is made of the resources of the Fire Guard and the N.F.S. in areas prescribed under the Fire Prevention Orders. Under this plan close working arrangements will be established between the Fire Guard and the N.F.S. and the main responsibility for reporting night-time fires due to enemy action to the N.F.S. will be transferred to the Fire Guard.

2. The part of the new plan providing for the summoning of N.F.S. assistance by the Fire Guard will apply only during "alerts" in the period from half an hour before until half an hour after blackout (for further details *see* paragraph 10). At other times the present methods for summoning N.F.S. assistance to fires will be continued.

3. The new plan is simple in principle, but before it can be applied to any district it will need a great deal of careful preparation, and the Fire Guard will have to be trained in its new duties. Regional Commissioners will determine in what local authorities' areas, or in what parts of such areas the preparations for the plan shall be first put in hand, and the date on which it shall be brought into operation in each area. In due course the new plan will be introduced into all areas prescribed under the Fire Prevention Orders.

4. The unit area for the purpose of the plan will be the area served by each N.F.S. fire station. Each fire station ground will be divided into a number of Fire Guard sectors, each of which for Fire Guard operations will be under

There were directions, also, about medical arrangements, burial of the dead, and dissemination of information(10).

The German preoccupation with the Russian front and in North Africa encouraged the authorities in Britain to tighten up various aspects of Civil Defence during the early weeks of 1942. Changes were made in training personnel, and steps were taken to increase numbers.

Particular attention was given to the firefighting arrangements. In Cambridge — which provides an example of what happened in every town — the Chief Air Raid Warden issued a memorandum in January defining the future structure and responsibilities of the Fire Guard Organization. It required all business premises, offices and shops to submit for approval their arrangements to prevent outbreaks of fire during air raids. Their employees were required to turn out at night to provide this protection, and this was considered to be voluntary duty, so that only a subsistence allowance of 4s 6d per night would be payable. If firms had insufficient personnel, they could seek reinforcement from a pool.

In most residential streets volunteer parties were already providing this sort of cover, but the whole system was now overhauled and gaps were filled. Cambridge was divided into three districts, and each district into sectors. A Head Fire Guard was appointed for each district, and a Senior Fire Guard for each sector. They reported to a Fire Guard Staff Officer with offices in the Guildhall, who was responsible to the Chief Air Raid Warden. These were paid personnel, but the general idea was that the whole Fire Guard operation should be performed by volunteers.

They were asked to perform duties "for not less than 48 hours per month, if called upon". Street parties were to consist of three persons. They were to be on duty together during the periods of blackout; but when no "alert" had been sounded by the air raid sirens only one of the three was required to remain awake and fully dressed. Women were exempt from the obligation, but were welcomed when they volunteered.

Other important innovations at this time included a scheme of mutual assistance between the Civil Defence services and the Home Guard, and a much greater flexibility in the Civil Defence organization as a whole. Whereas in the early part of the war there had been specialization, so that men trained as rescue parties or in ambulance work were expected only to carry out the duties for which their training had qualified them, now what was wanted were all-round civil defence men able to deal with any situation likely to arise.

Competition for manpower was acute, and difficulties often arose. The Norfolk ARP Emergency Committee made representations early in 1942 "regarding the indiscriminate recruitment of Home Guards from the ARP personnel, which, if persisted in, would render the ARP services incapable of affording any assistance to the civil population under invasion conditions". The Regional Commissioner, however, ruled that ARP volunteers should be encouraged to join the Home Guard. A compromise arrangement was arrived at; the ARP men could join a Home Guard Reserve, in addition to their Civil Defence work, and they would be called out only in the event of fighting in the immediate vicinity of their towns and villages.

In the course of the reassessment of the Civil Defence organization, it became clear that it had many shortcomings and every effort was made to put things right. Many of the personnel had not yet been issued with the standard uniform of serge battledress and beret. In Norfolk they began to get them early in 1942, but in Cambridge it was July before the town's Civil Defence Committee decided that wardens and those in the casualty service should have the uniforms — but not those in the rescue and decontamination squads.

The emergency water supplies which were stored in huge tanks at strategic points in each built-up area were found to be inadequate in many towns. Cambridge Corporation hastened to install twelve static water tanks in various parts of the borough, which between them provided an emergency reserve of 560,000 gallons. Ipswich was advertising for tenders to provide nine static water tanks, of capacities ranging from 20,000 to 100,000 gallons, as late as October, 1942. This was a serious business, but Cambridge undergraduates contrived to hit a lighter note when, one summer night, they carried four canoes and a punt from the river Cam and put them afloat on a reservoir on the lawn in front of King's College Chapel.

There had been delays in providing shelters for the public. The Anderson (outdoor) and Morrison (indoor) shelters designed for family use had been coming through only erratically, and more were still needed in most towns.

A great deal needed to be done to improve the street shelters. Cambridge had drawn up a plan for 268 surface shelters in various parts of the town, to accommodate 3,216 people. It had gone to the Regional Commissioner's office, where a "technical adviser" had made so many modifications to it that when it came back five months later, in March, 1942, the council's officers declared they would have to start again from scratch. The new scheme provided for more shelters, but smaller ones: 358 buildings, to accommodate 4,296 people. Each shelter measured 8 feet 6 inches by 6 feet 6 inches inside; there was no lighting and no sanitary provision. At night, each shelter was intended to sleep nine adults. Eventually, Cambridge provided shelter accommodation of one kind or another for 26,000 people — for about three in ten of its population.

Even towards the end of 1942 the shelter question was proving controversial. There were complaints at a Norfolk County Council meeting in October that many communal shelters lacked seats and that the Ministry had refused to supply timber for the purpose. One official declared that some of the communal shelters, which had been hurriedly built at the beginning of the war *without cement*, were unsafe — but he added that most of those had been demolished.

There was some public agitation during 1941 in favour of deep underground shelters. The official policy favoured dispersal of the public over a number of small shelters on or near the surface; these provided, at reasonable cost in labour and materials, good protection against blast, but little or none in the event of a direct hit.

The argument broke surface in Ipswich, and continued well into 1942. The town's lively, often provocative, Member of Parliament, Mr Richard Stokes (who was also chairman of Ransomes and Rapier, the Ipswich engineering firm) proposed a deep shelter tunnelled under Alexandra Park to provide sleeping accommodation for 672 people. He pressed this scheme with characteristic vigour and the borough engineer's department prepared plans. A tunnel was proposed, 1,000 yards long, lined with sectional concrete rings, giving an internal diameter of seven feet. But 400 feet of the tunnel would have been simply the approach gradients, leaving only 400 feet with overhead cover of 50 feet or more. The cost was estimated at £24,000 — £36 per person, which was far more than the surface shelters cost.

At about the time the MP made this proposal, Ipswich was winding up its shelter programme. The council claimed in June, 1941, that it had provided cover for ninety-five per cent of the population. There were over ten thousand bunks in school shelters, over a thousand Morrison shelters had been distributed, and the remaining five per cent of the public would be safeguarded, according to officials, when a programme of upgrading Anderson shelters and basements and trenches was completed.

Richard Stokes was not satisfied with this. He pressed the Ipswich Emergency Committee to submit the tunnel plan to the Regional Commissioner's office, and he asked questions in the Commons. The officials involved were not happy. The Town Clerk sent the plans forward to Cambridge under cover of a formal submission, but also included a private and confidential letter to the Regional Commissioner. Regional technical experts rubbished the plan; they said it was uneconomic and would require the type of skilled labour that was in very short supply. One civil servant minuted: "This scheme is almost as hare-brained as the one which formed the subject of [an earlier] Parliamentary Question. It is clear from the Town Clerk's confidential letter that it is being forced on a reluctant Emergency Committee by Mr Stokes, MP"[11]. The tunnel was never built.

With detailed anti-invasion plans committed to paper, and the Civil Defence services being rapidly reorganized, there took place a series of full-scale "invasion

Men of a battalion of the Queen's Royal Regiment taking part in a battle exercise at Shrublands Park, near Ipswich, round up some of the "enemy" wearing captured German uniforms. The exercise included simulated street fighting and the capture of a railway station. *Imperial War Museum*

At an exercise near Bury St Edmunds on 27th June every effort was made to simulate actual warfare conditions. The 6-inch howitzer in action during a full-scale artillery barrage was firing live ammunition.
Imperial War Museum

exercises" in every town in the Eastern Counties, involving the armed services, the Home Guard, every branch of Civil Defence, the police, and such public services as transport, communications and hospitals.

Great ingenuity was shown in trying to simulate the conditions of an actual invasion. The services provided "umpires" who assessed the way the battle was going, and light explosives and flares were used to represent bombs and artillery and mortar fire. As the fighting developed, the umpire-observers decided the probable consequences of each move, ruled what casualties there were on each side, which positions had been overrun, how many prisoners had been taken, and so on.

In a typical exercise of this kind British troops, playing the role of an invading army, would advance on the target town and probe its defences, where the Home Guard would have taken up battle stations. After this initial phase the "German" commander, finding the town to be strongly held, would send in dive-bombers — RAF planes would roar spectacularly overhead. At this stage the Civil Defence services would be brought into action to extinguish fire bombs, carry out rescue work, repair public services, and keep open the roads. The bombers would continue their attack until a full-scale assault by "German" infantry, supported by field guns, began. Probably the umpires would then rule that the attackers had overcome the defences, and the mock-fighting would continue through the streets of the town. British reinforcements might then arrive, the scales would be turned, and the "cease fire" would sound as the invaders fell back. Everyone, it was hoped, would go home, or back to camp, having learned a great deal about the dangers, but having become more confident about their ability to meet them.

Such an exercise was staged in Cambridge in May over a whole weekend and the *Cambridge Daily News* published information about it. The supposition was that the enemy had come ashore on the East Coast and was advancing on the

"ANGEL" EXERCISE.

ACTION TAKEN BY THE CHAIRMAN OF BURY ST. EDMUND'S INVASION COMMITTEE.

November 19th.

Hours.

09.00 Received "Stand-to" instructions from Military Commander. Police instructed to display Notices.

09.10 Bury St. Edmund's Invasion Committee summoned, arranged rota of attendance, and control taken of the civil population.

09.20 Bury St. Edmund's Information Bureau instructed to function.

09.30 Bury St. Edmund's Information Bureau instructed to display Notices on Notice Boards, charging the civil population to remain indoors, and to prevent the spreading of rumours. West Suffolk Police, Bury St. Edmunds instructed to arrange for the dissemination of the public.

12.00 Bury St. Edmunds Information Bureau instructed to display two sets of Notices on Official Notice Boards and by Loud Speaker, notifying the public what has happened, and urging the population [illegible]

A document signed by the Mayor of Bury St Edmunds, Mr E. D. L. Lake, relating to an invasion exercise in November.

university town, which was under heavy aerial bombardment. The public was told to stay indoors and not to be anxious if, during the night, they heard "unusual sounds", as of bombs and guns and planes overhead. If they had to go out, they should carry their masks, "in case gas is used".

Tear gas was, in fact, released, and some simulated dive-bombing took place. The exercise reached its climax between 11 pm on the Saturday and 11 am on Sunday. The "enemy" — some of them actually wearing captured German uniforms — tried to force their way into the town from two different directions. The umpires ruled that, after a great deal of street fighting, some strongpoints were captured, but at heavy cost.

In the town centre infiltrators captured some important buildings. Others, including four armed with tommy guns who tried to capture the borough police station, failed in their efforts and were "dealt with". At one stage three "prisoners" — two in the uniform of German paratroopers and the third dressed in Luftwaffe uniform — were observed being escorted down Milton Road by a squad of the Home Guard. A "fifth column" was introduced into the exercise; police and military rounded up most of them, but one woman, allowed to cross a guarded bridge after producing her identity card, suddenly swung round and "destroyed the bridge with a bomb" before she was "shot". During the course of these proceedings, several colleges were presumed to have been hit, including King's College Chapel, so that the Civil Defence units were given plenty to do.

At the conclusion of a similar exercise in Thetford, the umpires ruled that the "enemy" had penetrated the town's defences, occupied the town hall and control centre, and captured the Mayor, Mr H. W. Watling. It was afterwards announced that, from a military point of view, the exercise had been a complete success. Whether the Mayor and townfolk felt greater security and confidence was not disclosed! When King's Lynn staged its exercise, again the "enemy" captured most of the town, overcoming a fierce defence by the Home Guard, but this time the town hall was not captured. At Ipswich, the terse conclusion was that "all went well".

That was not always the case. After an anti-invasion exercise at Fakenham in January, the *Eastern Daily Press*, in an editorial comment, observed:

> The general public's response to the requests for aid — which were made on leaflets distributed several days beforehand — was disappointing . . . As a result of the poor response, the Invasion Committee were not in a position during the test to supply the personnel and equipment which were called for by the conditions. The attitude of apparently many people was the familiar one that, while they would not take part in what they regarded as play-acting, they would help if "the real thing" happened. Such an attitude cannot be too strongly condemned.

When Cambridge Civil Defence services staged a more limited exercise later in the year a spate of letters in the correspondence columns of the local paper suggested that mock casualties had lain around in the streets waiting to be dealt with for so long that some had got up and gone home.

Communities on the coast had an extra element to their defence exercises: they had to rehearse all the activities that would be necessary to repulse landings from the sea. Harwich organized a major exercise during April, and it lacked nothing; there were attacks from the sea, attacks by parachutists, gas attacks, bombing from the air. Every element of the Civil Defence forces was brought into action to deal with supposed circumstances which included roads blocked by bomb craters, victims buried under debris, gas and water mains fractured, electricity supplies cut, wounded requiring emergency treatment, homeless to be accommodated, confused public to be informed and instructed.

There were regular drills of a more limited kind, to test particular sections of the defence organization. The Civil Defence authorities in Great Yarmouth released tear gas in the streets on a couple of occasions, to test civilian readiness, and several elderly shoppers were minor casualties as crowds of people, caught without their respirators, dived into the nearest shops or offices. Clouds of gas billowed up the narrow Rows and a lot of eyes were left streaming painfully.

Norwich staged a firefighting exercise early in March just a few weeks before the city was hit by genuine catastrophe. The exercise extended over two nights and the intervening day. It was imagined that there were fifty different fires blazing simultaneously in the heart of the city, involving shoe factories, laundries, a brewery and scores of other business premises. Fourteen hundred firefighters took part, with fifty fire pumps, including fire floats on the Wensum.

Another example of a limited exercise was that conducted by the Cambridge Police, when the whole of the regular force was withdrawn from all duties for twenty-four hours of a busy weekend so that the Specials could take complete control of the police service in the town. Everything went smoothly.

The regular services were, of course, undergoing continuous training all over the Eastern Counties, but from time to time there were special large-scale exercises which representatives of the press were permitted to watch, as it was thought that publicity would be good for morale. One such took place at the end of March, on lonely stretches of heathland near Thetford, when the RAF demonstrated the capabilities of its fighter and bomber aircraft, gliders and paratroops. Eight thousand troops were involved and fifteen types of aircraft were put into the air at the same time.

Hurricane fighters swooped on lorries and tanks on the ground, each with a dozen Browning guns or a quartet of cannon blazing; American-built Douglas

Glider pilots under training with the General Aircraft Hotspur gliders on which they learnt to fly. Although built to carry a pilot and seven troops, the Hotspur was never used operationally; much larger gliders were employed for the invasion of Europe. *East Anglian Daily Times*

A low-flying Bristol Blenheim IV passes in front of watching army and Home Guard officers and NCOs during a demonstration near Thetford. More than 3,000 of these aircraft were built, but by 1942 Blenheims were being superseded by newer types of bomber, including the de Havilland Mosquito, which entered service with Bomber Command in May.
East Anglian Daily Times

Boston bombers made low-level attacks on a brigade headquarters, showering down hundreds of anti-personnel and anti-tank bombs, and some heavier ones. Single-engined Hawker Hector biplanes towed gliders carrying the newly-formed Airborne Division troops, which staged landings on rough ground. After the gliders came a cloud of paratroops, jumping from Whitleys behind a massive smoke-screen spread by other, low-flying aircraft. When the airborne troops had landed, they were fired on — "but by expert shots, making the nearest misses they dare", the *East Anglian Daily Times* correspondent wrote. The intention was to give the men an impression of "just what it feels like to face the reality of battle".

Ammunition was still in short supply at this time, but in some of these service exercises the public felt it was being used all too freely. Some villagers were afraid to leave their cottages, it was reported to the East Suffolk Standing Joint Committee in May. The committee's chairman, Lord Cranworth, observed: "The idea is to toughen the troops, but we don't want women and children toughened in that way". The Chief Constable made representations to the military. At about the same time, a Chelmsford women who stepped outside her front door to watch a Home Guard exercise in the street was killed when they lit a "smoke bomb" and it exploded, and a Wickham Market haulage contractor delivering cattle to a marshland area was shot dead.

CHAPTER FOUR

The Battered Coast

A LARGE proportion of the population of the East Coast towns had left their homes, many of which had been damaged by bombs. Visitors were not permitted to come into the coastal belt. None but official vehicles were permitted in the streets. Many of the shops, the small hotels and the bed and breakfast residences were boarded up. Some of the towns, particularly Harwich and Lowestoft, had become naval bases rather than civilian communities.

But the local authorities remained in office, and did their best to keep some sort of basic structure in place. With so many properties unoccupied, they had had to grapple with severe financial problems since early in the war. Great Yarmouth Borough Council began 1942 with another delegation to Whitehall to seek assistance so that the burden on the remaining ratepayers could be relieved. The delegation came away empty-handed. The council fixed a new rate of 18s in the pound, and the chairman of the Finance Committee remarked bitterly: "This must leave the impression that the last drop of blood is to be squeezed out of those authorities that have suffered by enemy action."

All of the coastal authorities were in similar difficulties. Felixstowe UDC, which on the eve of the war had had a general rate fund surplus of £13,865, found itself £2,986 in debt by March, 1942. Revenue from rates was down by thirty-five per cent, and income from other sources — mainly concerned with its peacetime holiday facilities — had dropped by sixty per cent, whereas the council's expenses had fallen by only twenty-eight per cent. The Ministry of Health had made a loan of £5,000 and repayment was due. If the loan was repaid, however, the council was going to be £7,100 overdrawn at the bank, and it had overdraft facilities for only £4,000. It was agreed that the treasurer would have to "nurse the accounts" for a little while, and somehow contrive to get through.

Despite such problems, morale was better than in some safer inland areas. The common suffering which German bombs had brought to these communities had had a unifying effect on the people who remained. One example of this, in Great Yarmouth, was the agreement of the three main political parties, for the first time ever, to hold a joint public meeting to hear their Member of Parliament, Mr P. W. Jewson, report on the war and proceedings in the Commons. "It was more than a token unity", the local newspaper reported. "The vote of confidence in the government was carried without a single dissentient."

Virtually all the East Coast ports were busy naval bases. Lowestoft had several wartime identities: as HMS *Europa*, it was headquarters of the Royal Naval Patrol Service; as HMS *Martello* it was the shore establishment of a minesweeping flotilla;

as HMS *Mantis* it was a base for Light Coastal Forces, motor torpedo boats and similar craft. Harwich was more often referred to as HMS *Badger* — its naval establishment — than by its peacetime name. Similarly, Felixstowe was HMS *Beehive*, a base for the motor torpedo boats which each night sailed out to attack enemy convoys off the Belgian and Dutch coasts. Brightlingsea was HMS *Nemo*, a base for minesweepers and lookout trawlers and a naval repair yard; Ipswich Docks had become HMS *Bunting*, another base for minesweepers.

Every estuary, almost every creek, it seemed, was home to a fighting ship of some kind. The yachts of peacetime had been provided with armament and assigned a role beside the minesweepers, minelayers, motor torpedo boats and air-sea rescue launches.

The minesweeping fleet had been built up steadily. At Parkeston Quay, for

Recovering the otter board, which holds the sweep away from the ship, on a minesweeper operating off the east coast. This vessel had in peacetime been a Yarmouth herring drifter; several such vessels were employed in searching for new types of mine so that the experts could design suitable countermeasures. *East Anglian Daily Times*

A coastal convoy under way, with kite balloons flying overhead to deter low-level bombers. These balloons, smaller brethren of the barrage balloons employed to protect British towns and cities, were taken out to the ships requiring them by former herring drifters at such places as Southend.
East Anglian Daily Times

example, there had been only three converted trawlers at the outbreak of war; by the beginning of 1942 there were two flotillas of minesweepers. A new underground combined operations room, plot and communications centre had just been completed and brought into commission.

In these towns, most of the waterfront was strictly out of bounds to all but service personnel, who had their own clubs and canteens and sometimes their own cinemas and theatres. The ratings and Wrens dominated the scene. At the celebration of United Nations Day in Harwich in April, it was an RNVR chaplain who conducted the service and a rear-admiral who read the lesson, and there was a dominant splash of blue among the two thousand who crowded the sports ground at Dovercourt. At other times, Harwich and the other naval towns were conscious of the visitors in less happy circumstances; two local authors have recounted that "it was generally believed that the most troublesome, and those who most frequently drew attention to their uniform and demanded special privileges, were those who never went to sea"[1].

The East Coast convoys — as well as all the traffic in the Thames — were controlled from Southend Pier. A. P. Herbert described the mouth of the Thames at this time as "the Clapham Junction of Eastern England, and this old Pier as the busy signal box, station master and traffic manager combined"[2]. The Naval Control Service station there issued information and instructions to the commodores of convoys, masters of merchant ships, naval officers in charge of escorts and all kinds of craft, Trinity House pilots, and representatives of all seafaring activities.

The Pier Solarium was used as the Convoy School. "Here, among the painted cut-outs, the cardboard palms and banana trees, under the blue Oriental sky and the tropical jungle blossoms, the cold and anxious, but undaunted masters met the Navy and received their orders," wrote Herbert. "Here came together more Merchant Masters than have ever come together in one place in all the world."

The naval men were not alone on the pier. In the glass-walled sun-trap at the pierhead, RAF men repaired and filled with gas the kite balloons with which, by 1942, all ships were given some protection against dive-bombers as they sailed in convoy. The Army were there, too; a machine-gun post and pill-boxes, and a store of depth charges and demolition charges for use in emergencies. The NFS had a presence, and the Observer Corps, and Trinity House, and Lloyd's, with its signal station. There was a mail office and a transport office, and a cafe and food stores, where a lady universally known as Mona presided.

At the peak, there were thirty-six small craft — tugs, drifters and trawlers — in the Southend Pier Fleet. Two East Anglian drifters, *Ocean Lover* and *Lord Anson*, were used throughout the war to pass orders and papers between the ships at anchor and the pier authorities. There were also salvage tugs, which were called on to do their work almost every week. The waters around the pierhead were a constant bustle of craft. And all day and all night the pier electric railway carried supplies and personnel, and at times sailors who were sick or wounded, or survivors of disasters at sea.

New dangers faced the East Coast convoys in 1942. After a quiet period, German E-boats* reappeared in force, and German aircraft laid extensive minefields off the coast. These mines were of a new design and could be laid in deeper water than the earlier types, so that the British minesweepers now had to sweep over a wider area. But the threat to convoys was, in fact, diminishing, because the defensive methods had improved, too. Airfields in East Anglia sent fighters to help protect the shipping lanes, and there was better co-ordination with these shore-based aircraft[3].

As the year progressed, the minesweeping fleet was further enlarged and

*The term E-boat was a British name, the E standing for enemy, for the fast, well-armed motor torpedo boats known to the Germans as S-boote or Schnell-boote (fast boats).

improved, with new vessels coming not only from British yards but also from the USA. At Brightlingsea, an Experimental Minesweeping Flotilla — a branch of HMS *Vernon* (the Portsmouth mine school) — was devising and testing new ways of sweeping German magnetic mines, which had a "reversed polarity" setting to counter the Royal Navy's "degaussing" techniques. A German bomber which crashed in Clacton in April, 1940, was carrying one of these mines, which did not explode; it was taken to Brightlingsea, and helped greatly in the research going on there[(4)].

The East Coast naval bases were part of the Nore Command, which by mid-1942 had six flotillas of MGBs (motor gunboats), two of MTBs (motor torpedo boats), and eight of MLs (motor launches). Each flotilla, at full strength, had eight vessels. A patrol line of MGBs and MLs was maintained about eight miles to seaward of the shipping lanes. During much of 1942 the patrols depended on visual sighting or on listening devices to detect the approach of the enemy, but with assistance from shore radar stations which gave them information by short-wave radio. By the autumn, however, the Coastal Forces craft and the convoy escort vessels had been equipped with radar and were able to keep a much more effective lookout.

As an additional deterrent to minelaying planes, two forts, the Roughs Fort and Sunk Head Fort, were positioned some miles off Harwich during the summer. Huge steel and concrete structures standing up from the sea, these forts had naval crews manning AA guns.

The position began to change significantly; now it was the RAF which was doing most of the minelaying in the North Sea. But the German planes and E-boats kept coming, and during January and February the mines they laid sank or damaged thirteen small ships and two destroyers, HMS *Vimiera* and HMS *Whitshed*.

In mid-February six destroyers based at Harwich and normally used for convoy escort, and also fighter planes from several East Anglian airfields, joined in the efforts to prevent the German battleships *Scharnhorst and Gneisenau* sailing from Brest to their home ports in the Baltic. They were no more successful than other British forces committed to this task. But at about the same time destroyers had a success when they caught a force of E-boats mining the waters off Yarmouth and sank three of them, taking seventeen German sailors as prisoners-of-war.

Over the third weekend of March a fierce naval battle was fought off the East Coast. The engagement began in the Channel on the Saturday morning, when a force of German E-boats attacked an Allied convoy; it continued through the night and well into Sunday, moving from the Channel to off the Norfolk coast. Destroyers and gunboats sank several of the attackers, and on the Sunday morning Spitfires joined in and damaged some others. But one British destroyer, HMS *Vortigern*, was lost in the battle; although the Sheringham and Cromer No 1 lifeboats went out while the fighting was still going on and although they searched

Gun crews on the alert for enemy ships and aircraft, a naval motor launch patrols in "E-boat Alley" off the East Anglian coast. The MLs were built in a number of boatyards in Essex and Suffolk and on the Broads. *East Anglian Daily Times*

for eight hours, they picked up only twelve men from the destroyer, and all were dead.

There were many fierce close-range attacks by the Germans in the so-called "E-boat alley" off Great Yarmouth during the summer months, and in mid-December E-boats penetrated the patrol line undetected and sank five ships in one convoy. None of these setbacks undermined the general belief that the Coastal Forces and the minesweepers had the advantage and that a turning point had been reached. About thirty-six ships sailed in convoy between the Thames and the Forth on six days out of every seven, and when the year ended twenty-one had been lost[(5)].

Much of the North Sea traffic during 1942 was of coal from the North-east. Part of the preparation for the coming invasion of Europe was the creation of vast stockpiles of coal in southern England, and every two days a convoy of about twenty-five colliers sailed along the East Anglian coast, moving southward. It was intended to have about ten months' supplies in hand in the south. There must be no other shipping in the Channel, it was planned, while an invasion and supply fleet was crossing to France.

The war at sea gave no respite to the East Coast lifeboat crews. Their operations called for meticulous planning on shore, as well as courage at sea. A good example of this is provided by the rescue of six Polish airmen by the Sheringham lifeboat, the *Foresters Centenary*, in October, 1942. A Coastguard reported to the Sheringham RNLI secretary that he could see men on a crashed aircraft that was sinking slowly. The secretary sent his daughter to the winchman's house to warn him to be ready to launch. Then, without delaying to get up from his bed to dress, he began telephoning. First he called the coxswain, then the two motor mechanics, then the messengers who cycled around to summon the other crew members. After that, he rang the officer in command of a company of soldiers

On the bridge of a British destroyer on convoy escort duty. Some hard battles were fought with E-boats, and one destroyer, HMS *Vortigern*, was sunk by torpedo off Cromer during a battle on 15th March. *East Anglian Daily Times*

standing by to act as launchers. They had to drag the boat, on her carriage, out of her house and across a sandbank over which the sea was flowing. Some of the launchers were almost up to their necks in water as they pushed and pulled the lifeboat from the carriage. Yet within fifteen minutes it was rescuing the six airmen from a dinghy, and after a further fifteen minutes it landed them on the beach. Meanwhile, the secretary went on telephoning; arranging for two doctors to go to the boathouse, for an ambulance to stand by on the cliff-top, and for his neighbours to have hot baths ready for the rescued men. In twenty-six minutes he sent or received twenty-one telephone messages.

The German attacks on convoys often took place so close to the coast that the noise of battle was clearly heard on shore, and fears were sometimes raised — particularly at night — that invading forces might be trying to land. The military authorities had assessed the greater danger now to be on the South Coast, and had decided to hold most of the defending forces well back from the East Coast.

There were extensive beach defences: miles of steel scaffolding and barbed wire in the shallow water, minefields laid on beaches, strategically-placed pillboxes. But otherwise the East Coast was not heavily protected.

During January the War Office sent a high-ranking officer to Harwich and the area around to inspect the situation, and he was not impressed with what he saw. He found the high ground at Ramsey, overlooking Harwich, unoccupied, although he thought it "a likely landing place for parachutists". The defended localities around Harwich were good, but the anti-aircraft guns were sited outside the perimeter "and the units seem to have done little or nothing towards turning the area into a good defensive locality". The defences of Shotley were "very indifferently constructed and wired. The sailors seem keen enough to get on with the job, but they obviously have had no advice on how to set about it". His other comments included:

> The Felixstowe front is very thin, and parachutists working from the rear would have a good chance of getting in . . .
> Ipswich itself is a very important place and an extremely difficult one to defend. The Home Guard in this area, and in fact in the whole of the area visited, seem to be rather weak and ineffective, but steps are being taken to get them to take over portions of the seafront . . .[6]

The same report lists the forces deployed for the defence of Harwich, as at 15th January, and reveals how thin on the ground they were. As defence against air attack, there was a ring of balloons trailing a barrage of cables, in charge of an RAF balloon squadron stationed at Dovercourt, a battery of light anti-aircraft guns at Trimley, and the headquarters of 121 Heavy AA Regiment at Felixstowe.

The Flag Officer in Charge at Harwich had just twelve officers and a hundred ratings of the Royal Navy at his disposal, quartered at Parkeston. The defence of Shotley was left to a training battalion of eight hundred RN recruits and the defence of Felixstowe to between seventy and eighty naval personnel. Revealingly, it was considered necessary in this document to note that the Shotley and Felixstowe sailors were "all armed".

There were several battalions of troops on coastal defence duties in the area, including Royal Artillery and infantry and the 9th battalion of the Essex Home Guard.

The Luftwaffe gave all the East Coast towns regular attention, but mostly it was "hit-and-run" bombing by single aircraft. The constant threat of such a raid was

Bomb damage on Lowestoft fish market after one of the many raids on the port. In fifteen raids during 1942 the town suffered ninety-three fatal casualties, nineteen of them servicemen.

as nerve-wracking for the civilian population, however, as were the occasional heavier attacks. Mrs Sarah Williams noted in her diary, when she was hearing air raid sirens every day:

> It is a funny feeling just now, living on the edge of England, particularly when it is cloudy and anything may drop out of the clouds. It makes me think of De La Mare's poem: "Look thy last on all things lovely every hour"[7].

Not many people had the literary background to seek solace in poetry. One of the first raids of the year — on 19th January — was on Sheringham, where Mrs Williams lived. Four people were killed and six injured, and four houses were demolished.

The local press reported on 14th January that an East Coast town had been raided the previous day, and that there had been casualties among shoppers. It was not until a month later that the town was publicly identified as Lowestoft, which had suffered one of its worst raids of the war. A plane had flown in from the North Sea in the late afternoon, while it was still daylight. As the AA artillery opened up the plane dived low, released its bombs, and flew off.

The high explosives fell in the heart of the shopping area and wrecked many of the town's best-known shops, including such "multiples" as Marks and Spencers, Boots and the Fifty Shilling Tailors. Some of the shopkeepers, as well as their customers, died beneath the wreckage. The young girl cashier in the tailors' shop, Beryl Bunn, was dug out after five hours' dangerous tunnelling through the wreckage by a rescue party; the manager, Mr Slater, saved her life and sacrificed his own by placing his body between her and the collapsing building.

The biggest deathroll was at Waller's Restaurant, where many had been having tea. Police Inspector George Arthur Read was on the scene within two minutes of the bombs exploding. He saw an arm protruding from a mass of debris, quickly organized a rescue squad, and five women were dug out alive. Elsewhere, a sailor was dug out after two hours, unhurt and cheerful. As darkness fell, flares were lit over the dreadful scene to assist the rescue workers. At intervals they stopped digging, to listen for cries from beneath the wreckage. The Mayor of Lowestoft, Major S. W. Humphery, stayed on the scene until overcome by exhaustion. The search went on without respite for a week, first for survivors, then for victims. The press reported that a large number had died, but never revealed the actual number, which turned out to be sixty-nine, of whom fifty-one were civilians and eighteen service personnel. These were the worst raid casualties East Anglia had experienced to that time.

Queen Elizabeth sent a letter of sympathy to the Mayor, with a supply of tea and "comforts" for distribution among those who had suffered. Later Inspector Read and two of the men who had led the rescue of the girl cashier, Mr William Bernard Eade and Mr Claude Edward Smith, were awarded the British Empire Medal; another rescue worker, Private Scott, of the Border Regiment, won the George Medal.

Lowestoft endured another serious raid ten days later, when again a lone raider dropped out of the clouds in daylight and bombed a congested residential district. Three houses were demolished, twelve people were killed, and others detained in hospital. The plane was glimpsed for only a few moments, and anti-aircraft gunners had no chance to sight it before it had disappeared out to sea.

On 18th February seven people were killed and two houses and a cottage completely demolished in Great Yarmouth. Just after midday, as people were going home to lunch, a lone bomber flew in from the sea, there was a rattle of machine-guns, and then hundreds watched four bombs detach themselves from the plane. Many victims were buried and rescue work continued for many hours. Bren-gun carriers were used to haul away some of the debris.

On 13th April ten or a dozen planes cruised over a wide area of East Anglia, and the bombs they dropped killed nine people.

During the summer months Great Yarmouth was a favourite German target, and the town suffered grievously. It was persistently attacked by single bombers, flying in one after the other, during the early hours of 30th May, and three people were killed and many houses badly damaged. Two large bombs exploded on the sea front. On 10th June sixteen high explosives fell on the town, and on 25th June, in one of the worst of its ordeals, three people died and enormous damage was caused. The parish church of St Nicholas, parts of which dated back to the early twelfth century, was burnt out, only the walls and the tower remaining. Members of a Boys' Brigade company had been fire-watching at the church, and they quickly summoned the fire services, but they had no chance. The Vicar afterwards described events:

> Hundreds of incendiaries were showered on the church and in five minutes the whole building was alight. Within fifteen minutes the tall spire collapsed inwards and the interior was a raging inferno. The cross and ornaments of the high altar were saved. Some of the bells crashed from the tower and others melted in the heat and the molten metal ran down the interior walls.

Eight high explosive and about 1,500 incendiary bombs were dropped. Apart from the parish church, the bombs destroyed several stores and warehouses and damaged the British Restaurant, the Liberal Club, a brewery, and houses in the congested Rows area. By this time three hundred of the houses in the Rows had been destroyed or damaged beyond repair.

Ipswich and Aldeburgh were bombed on the night of 1st/2nd June, and fires were started and business premises damaged in both places. Not many planes took part, but thousands of incendiaries and many high explosive bombs fell on Ipswich. Searchlights were active, but night fighters and heavy AA gunfire failed to beat off

The burned-out shell of St Nicholas' Church, Yarmouth, after the raid of 25th June.

A naval bomb disposal team with a large unexploded bomb which fell on the Pleasure Beach at Yarmouth during a raid on 30th May. The work of these teams was of the utmost importance, for unexploded bombs posed a threat which could bring other operations to a standstill for long periods.

the attack. The main destruction was of modest working-class homes, but a church and school were damaged. The German High Command claimed next day that its planes had scored direct hits on the harbour area, despite being repeatedly attacked by RAF night fighters.

On 4th/5th June a single Ju.88 attacked Lowestoft again, and there was a small number of casualties and some damage to houses. In that same night's raid, incendiaries fired a house in another, unidentified East Anglian town and a mother and her two sons, aged sixteen and six, lost their lives.

Raids continued over a widespread area during the summer. King's Lynn suffered two heavy raids during June. At breakfast time on the 12th a solitary Dornier flew over the town and released a stick of bombs. One hit and demolished the *Eagle Hotel* in Norfolk Street and damaged neighbouring shops on both sides of the street; another destroyed the auctioneers' market premises, and two others made giant craters in The Walks. Seventeen civilians and a number of service personnel were killed.

Eighteen days later (30th June) King Edward VII Grammar School was attacked by fire bombs, and part of the school and school-house were badly damaged. Five bombs lodged in the roof. Masters and boarders tackled the fires until firemen arrived, and there followed a stiff struggle to douse the flames. Two dormitories on the top floor of the boarders' quarters were gutted, and the other end of the block, containing the art room, general science and biology rooms, was damaged. Over a hundred incendiaries burnt out on the school playing fields. Elsewhere the town was machine-gunned, but there were no casualties in this raid[(8)].

In a coastal village near King's Lynn some incendiaries fell on a hospital, where nurses and some patients dealt with them, and so saved the building. The patients were then taken to dugout trenches but, as the raid seemed to be over, they quickly emerged and some again joined in fighting small fires. The Duke of Kent paid a surprise visit to Lynn soon afterwards and spoke to raid victims in hospital. The day after his visit there was a raid on Lynn Docks, and then on August Bank Holiday the town had fourteen air raid alerts up to 3 pm. Warden Hart noted:

> Somebody had arranged a sports day for the children and a running track had been marked out with flags. Plenty of children had turned up and the sports had started. In the distance we heard cannon fire. Within a few minutes, over the treetops flew a German bomber, low and steady. He must have seen us. We all were at his mercy. A burst of well-directed cannon fire and they must have killed scores of children and adults. But they flew straight on, and took no notice of us. Perhaps they were family men themselves.

Just before midnight on 21st July a stick of bombs fell across the main shopping centre of Cromer and twelve people, including one family of six, were killed. Offices and business premises were extensively damaged and the fine fifteenth-century church was severely damaged by blast, most of its windows being smashed. The Kursaal Fun Fair in Church Square was destroyed.

The following night it was Felixstowe's turn, its worst experience to date, when a plane twice circled the town at low altitude and then released a stick of high explosive bombs across its shopping centre. A family of six was killed when its home received a direct hit, others were injured, and business and commercial premises were extensively damaged. The Germans claimed their targets had been military installations and aerodromes, including an airfield at Orford Ness.

Early on 27th July nine were killed when a plane dive-bombed houses in Sheringham, and at breakfast time on 29th July two were killed in Great Yarmouth. In a small-scale raid on Ipswich during the night of 25th/26th August, a woman and her eight children were among twelve killed by a direct hit on an

Anderson shelter. The town was given the protection of a balloon barrage at about this time, but this did not spare it another attack on 15th September, when sixteen high explosive bombs damaged the railway sidings.

The coastal raids continued spasmodically during the rest of the year, but without any major attacks developing. Harwich was bombed on 16th September, Great Yarmouth and Cromer again in October. On 22nd October the village of Orford suffered catastrophe when a single Dornier Do.215 dived from the clouds and scattered high explosives. Eleven people, including five children, were killed and few of the houses in the village escaped damage. A direct hit on the grocer's shop demolished it completely.

On 15th December the Cottage War Emergency Hospital in Aldeburgh was partly demolished by a daylight bomb, but all the patients had been evacuated. Four high explosives fell in the High Street and the town was also machine-gunned. At the Post Office, which received a direct hit, nine people were killed and the telephone exchange was destroyed. Two were killed elsewhere and 129 people suffered injuries.

A week later a single hit-and-run raider flew over several areas. This was the last German air raid on the coastal towns during 1942, and Great Yarmouth suffered most severely: six people died when two high explosives and ten phosphorous incendiaries, released at almost roof-top height, destroyed a school and a number of houses. The German plane was brought down, but many in a working-class district found themselves homeless for Christmas. When the year ended, Great Yarmouth had been bombed twenty-six times in 1942, with twenty-seven killed and ninety-five injured. There had been sixty-nine high explosives, two parachute mines and 2,000 incendiaries. The sirens had sounded 324 times, plus 291 "crash" warnings, a total of 615 alarms.

Although, as we shall see later, the ordeal of Norwich in April and June was terrible, it was the population of the East Anglian coastal towns who suffered most frequently and most intensively during 1942. For them, there were few days in the year without either bombers overhead or guns firing and mines exploding at sea, or lifeboats being launched; sometimes all of these things occurred simultaneously. Their towns had a front-line appearance, crowded as they were with service personnel and equipment; their beaches were a tangle of fortifications. Few people in Britain were kept more constantly aware of the realities of war.

CHAPTER FIVE

Baedeker Blitz

GERMAN preoccupation with the war on the eastern front and in North Africa left the Luftwaffe with inadequate numbers of aircraft and trained crews to maintain a large-scale and persistent air offensive against Britain in 1942. As a result, most of East Anglia escaped sustained attack. As we have seen, the coastal towns, particularly Lowestoft and Great Yarmouth, were raided without respite, usually by single "sneak" planes using cloud cover until they were over the coast and then swooping down almost to roof level to bomb and machine-gun, but elsewhere in the Eastern Counties attacks were fewer than might have been expected.

The lone "sneak raiders", however, often cruised widely over Britain, dropping bombs almost haphazardly on villages as well as towns, even occasionally on trains; and during the summer of 1942 East Anglia also saw or heard passing formations of German bombers whose targets were further to the west, in the industrial Midlands. Occasionally these raiders dropped bombs on the Eastern Counties as they flew over, and there were many deaths.

The only East Anglian experience of a blitz on a major population centre, however, came with the spring series of so-called "Baedeker raids" (the name derived from a well-known series of German guidebooks), directed at towns containing some of Britain's most important national monuments: Canterbury, York, Exeter, Bath — and Norwich.

Norwich had suffered at an earlier stage of the war — between July, 1940, and August, 1941, there had been twenty-seven raids on the city, in which eighty-one people had been killed and many injured. But the big raids of April and May, 1942, which hit Norwich after it had enjoyed eight months of peaceful nights, were on a scale never before experienced.

There were three in a week: on the Monday, Wednesday and Friday nights. On the Monday, 27th/28th April, a moonlit night, the sirens wailed at thirty minutes before midnight. This was too late for the *Eastern Daily Press* to publish next morning anything more than a brief stop-press story that "high explosive and incendiary bombs were dropped on an East Anglian town late last night". Not until twenty-four hours later did the censors agree that there was no way of concealing from the Germans that they had found their target. The paper's front page then carried the bold headline:

VICIOUS NIGHT RAID ON NORWICH

and details began to emerge of what those in the city already knew to have been a

Above: Blazing shops in St Stephen's Street, Norwich, during the April "Blitz". A large part of the commercial centre of the city was destroyed by fires started by incendiary bombs. *George Swain*

Opposite: Flames light up the sky over Norwich during the raid of 27th/28th April, silhouetting the tower of St Lawrence's Church. The first attack resulted in an inferno engulfing 120 acres. *George Swain*

devastating raid. There were still restrictions which prevented publication of the number of casualties or the real extent of the destruction, and it was some time before the full story could be pieced together.

The raid had begun with the arrival over Norwich at 11.40 pm of two pathfinder planes releasing parachute flares, which hung in the air and lit up the streets, houses, shops, factories and public buildings. They then went into a shallow dive, dropping incendiary bombs and machine-gunning some streets in the city centre. The incendiaries set ablaze offices at the Midland and Great Northern Joint Railway's City Station and coaches standing at a platform. The flames spread to a nearby grain store and soon there was an inferno engulfing 120 acres, and quite out of control.

Only a few minutes after this first attack twenty-six more aircraft arrived in three formations which, one by one, flew across the city unloading high explosives and more incendiaries. The air vibrated with the throb of engines, and then came the sound of falling bombs, followed by explosions in series. Rows of terrace houses disintegrated, gas mains were fractured and set alight. For ten minutes the anti-aircraft guns roared into action, then became silent as RAF fighters arrived on the scene.

The attack lasted for sixty-five minutes. Later, it was computed that 185 high explosive bombs were dropped, most of them of half or quarter ton: a total of over 50 tons. There were 103 separate "incidents".

One bomb scored a direct hit on the Norwich Social Welfare Institution in Bowthorpe Road, where there were four hundred elderly patients; most of them had been taken to shelter in good time, but eight or nine old men who were in the infirm wing when it collapsed lost their lives. The Norwich Institute for the Blind was badly damaged, but everyone had been shepherded into a strongroom, and nobody was hurt there. Two new workshops, where they had been occupied during the day, were destroyed.

Another bomb blew the roof off the Regal Cinema. Other damaged buildings included the Hippodrome Theatre; several of the leading stores, Curl's, Woolworth's, Boots, and Bunting's, the drapers; Bowhill and Hubbard's and Edwards & Holmes's shoe factories; Coleman's Wincarnis Works; the City Station; and the Norwich Union insurance offices.

A number of public houses, churches, chapels, schools and a mission hall suffered badly, but most of the bombs, explosive and incendiary, came down on

residential areas, and whole rows of working-class dwellings in the most thickly populated part of Norwich were reduced to rubble. One bomb fell near an underground shelter in a public park, and people were trapped there. But none fell close enough to the Cathedral or the castle or any other important historic building to cause extensive damage.

The Civil Defence teams, firemen, police and all the other services got to work in the immediate aftermath of the first bombs, the scene around them illuminated almost like daylight by the German flares. An outstanding example of the courage displayed was the messenger service, composed of lads of sixteen to eighteen, on cycles: schoolboys, errand boys, factory apprentices. When telephone communications were cut, these lads rode through the shattered streets, through glass and debris, to deliver essential messages. Several of them were blown from their machines by bomb blast, and one who rode a motor-cycle plunged into a bomb crater before he could stop. They all got up, remounted and carried on.

Coleman's Wincarnis Works in Westwick Street, Norwich, ablaze during one of the raids. Wreckage blocks the street, preventing fire engines and other vehicles getting through. *George Swain*

Afterwards, it was discovered that one of them, John David Grix, was only fifteen and had been recruited because he had added a year to his age.

The other services performed similar feats of valour. While the raids were still going on, mobile canteens came out into the streets to serve hot drinks and snacks, staffed by the Church Army, the YMCA and the Salvation Army. Next morning the Women's Voluntary Service was quickly in action, distributing emergency clothing to those who had been bombed out, supervising the moving of any furniture that had survived, staffing rest centres and some of the canteens.*

In this first Baedeker raid on Norwich, 162 people died and over 600 were injured. The *Eastern Daily Press* reported that "all the defence services functioned admirably, and the dead included many of their number . . . Norwich has no reason to be ashamed of herself, on the morning after the night before." The Regional Commissioner, Sir Will Spens, visited the city on that morning to inspect the damage and to thank everyone who had been involved in the night's work.

There were many accounts of that first raid, but nothing better illustrated the calm courage displayed by most Norwich citizens than a letter hurriedly penned by a reader of the *Eastern Daily Press* and published immediately afterwards. It read, in full:

> 1.30 am, with our house intact, went across the city to my son and daughter-in-law. After frantic half-hour among debris, by God's mercy found them safe and sound in nearby dugout. Then to our place of business; found it alight from end to end. To ease the mind of our managing director, again went across the city to enquire of his sister. Back to the business to tell him her house badly damaged, but the lady quite safe. Carry on at business, doing my puny bit. Asked to take message to total stranger: "his son-in-law unable to return home last night, had to go out in the country". Found the old gentleman gazing at a heap of bricks and mortar that a few hours back was "four small tenements". Delivered my message and received a fervent "Thank you, my friend, we thought that he was under that lot!" Then, tired, filthy dirty, but humbly thankful, returned home and found everything the same as on any other morning — milk on the doorstep, letters and *Eastern Daily Press* on the mat. Messrs Milkmen, Postmen and Papermen, you are just or'nary people, but really you are rather wonderful.

After the first raid, mountains of rubble had to be shifted to rescue many who had been buried alive beneath it, and to recover the bodies of those who had been killed. Between 7 and 8 am pitiful queues of the bereaved and the destitute formed outside the City Hall. Loudspeaker vans toured the streets warning that water must be boiled, giving information about where various necessities could be obtained, and appealing to the able-bodied to remain at their posts.

Not everyone responded to this appeal, for some found it impossible to remain

*The WVS had been set up before the war to recruit women for "air raid precaution" work, with five people present at its first meeting. In January, 1942, its national chairman, the Marchioness of Reading, told a gathering in the Theatre Royal at Norwich that it had recruited well over a million women — one in every eleven. Nearly sixty thousand had enrolled in the Eastern Counties.

calm and controlled during the days of the Norwich blitz. One of the four members of the Norwich Emergency Committee provided this testimony:

> It was a pitiful sight to see old and young, often scantily dressed, trekking to the shelters at the sound of the siren: young mothers with their babies and children, the sick and aged seeking cover from the terror by night. There were also those who could not shelter, or who preferred the open country; the people who left the comfort of their homes to sleep out, often in wind and rain, in fields and woods. Those who saw it can never forget the trek out from the city. Some could only walk with difficulty, children tired and crying, their mothers in great distress, many with husbands away in the forces or transferred to other places of work. In the morning, the trek back again, to work or to school. Frightened people? Yes, but frightened people helping and encouraging each other, and with not a thought of surrender.[1]

The rescue and clearance work had not been completed, and dust and smoke still drifted over the wrecked city, which reeked of charred and sodden timber, when the Luftwaffe bombers struck again, just forty-eight hours later. On Wednesday night, the 29th/30th, the raiders followed the same pattern as before: they dropped flares, circled the city for a few minutes scattering incendiary bombs

in a huge and awesome semi-circle, and then several in succession dived under the curtain of anti-aircraft fire to release their bombs from a low altitude. As they pulled out of the dives, the planes machine-gunned streets and buildings.

The raid lasted just seventy-five minutes. Anti-aircraft guns raised a noisy barrage and the new RAF Mosquito fighter planes based at Castle Camps went into action for the first time, but they could not deflect the raiders. After their earlier experience, people took to the shelters very quickly; unfortunately, however, there were direct hits on some public shelters. One hundred and twelve high explosive bombs were dropped, and many more incendiaries than in the first raid — a total weight of bombs of 45 tons. There were sixty-nine deaths and eighty-nine seriously injured.

The damage was extensive. The main building and the chapel of the Norwich Diocesan Training College were destroyed, despite heroic efforts by the students, who had only two stirrup pumps and buckets of water available. Several big stores were demolished. Messrs A. J. Caley's chocolate factory was gutted by fire and burning chocolate flowed in the street. Clarke's shoe factory, the Barker Engineering Company works and St Mary's Silk Mills were damaged. Two cinemas

Left: A heavy bomb which fell in the middle of the road at St Benedict's Gates, Norwich, caused an enormous crater and destroyed many of the nearby buildings.
George Swain

Right: A solitary fireman walks down Brigg Street, Norwich, the morning after a raid. The cricket bats, ball and stumps marks the shop of R. G. Pilch, which soon reopened in smaller premises in Surrey Street.
George Swain

suffered direct hits and the Hippodrome variety theatre was wrecked. The stage manager and his wife and two of the visiting theatrical company who were with them in their caravan beside the main building were all killed; but Buddy, "the world's greatest comedy seal", who featured in an act in the programme, survived unhurt. Members of the touring company spent the next day salvaging as much as they could of £5,000-worth of theatrical props.

The ancient round-towered church of St Benedict's received a direct hit, leaving only the shell of the tower and the walls of the nave standing. Some of the most historic streets of the city were savaged by bombs. A thirteenth-century public house with a thatched roof was practically destroyed by fire, which broke out again time after time. There was great damage in residential areas. Firemen did a magnificent job, fought hard and successfully to keep the flames away from a hospital, and quenched all the fires within a few hours.

Mrs Sarah Williams, who was now working in Norwich and living at the hostel at the Diocesan Training College, made a diary entry next day which showed remarkable *sang froid*:

> The raid was short, but very intense, and in our area. There were some big fires started and the college to which the hostel belongs was burnt down. Only four or so fire bombs on the roof, but we couldn't put them out, and the whole place went. One trailer pump arrived, but there was no water. So we walked about and watched the fires, which — apart from the fact that they were burning places down — were lovely. I seemed to have odd conversations with people: soldiers, wardens, college lecturers and students. They were all upset at losing their college, but quite cheerful. We drank tea . . .(2)

The Women's Training College had arranged a reunion of old students for 23rd May, and they refused to cancel it. The gathering took place in the gymnasium, and those who attended brought picnic lunches with them. The college had lost its library and all its equipment, but was determined to carry on in temporary prefabricated buildings. This reflected Mrs Williams' attitude. She had lived in London during the early part of the blitz there. The day after she had watched the training college burn down — while drinking tea! — she worked all day at one of the Emergency Feeding Centres in Norwich and met many of the raid victims. There is a certain astringency about her diary comments over succeeding days:

> *1st May:* These raids were bad but, after all, only lasted two nights, whereas the London raids went on night and day for weeks, but the Londoners didn't make half the fuss that these people have done.

In fact there was a third before the week was out — beginning at 1.35 am on Friday, 1st May, but only one plane got through, of several which attempted to defeat the ground defences. It dropped a container which scattered seven hundred explosive incendiaries. There was a strong wind blowing and the many fires threatened to gut the main shopping centre of the city, but wardens and fireguards

EASTERN EVENING NEWS, Apl. 30, 1942

JUST ARRIVED
Large consignment of Ladies' High-grade Hand Bags
ALL COLOURS
GREENS of NORWICH

Black-out—
9.49 p.m. to 5.55 a.m.
WIRELESS—Page 3, Col. 3.

Eastern Evening News

FINAL

No. 18,506—Three 'Halfpence

Thursday, April 30, 1942

TWILL WEAVE SUEDELEINE
FOR SMART DRESSES
Rose, Petrel, Saxe, Gold and Moonlight Blue. 36 in. wide
Per 5/1½ Yard
BONDS - NORWICH

SECOND 'REPRISAL' RAID ON NORWICH

Much damage to shopping centre

A.A. GUNS PUT UP HEAVY BARRAGE

ANTI-AIRCRAFT GUNS PUT UP A HEAVY BARRAGE WHEN NAZI RAIDERS MADE THEIR SECOND "REPRISAL" ATTACK ON NORWICH LAST NIGHT.

Though the raid was on a smaller scale than that on Monday night, considerable damage was done, particularly to a large shopping centre.

It is feared that there were numerous casualties, including some killed in public shelters.

Several of the raiders were badly damaged, but their destruction is not yet confirmed. Night fighters finally drove them off.

Civil defence services from outside were rushed to help the local A.R.P., and the firemen successfully concentrated in preventing the spread of flames in the direction of a hospital.

A large block of shops was gutted by fire after direct hits with heavy high explosive bombs.

Damage to old and new Norwich

ONE of the oldest churches in the city—Early English—has only its round tower standing, and one of the newest churches, built a few years ago, was destroyed by fire in last night's raid

One of the oldest public-houses in the city and a modern milk bar are among the buildings which have disappeared.

Low level raid on aero works

Independents win two by-elections

RUGBY AND WALLASEY RESULTS

THE Government has lost two seats to Independent candidates in the Rugby and Wallasey by-elections.

At Wallesey, Mr. George L. Reakes (Independent) obtained a majority of 6012 over the National Government candidate, Alderman John Pennington, chairman of the local Conservative Association.

A second Independent candidate was Major L. H. Cripps, shipowner brother of Sir Stafford Cripps, polled only 1597 votes and lost his deposit.

Then, about an hour later at Rugby, a close fight ended in a victory by Mr. W. J. Browne, Independent, with a majority of only 679, over Colonel Sir Claude Holbrook, the Government nominee, and chairman of the local Conservative Association for 15 years.

The the General Election the figures were: Lt.-Col. J. T. C. Moore-Brabazon (C.) 27,949, Mr. J. Airey (Lab.) 13,491; majority 14,458.

Mr. Reakes, who is a journalist, was a member of the Labour Party until a difference of opinion over Munich. He was Labour's nominee when elected Mayor for Coronation year.

Wallasey became a separate division in 1918, and since then, until to-day, has always returned Conservative with a substantial majority.

Mr. Reakes said after the result to-day: "It is a victory for Churchill, and our enemies will now know that Wallasey wants a vigorous prosecution of the war with a fight to the finish."

RUGBY REVERSAL

The by-election at Rugby was caused by the elevation to the peerage of Capt. David Margesson.

At the general election the figures

Above: The front page of the *Eastern Evening News* of 30th April tells of the previous night's raid.

Right: The ruins of the Norwich Diocesan Training College in College Road after the raids.
George Swain

went into action and the NFS was quickly on the scene; the situation was contained. Mrs Williams' diary recorded:

> *6th May*: Everyone is in a dreadful pickle because the laundries have been bombed and hardly any of our people have facilities for washing clothes.
> *7th May*: The warden was bitter today because so many men living in the district had handed him their keys and told him to put out their fires (if any), as they were going to sleep in the country. He said their houses could burn down, for all he cared.

To be fair, we must balance against this view the impressions of a part-time Cambridge fireman whose unit was among those summoned to Norwich to help. Afterwards he wrote of the remarkable spirit of those who suffered:

> Norwich is a much-damaged city and piles of debris and irregular buildings tell a sad story. Hundreds of humble homes have been blasted beyond habitation. Yet the people are determined. For instance, our first visitors after getting to work were two young women in their teens in a private car. The doors opened and revealed an urn of tea . . .
>
> The courage of the people is beyond belief. As we toiled, there was the pitiful sight of tots in arms and the aged. They carried bundles in their arms, on pushchairs, prams, cycles and handcarts — their few rescued personal belongings. None wore an expression of despair, and many were the cheerful exchanges of comments with us. A man and his wife and little boy walked along. The boy carried some toys, the woman a birdcage covered with a cloth.
>
> "How's the bird?" I asked.
>
> Back came the woman's reply: "Our canary is alive anyway, thank goodness."
>
> That sort of incident happened repeatedly and many were the sights we saw — a motor-car parked on a rooftop, a chimney-pot lying sideways on the chimney stack . . .[3]

"All safe at Tasburgh" says the chalked message on the wall—and some wag has stretched a "bed and breakfast" sign across the gaping window opening; a scene in Exeter Street, Norwich. *George Swain*

There can be no doubt, however, that morale was not high, for a wave of wild rumour swept across East Anglia, such that the Regional Commissioner, Sir Will Spens, felt a need to issue a special statement through the Ministry of Information:

> Last week there were a large number of rumours in the Region. Many of these had no foundation in fact. What was alleged to have taken place or to have been said had not taken place or been said. Where there was foundation on fact, they were grossly exaggerated.

The statement went on to elaborate. Heavy attacks had been alleged to have been made on towns which, in fact, had not been attacked at all. Broadcasts were alleged to have been made which were not made. The number of persons killed at Norwich was, in some cases, multiplied tenfold by the rumour-mongers. Sir Will went on:

> I appeal to all persons in the Eastern Region to set an example by dispelling rumours, by not passing these on, and by being pretty short with those who do. They can in that way be of real service to the country.

When Tom Driberg, an MP recently elected as a critic of the government, made his maiden speech in the Commons on 7th July he attributed some of these problems to the government's "excessive addiction to secrecy". When a city was blitzed, he said, the names of those killed and the details of casualties were posted next day outside the town hall, but were not published in the press. "Say twenty people were killed", he said. "Twenty miles away one heard next day that 200 were killed, and thirty miles away the figure was probably 2,000."

On 4th, 5th and 7th May Norwich buried its dead in a special avenue of the cemetery; three "united burials" in a mass grave, conducted with full civic and religious ceremony. The full extent of the damage, and its consequences, were still being assessed. Both theatres, the Hippodrome and the Theatre Royal, and two cinemas, the Odeon and the Carlton, were closed. Many of the leading businesses had to find new premises. The department store, Curl's, for example, reopened many of its sales counters on the first floor of Jarrolds' premises, and others on the ground floor of Garland's. Another store, Bond's, did not reopen most of its departments until 11th July, and then they were spread over four different addresses.

Many churches had been destroyed or heavily damaged. The Cathedral had escaped fairly lightly: a bomb which fell in the Close, but some distance from the east end of the Cathedral, damaged many windows, but the older stained glass was unaffected. St Peter Mancroft had lost glass and mullions. But St Benedict's and St Bartholomew, Heigham, were in ruins, and St Anne's, a new church on the Earlham Estate, had been destroyed. St Martin-at-Oak, the ancient flint church in Oak Street, had been saved from destruction, but its interior had been damaged by fire-bombs. St Stephen's had been badly blasted, but fortunately its valuable stained-glass east window had been removed to safety in the early days of the war. St Andrew's had a hole in its roof. The Dereham Road Baptist Chapel was

extensively damaged. The Friends' Meeting House in the Gildencroft, which dated from 1699, had also suffered badly.

As for the public houses, the *Fountain*, an eighteenth-century posting tavern near St Benedict's Gate, had received a direct hit; the *Surrey Inn*, in Grove Road, and the *Buck* public house in Oak Street had also been completely destroyed; the fifteenth-century *Boar's Head* in St Stephen's Street and the *Anchor of Hope* beerhouse in Oak Street had both been destroyed by fire; and only the south front of the *Old Dolphin*, which was a scheduled ancient monument, survived, blackened and scarred.

Although nothing subsequently matched the horror of this week of raids, the ordeal of Norwich was not over. By the time of the next German raid, however, shortly after midnight on 9th May, the defences had been greatly strengthened. A barrage of thirty-five balloons had been provided and this was raised quickly; RAF fighters made thirty-seven sorties. Newly-installed heavy anti-aircraft guns sent up a non-stop thirty-minute barrage. These carefully co-ordinated measures were successful. Many of the bombs fell outside the city; a communiqué reported that they had fallen in or near villages around Norwich, where they caused little damage and no casualties. In one case most of the dozen houses in a hamlet were damaged and the blacksmith's forge was destroyed. Flying glass injured three of the residents, and five cows, two pigs and a considerable number of chickens were killed.

In Norwich, one bomb fell on the boiler-house of the Woodlands Hospital and caused heavy damage, but no casualties. The evacuation of the old and bedridden patients presented a problem. Twenty-five of them were accommodated at Crown Point, the residence of Mr and Mrs Russell Colman, and others went to St James' Hospital at Shipmeadow. The damage at the Woodlands Hospital deprived the authorities of the use of six hundred beds.

There was another raid during the night of 26th/27th June, lasting only forty-five minutes, but a frightening attack which caused sixteen deaths and many injuries. The bombers released flares to light their target, then showered down over thirty high explosive bombs and an estimated 20,000 incendiaries. Some devastating fires were caused. The raiders were again greeted by heavy fire from the AA guns, and RAF night fighters could be heard above the deeper roar of the Luftwaffe planes. The noise was tremendous, and soon the glare of big fires spread above the rooftops.

One was at the Norfolk and Norwich Hospital, which was straddled by bombs, and one wing of which was burnt out. When the raid began patients had already been moved to the basement, but after hundreds of incendiaries had rained down it was decided that they must be brought out of the building. Nurses carried them out

Charred debris litters the chancel of the Victorian church of St Thomas in Earlham Road, Norwich, a victim of the "Blitz". *George Swain* and laid them, in long rows, on a lawn close at hand; there they had to wait until ambulances and coaches could be brought up to remove them to another hospital. They lay there watching the flames spread to the wards they had occupied a short time before. The main building escaped serious damage, but the operating theatre was destroyed. Men of the Scottish Horse, who were stationed nearby, helped to carry out valuable equipment from the theatre, and nurses, grimy, dishevelled and wet, rescued linen and blankets.

The Norwich Maternity Home also suffered a direct hit by a high-explosive bomb, but all the patients there had been moved to a protected room, and they escaped unhurt.

It was in this raid that the Cathedral narrowly escaped serious destruction. Over a thousand incendiaries fell within the precincts, many on the Cathedral roof, where they set fire to the main supporting timbers. Two fireguards, one of them a member of the Cathedral clergy, climbed precariously to the roof, hauled up a hose, and dealt with this blaze. Several houses in The Close were destroyed by fire.

During this night, too, the King Edward VI Grammar School in The Close was heavily damaged, and Bond's, the drapers, was burnt out. The damage was widespread, with three churches destroyed and many public buildings, shops, offices and factories, schools, and hundreds of private dwellings destroyed or badly damaged. One of the most terrifying features of this attack was the manner in which some of the raiders appeared to be skimming rooftops as they dived towards their targets.

A month passed before Norwich was raided again — at 1.20 am on 28th July. Only one high explosive bomb fell, and it did little damage, but a shower of incendiaries started a number of fires. Other raids followed later in the year: on 2nd August, when a small force of bombers dropped a few high explosives and many incendiary bombs (including a new type with an explosive charge, which caused several deaths) on business and shopping areas; on 13th August; on 5th September, a busy Saturday morning, when a high level attack with HE bombs killed six people and left several industrial targets damaged; on 19th October, when one of four high explosive bombs scored a direct hit on Edwards and Holmes' shoe factory; on 3rd November; and on 5th December.

When, at the end of 1942, a reckoning was made, it was found that Norwich had had 106 alerts, covering a total of ninety-nine hours. Some 30,000 dwellings had been damaged, and 2,082 had been demolished or were beyond repair.

There could have been no city in the country which had more conscientiously tackled its air raid precautions preparations. A committee had been appointed back in March, 1936. When war began, a four-man Emergency Committee met almost daily for three months. Men and women were trained. By 1942 the city had public shelters for 122,000 people out of a population of 126,000.

There were seventy-four wardens' posts, all connected by phone to the Central Control Room, which also had direct lines to each of five Rescue Party Depots and four Ambulance Depots. The Central Control Room had twenty-four phone lines, plus messenger service. On duty there during the raids were the ARP Controller, the City Engineer, the Medical Officer of Health (or their deputies), the ARP Officer, a Rest Centre Officer, a representative of the Warden's Service, representatives of the Post Office telephone service, the gas, electricity and water undertakings, a gas identification officer, liaison officers from the police and the fire service, the City Treasurer acting as Operations Officer, and the City Architect plotting incidents on a large-scale map of the city.

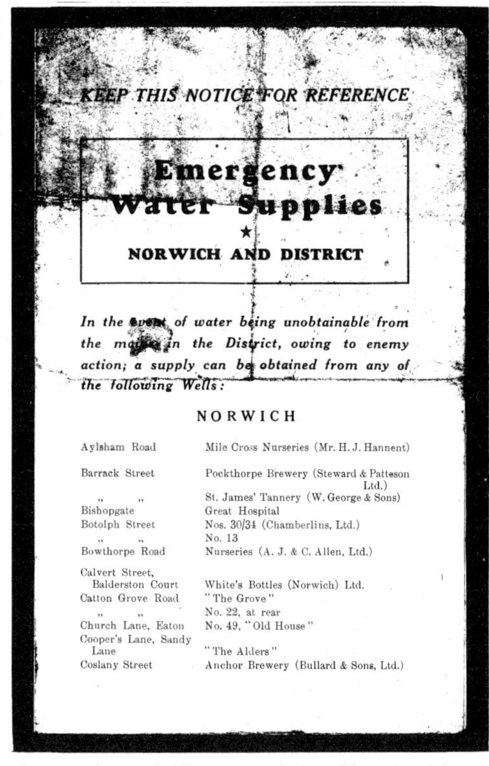

KEEP THIS NOTICE FOR REFERENCE

Emergency Water Supplies

★

NORWICH AND DISTRICT

In the event of water being unobtainable from the mains in the District, owing to enemy action; a supply can be obtained from any of the following Wells:

NORWICH

Aylsham Road	Mile Cross Nurseries (Mr. H. J. Hannent)
Barrack Street	Pockthorpe Brewery (Steward & Patteson Ltd.)
,, ,,	St. James' Tannery (W. George & Sons)
Bishopgate	Great Hospital
Botolph Street	Nos. 30/34 (Chamberlins, Ltd.)
,, ,,	No. 13
Bowthorpe Road	Nurseries (A. J. & C. Allen, Ltd.)
Calvert Street, Balderston Court	White's Bottles (Norwich) Ltd.
Catton Grove Road	"The Grove"
,, ,,	No. 22, at rear
Church Lane, Eaton	No. 49, "Old House"
Cooper's Lane, Sandy Lane	"The Alders"
Coslany Street	Anchor Brewery (Bullard & Sons, Ltd.)

Norwich was better prepared for the air attacks of 1942 than many British towns. This leaflet listing places where emergency water supplies could be obtained proved invaluable to many of those who obeyed the instruction "keep this notice for reference". *L. W. Malster*

The Norwich City Engineer, Mr H. C. Rowley, had visited Coventry after its terrible blitz ordeal in 1940, and as a result of what he learned there he had made detailed plans for the action that might be called for if Norwich suffered a similar fate. These plans were agreed with the Norwich Master Builders' Association, and a mutual assistance scheme was worked out with nearby local authorities.

When the raids occurred, the well-laid Norwich plans proved their value. To assist the city's own Civil Defence workers fire, rescue and ambulance units were rushed in from Bedford, Brentwood, Braintree, Bury St Edmunds, Cambridge, Chelmsford, Colchester, Dunstable, Hoddesdon, Ipswich, Letchworth, St Albans, Southend and Watford, as well as from the RAF.

After the second big raid, the situation was studied on 1st May by a government Minister, Miss Ellen Wilkinson, who spent the whole day in the city. The business of repairing damaged houses was well in hand, she declared, but problems of billeting the homeless remained to be solved. The city's MPs, Mr Geoffrey Shakespeare and Mr H. G. Strauss, also arrived on the scene, stayed the weekend, and toured the blitzed areas.

The priority task was to repair as many homes as possible as quickly as possible. The city was divided into sectors. At daybreak after the first raid, each sector was visited by a member of the Engineer's staff, each accompanied by a master builder who acted as his deputy, and they surveyed the damage and set things in motion. Within twenty-four hours one thousand men were at work, many of them brought in from outside the city. Then came the second raid. For the first time during the war, compulsory powers were applied to draft in more workers, and within a week nearly 2,000 men, including some from London and Birkenhead, were repairing houses.

Nevertheless, when the Duke of Kent visited Norwich on 26th May he found many people still searching the wreckage of their homes. The Duke's presence was intended to boost morale. He inspected the Civil Defence services and the Home Guard, who were paraded in front of the City Hall, and visited the Norfolk and Norwich Hospital and the Norwich Institution for the Blind.

Repair and clearance went on for many weeks. At the end of June a further 250 London builders arrived as reinforcements; the locals dubbed them "Cockney sparrows". They were billeted in Norwich homes, and they regularly worked eleven-hour days, beginning at 7 am.

Until homes still standing could be made habitable again, the bombed-out had to be billeted and the organization which made an enormous contribution to this task was called "MAGNA" — the Mutual Aid Good Neighbours' Association. It had been launched in November, 1941, with Mrs Ruth Hardy as its organizer. Its purpose was to enrol everyone who was prepared to offer warmth, shelter, sympathy and kindness to the victims of bombing, until such time as they could be removed to hospital, hostel, rest centre or other appropriate place. The object was to get this reservoir of goodwill and practical assistance on a properly organized basis. That meant having an organizer attached to each of the eighty warden's posts in the city, and a "street mother" for each of the 1,500 streets and 715 yards and courts. The plan was a great success; 30,000 Norwich women were enrolled and each had a small yellow poster in a front window announcing that "a good neighbour lives here." After the raids, MAGNA arranged billets for four hundred of the homeless.

In due time, there was official recognition of individual bravery during the blitz. The Deputy Chief Constable received an MBE and four British Empire Medals were won by those who dealt with the Norwich damage. One of those honoured was the fifteen-year-old Boy Scout, John David Grix, who had cheated

King George VI talking to Civil Defence messengers during a visit to Norwich in October.

about his age to enrol as a Civil Defence cyclist-messenger. He had spent the two nights of the biggest raids riding through the thick of the chaos and on one journey he had been blown from his bicycle by bomb blast five times. When the King paid a surprise visit to Norwich in October, Grix was among the Civil Defence workers presented to him. The King then made a twenty-five-mile tour of the city, visiting the hospital, the Cathedral, the Services Club and a factory, and driving along forty-eight different streets. He lunched at the *Maid's Head Hotel* as the guest of the Lord Mayor.

A fortnight later Grix went with his parents and the other local heroes to Buckingham Palace, where crowds pressed around him to see his medal. "Look here", he exclaimed, "this is a jolly sight worse than any blitz."

No other inland centre in East Anglia faced an assault like that on Norwich, though most suffered one or more raids during 1942. There was daily Luftwaffe activity over East Anglia in July, when the main German objectives were Birmingham and the Midlands, but when Peterborough was a subsidiary target.

Four high explosive bombs fell on the west end of Cowgate and around the station and damaged a great deal of property, including Robert Sayle's stores, the Salvation Army headquarters and the *George Hotel*. Nobody was killed.

Cambridge became a target on 27th July, when about thirty planes cruised over a wide area of England and took whatever opportunities they found to sneak briefly out of cloud cover to unload their bombs. Four people were killed and seven injured when a residential quarter was bombed and streets machine-gunned, shattering shop windows. Only a single plane was involved. It appeared suddenly in daylight, and dived to less than 100 feet over the town. Hundreds of people in the streets, as fascinated as they were frightened, saw the dark shape roar above the rooftops and release its load of bombs, a mixture of incendiaries and small HEs.

The Cambridge Union building suffered most seriously: a small high explosive bomb fell in one corner of the library, and incendiaries on several other parts of the premises. Three fire-watchers were on duty, and with the help of wardens they fought the flames until the NFS men arrived with pumps. In the end, the water did almost as much damage as the fire. Some valuable musical books were destroyed, all the windows at the front of the building overlooking Round Church Street were blown out, but damage to the famous debating hall was slight. The Round Church escaped almost undamaged, with just one stained glass window blown in. Another HE bomb from the same plane blew in the windows of Whewell's Court at Trinity College, and splinters extensively scarred the outer wall of the Court.

Five people were killed when March was bombed during the night of 28th/29th July.

In August, as a record harvest was waiting to be cut, the Germans began to drop large numbers of incendiary bombs over the fields, hoping to destroy the standing crops. These tactics were pursued throughout the month, and villages and hamlets remote from towns and targets became used to the scattering of bombs close at hand.

There was a particularly distressing attack on Colchester in the early hours of Tuesday, 11th August, when four 500lb bombs scored direct hits on two wards in the west block of the Severalls Mental Hospital, which accommodated senile and infirm patients, and on the laundry building. Thirty-eight patients were killed, and twenty-three others and two nurses were injured. All night and all next day the rescue workers searched for bodies under the debris. There was a mass funeral, with victims buried in a common grave on 14th August.

Colchester was attacked again on 17th September, when six raiders dropped combined HE and incendiary bombs and damaged a large number of residential properties; and on 28th September, when a single Dornier Do.217 swept in low at mid-morning and dropped four bombs on a working-class area in the heart of the town, shattering buildings, killing eight people, and putting twenty-eight others into hospital. Many houses and shops were damaged and rescue workers had to search through masses of debris. On 30th September another Dornier, at about the same time of day, bombed St Botolph's Goods Station and machine-gunned some streets; and on 19th October a bomb landed on the Arclight factory of E. N. Mason and Sons.

The air attacks grew less frequent as the autumn set in, but they did not cease. Nobody knew when an enemy plane would appear suddenly with its bomb doors open or its machine-guns blazing. It was difficult not to feel constantly "on edge". Bombs were dropped on Downham Market in Norfolk, near Clare in Suffolk, and at several other rural locations on the last day of June. Many smaller towns were visited: Wymondham in late July; Dunmow and Clare again in September; Needham Market, Wickham Market and Tiptree on 19th October, when a number of planes spent the whole morning cruising widely over the region, taking advantage of low cloud from which they swooped almost to the rooftops of several towns and villages to machine-gun streets; North Walsham on 31st October. Casualties were light in these raids, and on 19th October one of the raiders, a Junkers Ju.88, was shot down by the guns of HM trawler *Lovania* and AA guns on shore; it crashed and exploded in a field near Lowestoft.

The anti-aircraft gunners and the RAF fighters were by this time having

Not all the raiders returned home safely. This Dornier 217 crash-landed on the edge of a Fenland drain in the early months of the year. *East Anglian Daily Times*

considerable success in shooting down raiders. British planes, too, sometimes crashed in East Anglia. In the north-western area of Essex alone, there were nine such incidents during 1942: three fighters down during April and May, at Wickham St Paul, Bulmer and Helions Bumpstead; two more in July, at Birchwood and Ovington; two Wellington bombers down at Finchingfield, in June and October; another, at Gestingthorpe, also in October; and an RAF Oxford down at Sible Hedingham in November. One of the worst disasters of 1942 was the result of a British plane crashing in the middle of the village street at Somersham, a few miles north of Cambridge, on the night of 5th October. A flare on board the aircraft ignited and set fire to the machine, and the crew baled out and landed safely. The plane completely destroyed seven cottages in the village, others were badly damaged, and eleven people lost their lives. A tremendous blaze was visible for miles around.

During the early months of 1942 RAF Bomber Command maintained a steady programme of raids on targets in Germany. A directive of 14th February, 1942, designated the primary objective as "the morale of the enemy civil population and, in particular, of the industrial workers"[(4)]. At the end of March RAF bombers laid waste 200 acres of Lübeck with 300 tons of HEs and incendiaries, and more than 15,000 were reported to have been made homeless. No German city had previously suffered so. Hitler ordered retaliation: "Besides raids on ports and industry, terror attacks of a retaliatory nature are to be carried out against towns other than London." Indeed, the enemy propaganda insisted that the Baedeker raids on Norwich and other cultural centres in Britain were a direct reprisal for RAF raids on similar historic cities in Germany such as Lübeck. On the day preceding the first big Norwich raid Mrs Sarah Williams had written in her diary about the RAF bombing of Germany:

> The news of the big raids seems to be heartening people and all kinds of people said "The war will be over this year". A sudden wave of optimism, in fact . . .

Air Chief Marshal Sir Arthur Harris, who was appointed C-in-C of Bomber Command in February, 1942, was a vigorous advocate of concentration bombing by a thousand planes at a time. As soon as he was able to get together such a force he despatched it to Cologne — on 30th May, just twenty-four hours after the second big raid on Norwich. The marshalling of such a force in the air was a formidable undertaking and the East Anglian skies were full of planes as never before. The huge fleets crossed the coast on their way to Germany over Great Yarmouth, Orfordness and Cromer. In Sheringham Mrs Williams noted in her diary:

> It is full moon . . . I went out and looked and saw bomber after bomber going over . . .

The air bases in the region supplied many of the planes and their crews, and everyone who lived near them was immediately aware that something new was going on. Wellingtons from Alconbury, Bassingbourn, East Wretham, Feltwell,

Honington and Marham, and Stirlings from Oakington and Marham, were part of the force. The first public reaction was favourable. On the morning after, readers of the *East Anglian Daily Times* read a front-page lead story headlined:

3,000 TONS OF BOMBS DROPPED IN 90-MINUTE COLOGNE RAID

R.A.F. HAVE 1,250 AIRCRAFT ENGAGED IN BIGGEST ATTACK OF WAR

DEVASTATION FAR GREATER THAN AT LUBECK AND ROSTOCK

CITY ENSHROUDED IN SMOKE CLOUD OVER 15,000 FEET HIGH

Mrs Williams noted:

> Everybody feels quite jubilant today because of the raid on Cologne. Definitely, everybody's spirits have risen sharply since the news of such a big attack, though mingled with this is the fear of retaliation and reprisal.

The Ipswich MP Mr Richard Stokes felt differently. "The bombing of Cologne was morally wrong," he told an audience at one of his public meetings. "No real effort was made to limit the targets to military objectives." When Mrs Williams went back to Norwich after her weekend at home in Sheringham, she heard echoes of this view:

> The train, as usual on Monday, was very full, mainly of Service personnel. There was quite a lot of talk about the big Cologne raid, and much rejoicing . . . But when I started to meet the people from school there were different comments. Mrs G. thought it was awful. Mrs L said she was glad she had lived through the Norwich raids to be able to sympathize with the people of Cologne.

Principal German Air Raids on East Anglia during 1942

JANUARY

11th	Aldeburgh.	Showered with propaganda leaflets, despite the fact that most civilians had left the town.
13th	Lowestoft.	Lone plane drops 4 HE bombs on London Road shopping centre in late afternoon. 69 killed and 114 seriously injured, and much damage to commercial property in town's worst raid.
19th	Lowestoft.	2 HEs.
	Sheringham.	2 HEs kill 4 and injure 4 in Cremer Street.
21st/22nd	Gt Yarmouth.	4 HEs dropped from about 50 ft.
23rd	Lowestoft.	Lone plane drops 4 HEs on area around railway station. 12 killed.
31st	Cromer.	Late-night raid.
	Reedham.	4 HEs at mid-morning.

FEBRUARY

2nd	Lowestoft.	Bombs on harbour area.
	Southwold.	Daytime raid.
18th	Gt Yarmouth.	Lone raider drops 4 HEs. 7 killed.

There were no raids on East Anglian towns during March.

APRIL

19th	King's Lynn.	
27th/28th	Norwich.	First Baedeker raid, around midnight. Heavy damage, extensive fires, 158 killed, 1,200 homeless.
29th/30th	Norwich.	Second Baedeker raid, again around midnight. Extensive damage and fires, 68 killed.

MAY

9th	Norwich.	Premises damaged, but no casualties.
30th	Gt Yarmouth.	4 killed.

JUNE

1st/2nd	Ipswich.	Fires started.
	Aldeburgh.	Fires started.
4th/5th	Lowestoft.	
10th.	Gt Yarmouth.	16 HEs.
12th	King's Lynn.	
25th	Gt Yarmouth.	8 HEs and 1,500 incendiaries across town centre. 4 killed and extensive damage. St Nicholas' Parish Church destroyed.
26th/27th	Norwich.	Norfolk & Norwich Hospital, Norwich Maternity Home and Cathedral damaged. 70 major fires and many smaller ones.
30th	King's Lynn.	King Edward VII Grammar School damaged.
	Peterborough.	4 HEs on Cowgate and around station. Heavy damage to property, but no deaths.
	Bedford.	

JULY

early days	Peterborough.	
	March.	
	Bedford.	
	West Dereham.	
12th	Gt Yarmouth.	4 HEs. 2 killed.
	Lowestoft.	Bomb on the Naval commander's office. 1 killed.
19th	Chelmsford.	Low level attack.
21st/22nd	Cromer.	11 killed and 15 injured in pre-midnight raid; Kursaal Fun Fair in Church Square hit and heavy damage elsewhere.
	King's Lynn.	Docks area bombed.
	Felixstowe.	Naval equipment damaged.
23rd	Eight different areas stretching from the East Coast to Hunts.	Two bombs on R.N. Barracks in Gt Yarmouth, and others on the docks at King's Lynn.
Last days	Sheringham.	9 killed.
	Cambridge.	12 HEs. 3 killed. Union Society building hit.
	Wymondham.	
	Near Ely.	
28th	Norwich.	1,000 kg HE in Trafford Road area, no casualties. Incendiaries cause numerous fires.
29th	March.	6 killed.
	Halstead.	
	Gt Yarmouth.	4 HEs. 2 killed.

AUGUST

1st/2nd	Norwich.	Extensive damage to property.
7th	Cambridge.	Precision attack aimed at the Unicam Works in Arbury Road, making optical equipment for guns and submarines.
10th	Peterborough.	Power station is intended target, but is undamaged.
11th	Ipswich.	HEs and incendiaries damage property.
13th	Norwich.	Small-scale raid.
14th/15th	Ipswich.	Small-scale raid.
16th/17th	Colchester.	Small-scale raid.
18th/19th	Norwich.	Small-scale raid.
22nd/23rd	Gt. Yarmouth.	4 HEs.
25th/26th	Ipswich.	Direct hit kills mother and 8 children in Anderson shelter.
26th/27th	Ipswich.	
28th	Lowestoft.	
29th	Cambridge.	High-level attack.

SEPTEMBER

5th	Norwich.	HE raid on busy Saturday morning; 6 killed and industrial targets hit.
	Chelmsford.	High-level attack.
	Cambridge.	High-level attack.
7th/8th	Dunmow.	
	Clare area.	

15th/16th	Ipswich.	16 HE bombs damage railway sidings.
16th	Aldeburgh.	Bombed and machine-gunned.
16th/17th	Colchester.	Property damaged.
17th/18th	King's Lynn.	Property damaged.
28th	Colchester.	4 HEs.

OCTOBER

19th	Gt Yarmouth.	Early morning raid. 4 HEs.
	Norwich.	Two raids. Direct hit on Edwards and Holmes' shoe factory.
	Ipswich.	2 HEs.
	Needham Market.	2 HEs. High Street explosion kills 4, with 9 seriously injured. Extensive damage, including two schools.
	Cromer.	Hotel hit. 1 killed, 3 injured.
	Colchester.	2 direct hits on Mason's Arclight Works, 6 killed and extensive damage.
	Wickham Market.	Bomb in High Street kills 3 and injures 7 and demolishes many homes.
	Tiptree.	
22nd	Orford.	5 killed on Market Hill.
31st	North Walsham.	60 houses damaged.

NOVEMBER

3rd	Norwich.	Streets machine-gunned. Bomb on Surrey Street bus station fails to explode.

DECEMBER

15th	Aldeburgh.	4 HEs hit High Street, destroy telephone exchange, and damage Cottage Hospital. 11 killed, 129 injured.
22nd	Gt Yarmouth.	2 HE and 10 phosphorous bombs dropped by lone raider, which was then brought down.

CHAPTER SIX

Women and Children, too

BY the beginning of 1942 the mobilization of manpower had been pushed almost to the limit. Of all the things that were in short supply — food, clothing, weapons, raw materials, and indeed practically everything else — nothing was more serious than the shortage of men and women available to complete the job in hand in the time available.

Two and a quarter million men had been called into the armed services and were being trained for the battles ahead; but that meant they were unproductive. They could not be properly trained until more weapons and equipment reached them, but the factories, although they had drawn in large numbers of single women, were still short of the labour they required to maximize production. The farmers, under instructions to grow more crops on more land, complained that they were seriously hampered by lack of labour. Those who were trying to maintain the basic civilian activities of the nation were overworked and under strain. On every side the government was beset by problems of scarce manpower and womanpower. In the early months of 1942 it made another, more determined, effort to move every man and every woman into position to make a maximum contribution to the war effort.

Voluntary appeals had limited success. When, during January, Cambridgeshire County Council circulated householders asking who would accommodate unaccompanied children under five should it become necessary to evacuate them from heavily bombed areas during the following autumn and winter, no accommodation was offered. When Haverhill Urban District Council asked for volunteers for fire guard duty in the town, only sixty-one people came forward, and an appeal by the council chairman for volunteers to form "utility squads" to serve in the event of an invasion brought only four enrolments.

In May the Mayor of Saffron Walden, Alderman Ellis Rooke, complained: "The women of this town have not come forward to give their services for training in Civil Defence work . . . When young people recently registered, of the 80 boys, some 68 presented themselves afterwards for interviews, with a view to being placed in some useful spare-time work. This was not so with the girls. Out of 65 who registered, only 22 attended afterwards for interviews. It is disgraceful to think that at dances at the Town Hall — there have been four this week — they get full houses, yet these girls will not offer themselves to train in useful work."

In mid-March, the Eastern Regional Commissioner, Sir Will Spens, told a meeting of members of the Women's Voluntary Service in Cambridge: "There are many people who are not taking any significant part in the war effort and I ask you to help to remove that feeling of apathy which exists and to do all you can to get other people to make efforts."

If the emphasis in these comments was on women, that was because the supply of able-bodied men had run out.

Local authorities, which had to administer most of the schemes involving voluntary war workers, had lost nearly all their younger men to the forces. In February Newmarket UDC decided to suspend all council committee meetings for a month "to relieve staff and to give an opportunity to progress with the invasion scheme". By the beginning of May, Cambridgeshire County Council had lost more than half of its male staff to the armed forces. When Chesterton RDC was asked to release its Deputy Surveyor for other work of national importance, after it had already lost its Engineer-Surveyor, it refused, insisting that it would be left with nobody with essential technical qualifications. Most local authorities and others with public responsibilities declared that they could not spare another man for the fighting forces.

The Board of Visitors at Fulbourn Mental Hospital, in Cambridgeshire, was told that when a nineteen-year-old member of its staff was called up it would be left with one man, one woman and a fourteen-year-old boy to cook for nine hundred people seven days a week. Cambridgeshire Public Assistance Committee, at about the same time, debated the position of the Master of the County Infirmary; he was thirty-seven and had been keen since the outbreak of the war to volunteer for armed service. Should the committee withdraw its application for his deferment? Seven thought he should be allowed to go; six were seriously concerned that he was more urgently needed where he was; as one of these six pointed out, eight hundred children had been brought into the world at this infirmary during the previous nine months.

When seven Cromer lifeboatmen, all aged between twenty-one and thirty-three, were summoned for medical examination in February and told they would soon be called up to the services, there was a popular revolt in the town. Three of the crew had already been called up and most of those left were in their seventies, or closely approaching seventy. One was seventy-eight. Two lifeboats were stationed at Cromer. The number one boat had been called out over a hundred times since the outbreak of the war, the number two boat sixteen times. Sometimes they had both been out at the same time. So the men felt they could not do their job without their younger colleagues, and some talked of resigning. A local newspaper explained:

> The lifeboatmen, whose gallant deeds have made Cromer known all over the world, do not object to doing their bit for their country, but, being experienced men, they consider they can better serve it by remaining in the town, ready to face the many risks attendant upon their work in the lifeboat crew.

In the end, despite representations to Mr Ernest Bevin, the Minister responsible

Coxswain Henry Blogg, of the Cromer lifeboat, sitting for a portrait by T. C. Dugdale, ARA. Blogg was in charge of the lifeboat throughout the war and became something of a national hero.
East Anglian Daily Times

for manpower, the men were called up. This left twelve men to man the two lifeboats. Mr Henry Blogg, the veteran coxswain who had led many East Coast rescues, had only recently been awarded his third RNLI Gold Medal and was something of a national hero, remarked grimly: "That is not enough, but we shall have to do the best we can". This episode did no good to morale along the north Norfolk coast.

As these examples indicate, the competition for manpower was so acute that there were appalling difficulties on all sides. The government resolved to reduce the demands for labour in civilian occupations by every possible means. One example of the measures it introduced as the year opened was a scheme to cut back on deliveries of goods made by shopkeepers to their customers. This led to a profound change in the shopping habits of large numbers of people who were used to giving lists of their requirements to their grocers, their butchers, their bakers and their various other suppliers, and having them promptly delivered to their homes. Before the war, there had been a veritable army of delivery boys on specially-designed cargo-carrying bicycles, as well as large numbers of horse-drawn and motorized delivery vehicles. Their numbers had been reduced by 1942, but, in the official view, there were still far too many. For example, in Royston there were ten

PUBLIC NOTICES

Ipswich Grocery and Provision Trades.

Retail Delivery within the Borough.

In the interest of
National Economy
and the **WAR EFFORT** it has been decided that all methods of delivery will cease on and after **MONDAY, MARCH 9th.**

We as traders ask the public to still support those whom they are already registered with, and to remain loyal with them in these difficult and strenuous times.

AGED AND INFIRMED.
Special consideration is being given to these cases, and an announcement will be made in these columns in the very near future.

This decision has been approved by both the Ministry of Food and Transport.

W. WHITEHAND,
Chairman.

LEGAL NOTICES

JOHN WILLIAM ALBERT CHURCHYARD, Deceased

An announcement that "in the interest of national economy and the war effort" there would be no further deliveries of groceries in the Ipswich area.
East Anglian Daily Times

vehicles delivering bread, eleven for milk, six used by butchers, three for wines and spirits, four for groceries, two for greengroceries, six for coal, and eleven for other retail deliveries of one sort or another: a total of fifty-three.

Traders were told that they must co-operate and arrange to deliver groceries and provisions on only one day each week; meat, fish and greengroceries might be delivered on two or three days in each week. They were ordered to pool their vehicles, and the areas in which those vehicles operated were severely restricted. Apart from saving manpower, the government argued, the scheme would save ten million gallons of petrol a year.

The retail traders in the Eastern Region thought these proposals were draconian. At a conference in the Cambridge Guildhall on 16th January they raised problems, but it was quickly made clear to them that they were there to be told, rather than to discuss. They were sent away to arrange district meetings as a matter of urgency. Cambridge retailers met a few days later and were told that their scheme must be in operation within three weeks. "There is no boloney about this — it has got to be effected," the District Transport Officer told them bluntly. They complied, and laid up one in four of their delivery vans.

The limitation of deliveries, so that housewives had to go to the shops to see what was actually available, caused another significant change in shopping habits.

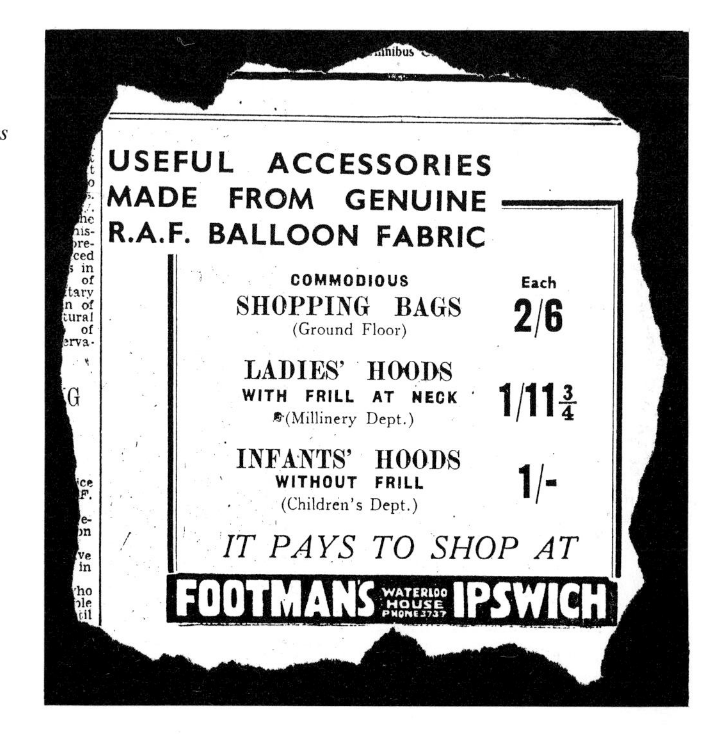

Rubberized balloon fabric could be used for other things besides balloons, as this advertisement shows.
East Anglian Daily Times

Credit was sought, and given, less than ever before. Before the end of the year a revolution had taken place, and the vice-president of the Cambridge Chamber of Commerce, Mr G. A. Heyworth, was able to say that "cash and carry has probably come to stay".

The range and variety of goods of every kind was steadily reduced, not simply because of shortage of materials but as a deliberate policy to save manpower and womanpower. The President of the Board of Trade, Dr Hugh Dalton, told the Commons that the policy of producing standardized, so-called "utility", goods would release 30,000 additional workers to the services or the munitions factories, while at the same time increasing overall supplies.

Production of pottery and hollow-ware was cut back to standard utility lines; domestic crockery could be only white or light ivory in colour, and it came in three grades, at controlled prices. By this means, it was claimed, half of the country's 42,000 pottery workers had been switched to war work.

Clothes became much more austere. It was made illegal to decorate women's underwear or nightwear with lace or other forms of embroidery, and "austerity cuts" were prescribed for the manufacture of men's shirts and pyjamas. Utility skirts were permitted only four pleats. Women's dresses had to be manufactured in a range of thirty-six standard sizes, "to suit all shapes and sizes". The public was assured that this would be "an immense improvement on the ready-made dress sizes to which we have been accustomed".

Some indication of the resultant hunger for glamour was given when a Norwich department store announced, after the raids on that city, that 30,000 yards of cloth

Towels go "on the ration"; an announcement from the Board of Trade.
East Anglian Daily Times

had been salvaged and could be sold without coupons — and at eightpence a yard! Only one small advertisement was published, but it mentioned "beautiful silks and cottons, some of prewar standard and hardly damaged". Girls in nearby country villages got out of bed at 4 am and cycled into town. By 6 am there was a big queue outside the shop, many with camp stools, flasks of coffee and sandwiches. The queue lengthened. The police instituted crowd control. Eventually, 2,000 women filled the pavements for a quarter of a mile. When the doors opened, customers were each given fifteen minutes and allowed one length of lingerie material, one of cotton, and one of silk. By midday it had all gone, and large numbers went home disappointed.

Utility household textiles appeared in the shops, and the Minister announced that utility footwear would shortly become available in substantial quantities, followed by utility furniture at fixed prices, and later by utility cutlery, clocks and watches. He made it clear that Britain was moving into a "utility" existence all round. There were going to be utility pencils, utility cigarette lighters, utility suitcases, even utility wedding rings. "With regard to utility umbrellas", he added, "we are standardizing down to two sizes and taking out half their ribs." MPs laughed, but Dr Dalton was not joking.

The utility ranges were manufactured to the best standard possible with the limited materials available and, in the circumstances of the time, represented good value for money. Not everyone was able to buy these goods, however. When utility furniture went on sale it was available only to the newly married, expectant mothers, growing families, and those whose homes had been destroyed in air raids. They had to apply for "buying permits". From 1st November, 1942, no furniture other than utility was permitted to be made.

And not everyone thought the controlled prices a sufficient attraction, so long as alternatives were available; William Stock, the Chelmsford shop assistant, noted in his diary:

> Bought a pair of new shoes, which cost twice as much as the last pair I bought. However, I thought they were good wartime value. The utility shoes, though cheap, do not look very hard-wearing. Their soles are thin and their designs are not attractive. These I would not buy[(1)].

Throughout the year the Board of Trade pushed ahead with the policy of "concentrating" the less essential industries in order to provide additional labour (and materials and factories) for more urgent war needs, and there was a virtual prohibition of the manufacture of a wide range of non-essential goods.

Some small cars were still being turned out of British factories in July, but they were only for the police and others who held special permits, and the Commons was told that the manufacture of civilian motor vehicles in Britain was to cease "in the near future".

Industry and commerce, trade and the professions were all brought under close scrutiny in this sweeping reassessment of Britain's resources. Raw material supplies to factories in Norfolk, Suffolk, Essex, Hertfordshire, Bedfordshire, Cambridgeshire and Huntingdonshire were supervised by a regional office in Cambridge of the Raw Materials Department of the Ministry of Supply. The Ministry of Labour and National Service set up a new Appointments Department, with three offices in the Eastern Region, to sort out "people with administrative, managerial, professional or technical qualifications . . ." and anyone else whose normal salary exceeded £420 a year.

We have seen in an earlier chapter how the Civil Defence services were reorganized at this time. Attention was also paid to the Home Guard, and it was decided that men who were still civilians should be liable, from March, to compulsory enrolment. At first this was restricted to the most vulnerable areas of the country, which included Norfolk, Suffolk, Cambridgeshire, Huntingdonshire, the Isle of Ely, Bedfordshire and those parts of Essex and Hertfordshire which lay outside the Metropolitan Police area, but soon afterwards it was extended elsewhere. The introduction of compulsion upset some of the older hands who had been proud of their promptitude in volunteering, and some of them resigned. An historian of the Home Guard in Cambridgeshire wrote:

> There was at the time some apprehension lest compulsion might alter the whole tone of the Home Guard. It was felt by some that a force originally raised in the old yeoman tradition might deteriorate once it was diluted with conscripts, as they were at first called. These fears were not justified. Compulsion brought in a large amount of fine material. Men holding responsible positions and who were already serving their country for long hours were drafted into the ranks and made excellent soldiers . . .[2]

Major-General Viscount Bridgeman, Director General of the Home Guard, in a message on 14th May marking the second anniversary of its formation, declared:

> The resignations which took place in February last, on the application of compulsion, are proving a source of strength rather than weakness . . . Many who have borne the burden for so long must now give place to the younger men whom they themselves have trained . . . It is now possible to allot more Regular officers and NCOs for permanent duty with the Home Guard.

Full-time officers were appointed as adjutants and quartermasters, and administration was organized more efficiently than it had ever been before. Each platoon now had its HQ organization, with expert signallers, intelligence, first-aid, gas squads, assistant quartermasters and clerks. Company HQs were at last developed into the form and organization of the Regular Army. The 2nd Cambs and Suffolk Battalion, for example, had been meeting in the Doric Cinema in Newmarket every Sunday for months, simply watching training films; its real battle training began with the arrival of an adjutant and equipment in July. Similarly, the arrival of a quartermaster had a big effect on the supply of equipment to the 4th battalion: "Every man was at last equipped, and order brought from chaos in the administrative side of the companies"[3], and the battalion was able to hold regular weekend camps at Thriplow. The 7th Cambs (Mobile) Battalion ran full-time ten-day courses four times a year for 150 to 200 men at a time, during which they went on five-day hundred-mile route marches carrying full equipment and sleeping in bivouacs in varied type of country in the fens and the heaths east of Cambridge. The men practised anti-tank tactics by night and new battle drill by day.

Eventually all men between the ages of eighteen and sixty had registered with the authorities and all under forty-seven who were fit were settled in the armed forces or the Civil Defence organization, or in essential war production work in the factories, shipyards or mines, or were combining some other form of civilian war work with part-time Home Guard or Civil Defence service. The authorities then turned their attention to women and to the under-eighteens of both sexes.

Lieutenant-General K. A. N. Anderson inspecting the Cambridgeshire Home Guard at their anniversary parade at Cambridge in May, 1942.

Since the outbreak of war, women had been steadily taking over a wide range of jobs for which, previously, they would never have been considered. Even mothers, who were not under compulsion to do so, took employment when there were nurseries to look after their children. Cambridge had half a dozen such nurseries, able to accommodate 167 children, aged two to five.

Women were working in factories in large numbers; they were manning buses, delivering mail, driving tractors. Now they were accepted for training for skilled technical tasks. The Post Office had introduced a scheme to train women telephone engineers and by the summer of 1942 there were 490 of them in the Home Counties Region, working a forty-eight-hour week, for which they were paid 41s to 59s 6d. In Cambridge, by June, thirty-seven such women had replaced men, and some of them were installing equipment at the new aerodromes being built in the area. But when the *Cambridge Daily News* reported on their activities there was more than a hint of chauvinist condescension:

> In the matter of sorting and lacing cables, some of the women are as efficient as the men, and others show aptitude in following diagrams. New trainees, when first confronted with the enormous numbers of different coloured cables, are apt to bestow weird and wonderful names on them, more reminiscent of the summer sales than the official designations of the colours. The Post Office does not recognize eau-de-nil, petunia, or autumn glow.

Why Married Women
(AS WELL AS SINGLE)
are asked to volunteer for the Services

THE Government is asking *every* married woman who has no young children and is not doing vital work, to volunteer for the ATS or WAAF. Some people wonder why. "Why *married* women? Why not the single girls?" they ask.

The reason is simple. Here it is:—

Of the women aged 18 to 43 in this country, only four out of ten are single. These single girls, as you know, were the first to be called upon for the war industries and the Services. The records show that *almost all* of them are now in vital work that they cannot leave, or already in the Services. This is true even though you may know a few single girls who you think are not in important work. Every unmarried woman who *can* be spared from industry *will* be released. *But there are not enough of them.* That is the simple truth.

Of course, all *married* women cannot go, either. Mothers of young children cannot go. Nor can wives who are cooking and running the house for their families and at the same time

FAMOUS FOR HER PASTRY. *Here's someone who has a really important war job. She is a cook in the ATS, and constantly receives messages saying: "Compliments to Pte. S—— for her pastry to-day!" It makes a difference to the men in the Forces to get good food!*

SINGLE

"The records show that almost all of them are now in vital work that they cannot leave, or in the Services .... There are not enough of them."

MARRIED

"Married women, including Servicemen's wives, are asked to volunteer unless they are doing vital work that really helps the war effort. Of course, mothers of ... ldren cannot go ...."

Left: A call to women, married as well as single, to volunteer for the ATS or the WAAF. *East Anglian Daily Times*

Right: Women were called upon to do many different jobs. These three were employed on the making of concrete railway sleepers at the LNER sleeper depot at Lowestoft. *East Anglian Daily Times*

The Norwich shoe industry was still managing extremely well at this stage of the war, largely because of the skill and ability of local girls who were doing jobs previously done by men. The *Eastern Daily Press* commented proudly:

> The Norwich shoe industry has so successfully put its house in order that it is now better equipped to meet a resumption of normal trading than it has ever been in the last 25 years. The Norwich firms, it seems, have, while retaining their hold on the temporarily less important fashion footwear, made a new name for themselves since the war in the utility and what are termed "fashion-utility" ranges, which have naturally come to the fore under clothes rationing.

East Anglian farmers, however, were extremely slow to take up the offer of help from the Women's Land Army, although many of their wives were doing the paperwork which resulted from all the new government regulations. During 1942 hostels were built for the WLA, but most young women who left home to take war work elsewhere lived in billets or lodgings. For some of them this proved to be a very depressing business.

Miss Winifred Last, a civil servant in her mid-forties, had taken a job — and accommodation — in Bury St Edmunds. She was paid £170 a year, with a small

bonus, and she paid thirty shillings a week for rooms in Guildhall Street. She described vividly in her diary the conditions in which she lived:

> I lay awake for hours listening to mice as they scratched and bumped into things. I have to share the lavatory and water tap downstairs. The tenant downstairs asked if I would only go through her rooms to the water tap and lavatory once a day at 8.45 am, as she liked to be private. Felt very annoyed, and said I'd do what I could, but could make no definite promise.
>
> I look at the dust on things. I feel I need a bath and haven't even water enough for a decent wash . . . I think there is some virtue in the village pump, to which all would have unrestricted access. I've some washing wants doing, but I've nowhere to hang it to dry. I am no longer able to hang out laundry in the bit of back yard because I know it would offend the tenant downstairs. It might dry in the cupboard where the plaster has vanished and the wind blows from outside through the laths.
>
> I have nowhere to shake rugs, unless out of the front windows into one of the town's main thoroughfares! And passers-by might object to that, particularly if I used the attic window, in which case the window frame with its remnants of glass (it is tied together with string) would possibly drop into the street.
>
> The wireless has been on downstairs all evening. Mine won't go because the Electricity Company won't let me have a meter, because I'm not in a self-contained flat. As no gas is laid on, I burn paraffin in lamps and stove[4].

The conscription of childless women had begun in December, 1941, with a choice of services or factories. No other country had taken such a drastic step. The first women to be called up for the auxiliary forces under the terms of the new National Service Act registered early in January, 1942, had their medical examinations in the last week of February, and were in uniform early in March. They were all aged twenty-one or twenty-two, but by the middle of the year, single women aged twenty were being called up as well, and all between eighteen and thirty were subject to the Control of Employment Order, which meant that they could be directed to work essential to the war effort. By June girls of the ATS were being trained at a Mixed Heavy AA Practice Camp in East Anglia. There they were "broken in" to the noise and vibration of heavy guns, before they were posted to duties at gun sites. When posted, their duties were to spot approaching aircraft and find their height and the range of the target.

Mrs Sarah Williams noted on 7th January:

> Women seem extremely eager to evade the National Service Act. I heard of two cases today: one of a girl getting married and another of a girl whose mother had been perfectly well and healthy until her daughter had to go — or it seemed likely — when the mother developed chronic invalidism[5].

A large number of young women had volunteered for the forces, and were already serving, but the *conscription* of women disturbed many people. Their emotions found expression when, in April, the first ATS girl was reported killed in action. Mr D. L. Perkins, of Cambridge, wrote to the *Cambridge Daily News* indignantly:

> A young girl of five months' service dies protecting businesses in which young men lead comfortable reserved lives, protecting cafes where young men eat their cakes and sip their coffee, protecting cinemas, theatres, dance halls, public houses, all containing a large quota of civilian young men whose main interest in life appears to be their own pleasure and comfort . . . Let the civilian youth of England beware lest the fighting men and women of the Services find a bitter label for them — "they fought — to the last English girl".

This produced a series of letters to the editor. The Perkins letter was an interesting document of its time for, as another (apparently neutral) correspondent pointed out, "such remarks are being made daily, in fact hourly, by many such as Mr Perkins". The letters published were evenly balanced between those who shared Mr Perkins' sense of outrage and those who thought he had misjudged the whole situation. Representative of the first school was the correspondent who declared:

> It is an undoubted fact that this town abounds in shirkers of all ages, who can advance all sorts of excuses for sitting back and leaving it to the other fellow, and whose war effort is nil.

The opposite view was put by a man who pointed out that factory workers were working twelve to fourteen hours a day and then doing voluntary Civil

Defence duties. He thought Mr Perkins was "totally unaware of the existence of Manpower Boards, who carefully sift the credentials of every civilian in a reserved occupation".

The *Cambridge Daily News* permitted Mr Perkins the last word. He said he had received letters and messages from servicemen with emphatic views, and he declared his own conviction that "a gun-site is no place for a young girl".

Inevitably, some of the critics were irritated by the sight of undergraduates of military age walking the streets of Cambridge. In February the Censor of Fitzwilliam House, Mr W. S. Thatcher, was reported to have criticized them at a meeting in the town. "He would like to see a detailed account of how their hours were spent," it was reported. "However 'necessary' cinemas, 'high conversation'

The Chief of Air Staff, Sir Charles Portal (later Lord Portal), speaking to WAAFs on a barrage balloon site during a tour of inspection. *East Anglian Daily Times*

and the social life of cafes might be from their point of view, it was now dangerously futile."

This was no sooner in print than Mr Thatcher dashed off a letter to the editor explaining that "my indictment was against all classes in the country, and not particularly the undergraduate. Further, even when taking the undergraduate as an example, I did not criticize the great bulk of men, who are doing their duty." It turned out that the paper had not covered the event with a staff reporter, but had had its report supplied. We are left to guess whether Mr Thatcher was in retreat before the ire of the university authorities, or whether his hearer who recorded what he thought he had heard had allowed his own prejudice to distort the facts.

The chairman of Cambridgeshire County Council, Alderman W. J. Taylor, tried to cool things, remarking: "When things do not go quite right, stop finding fault with one another — but carry on."

There were some men — and women — who resisted conscription because they declared their consciences forbade their participation in war. When they appeared before tribunals in Cambridge and Norwich they often attracted sharp criticism, but overall there was a surprising degree of tolerance of their position.

Most were granted exemption from service in the armed forces on condition that they did some form of noncombatant service or worked on the land or in Civil Defence. At the tribunal at Cambridge Guildhall on 21st May, for example, nine applications for exemption were made by university students. Three were ordered to perform noncombatant duties, two were registered on condition they served in a Friends' Ambulance Unit, one on condition he joined the FAU or worked on the land, two others were ordered to do land or forestry work, and one was permitted to continue with the research work on which he was engaged.

There were four women objectors at the same tribunal. A twenty-one-year-old woman whose home was near Fakenham appeared in Salvation Army uniform and said she had worked at a canteen in Norwich throughout the bombing raids there; she was ordered to continue with that work, full-time, with the Salvation Army. The next was a twenty-one-year-old domestic servant from Elmswell, who was ordered to work on the land or on civilian hospital duties. The other two were sisters, and both dedicated Jehovah's Witnesses; the elder was twenty-four and had already been to prison for refusing a direction to do hospital work. Both were registered unconditionally.

A number of conscientious objectors who failed to comply with conditions imposed by the tribunals were sent to prison by East Anglian magistrates, the usual charge being that they had refused medical examination, and the usual sentence being three months. A thirty-two-year-old woman, a Jehovah's Witness who claimed the status of a full-time minister, was sent to prison for three months at Essex Quarter Sessions in July because she refused to work on a farm.

The practice, familiar during the 1914–18 war, of sending white feathers to men who would not fight was rare in the Second World War, but after a few had been sent to men who had been discharged from the services on medical grounds a Minister, Mr Osbert Peake, told the Commons: "Everyone will sympathize with the desire to put a stop to this mischief . . . In this war, in which the whole energies of the nation are engaged, a man's patriotism and courage cannot be gauged by reference to the clothes he wears. Civilians, whether ex-servicemen or not, are required to perform the work for which they are best qualified and can best serve their country. I hope the publicity that has been given to this matter will put a stop to this stupid and objectionable practice."

A spate of letters in the *Cambridge Daily News* in July illustrated the exceptional degree of tolerance of dissident opinion which was characteristic of Cambridge. In response to an initial letter highly critical of COs, a serving soldier wrote:

> I joined the Army on the day this war commenced in support of my ideals, but I am not condemning the conscientious objector because he feels that joining the Army is contrary to his ideals . . . I think the tribunals carry out their duties in the correct manner as instructed. I would beg for tolerance . . . I detest any person who isn't prepared to make a sacrifice for an ideal, but I respect the person who is, whichever way he makes it.

During the early months of 1942, the net was being thrown wider to catch teenage youths. On 31st January those aged seventeen were required to register for call-up to the regular forces, and a month later boys of sixteen. The National Service Acts made young men *liable* to be called up when they were eighteen. During the early part of the war they were not called until they were twenty; then, later, it was when they were nineteen. Now, as 1942 began, they were getting their call-up papers as soon as they were eighteen and a half and before the year was out when they were just eighteen. The government promised that nobody would be sent overseas under the age of nineteen.

The government also wanted boys and girls of a much more tender age. The War Office had established an Army Cadet Force, in which youngsters received basic training for two sessions each week, so that when they were later called up they would already be familiar with some features of service life. From 1942 the Home Guard accepted responsibility for this Cadet Force, and when the lads were seventeen they transferred automatically to the Home Guard.

Cambridge was asked to enrol a force of three hundred. On 24th February an advertisement appeared in the local press calling on youths between fourteen and seventeen to apply to Lieutenant-Colonel J. G. Grace, of the Home Guard. The schools co-operated closely, and four hundred were enrolled immediately, so that the first parade took place in the Guildhall only five days later, on 29th February. The response was such that the War Office was asked for permission to enrol 1,000 in the whole county, and later 2,000. By the beginning of April 1,800 had signed up, nearly 1,000 uniforms had been issued, and there was a new target of 2,400. Soon afterwards the Suffolk Army Cadet Corps reached its full establishment of twelve units with 1,600 youths, and every unit had a waiting list. There were two seven-day

Members of the Holbrook squadron of the Air Training Corps photographed outside the Royal Hospital School, Holbrook. Many later joined the RAF. *Mrs M. Leeson*

summer camps under canvas and the 690 who attended received instruction from Regular Army and Home Guard officers.

An Air Training Corps, and later a Sea Cadet Corps, were also formed. When they registered for call-up to the regular forces, then, most lads were already serving in one or other of these junior organizations. Those who were not were pressed to do so.

The same thing was happening throughout the Eastern Counties, with every possible effort being made to bring young people voluntarily into the services. During the summer several hundred cadets of Norwich wing of the ATC, aged sixteen to eighteen, camped at different aerodromes to get experience of actual conditions of life in the RAF. Many were given some flying experience, and the Link Trainer was very popular. They were also given a chance to get used to the feel of parachute harness — but they were not allowed to jump. At one of the parades of the 104th Cambridge Squadron of the ATC an RAF officer who had taken part in thousand-plane bombing raids on Cologne and Essen gave them a pep talk, declaring that both "shows" had been "absolutely wizard".

Empire Youth Sunday in April was the occasion of big parades in most towns. In Ipswich, for example, the Mayor, Alderman R. F. Jackson, took the salute outside the Town Hall as units of the Home Guard, the Army Cadets, the Sea Cadets, the Air Training Corps, the Scouts, the Guides, the Boys' and Girls Brigades, the St John Ambulance Cadets, the NFS and the ARP Messengers marched past. Later Ipswich saw its largest-ever parade of the ATC when four Ipswich squadrons, plus detachments from Felixstowe, Woodbridge, Hadleigh, Stowmarket, Samford, Sudbury and Leiston squadrons — a total of eight hundred officers and cadets — attended a drumhead service and then took part in an inter-squadron sports meeting.

Similar efforts were made to get the girls involved in a Girls' Training Corps, a para-military organization for those aged fourteen to eighteen, with the simplest of uniforms — blue side-cap, white shirt and blue tie and skirt — and the declared purpose of "training girls to citizenship and service to the community". At a crowded inaugural meeting in the Ipswich Library they were promised a programme of physical training, first-aid, firefighting and anti-gas drill, and told that it would be useful training for those of them who would be going into the services shortly, when they were eighteen. Two clergymen who were present were unsuccessful when they moved a resolution that training should not intrude on Sunday. When three companies of the GTC were formed in Cambridge, the proposed training was given a rather different emphasis; it would range, they were told, from car maintenance to cookery and child welfare.

The majority of children left school and started work when they were fourteen, so that these other activities had to be fitted into their leisure time. In October, 1942, the Ipswich Youth Committee received a report on the registration of sixteen to eighteen-year-olds in the town. It contained this passage:

> Many young people are working too long and too hard. There is some danger of devitalizing the nation in the earlier years. The effect of strain was manifest, both with the girls and the boys, but especially in the case of girls, who declared they were too tired to go out at night . . .

It was discovered that some youngsters were working twelve to fourteen hours a day, doing firewatching duties as well, or travelling long journeys. Those with sufficient leisure were regular cinemagoers — some went five times a week. There was a small core of the boys, estimated at about five per cent, whose attitude was reported to be that they would undergo training only when they were forced to.

By the summer the government had introduced a new scheme to employ children in agriculture, and local education committees were asked to make necessary arrangements to release them from school. The scheme was discussed by Cambridge Borough Education Committee on 2nd June. It excused children of twelve and over from school attendance for not more than twenty school sessions in one year, and approved their employment for up to thirty-six hours in any one week, or seven hours in one day, or four hours continuously.

One member, Alderman Mrs C. D. Rackham, attacked the whole idea, calling it disgraceful that children so young should be employed for so many hours. But hers was a lone voice. The chairman of the committee concerned, Councillor G. Wilding, said he had watched children at work; they seemed to enjoy it and not to regard it as work at all. The children employed under the scheme would mainly be called on to lead horses, gather potatoes and pick fruit. The Education Committee approved the scheme. Three weeks later Mrs Rackham, who had been a member of the local Juvenile Bench for twenty-two years and was recognized as an expert on eight- to sixteen-year-old children, returned to the attack. The safeguards surrounding the scheme were wholly inadequate, she insisted, and were impossible to ensure. She pleaded that, at least, children should be medically examined before being put to work. Another woman member of the Education Committee was perturbed because she had observed children being kept out working late at night, but nevertheless she supported the employment scheme, hoping that farmers would behave reasonably. Other, male, members were sharply critical of Mrs Rackham. Councillor M. C. Burkitt declared that children loved doing most of the jobs to which they would be put; they would not in the slightest be injurious to their health, but rather the reverse.

The plan to use children of twelve for the harvest was also strongly criticized by the president of the National Union of Agricultural Workers, Mr Edward Gooch, who was a Norfolk man. He told his county committee: "It is a crime against the children and, despite the government's attitude on the question, I do not intend to give my approval to the employment for profit of children under fourteen years of age." Norfolk Education Committee, however, when it considered the question in May, agreed to co-operate by releasing children aged twelve and over for a maximum of ten days' farm work during the year. Some members of the committee objected, but others argued that youngsters had always been employed on fruit picking. One declared that mothers looked on it rather as a holiday than anything else.

Mrs Sarah Williams, in Norwich, noted in her diary in June:

> The Headmaster asked for boys to go to a farm tomorrow to single sugar beet. The farmer has 30 acres which have to be singled in the next ten days, or ploughed under. There were plenty of volunteers. They are to be paid sixpence an hour.

The *Cambridge Daily News* London Letter in August reported that "The attention of the Ministry of Labour and the Ministry of Agriculture is being called to reports of over-working of boys on farms . . . On some farms it appears the boys have to work 60 hours a week . . ." The paper did not follow this up with any investigation of what was happening in its own area.

By this time there was a new source of labour for the farms, Italian prisoners of war. The first of these had arrived in Britain the previous autumn from North Africa, where they had been captured in battle, and five hundred had been sent to Ely and three hundred to Royston. In each of these places a fifth of them were set to work building the camps in which they were to live, while the others were sent to work on local farms[6]. From May, 1942, they arrived in Britain in monthly batches of five thousand, and two-thirds were directed into agriculture, the others being classified as "tradesmen" and "builder's labourers".

Initially these POWs were put into camps which each held five hundred, with 120 guards, and were taken each day in lorries to workplaces within twenty miles and collected again at dusk. Soon it was considered safe to let them work unguarded, leaving their employers with the responsibility of keeping an eye on them. Later again, it was decided that POWs who had earned a reputation as "good conduct" men might be allowed to live, singly or in twos and threes, on the farms which employed them. In fact, farmers were slow to recruit them, not entirely because they had so recently been fighting against British troops but also because they did not understand English and most of their working experience had been with a different kind of farming.

During the course of 1942, however, this situation changed and the Italians were not merely accepted but often were popular with those who got to know them

Women worked on the farms. This gang of women is engaged in harvesting rye on an East Suffolk farm, where more than 200 acres were down to the crop. *East Anglian Daily Times*

well. At the end of the year there were over eight thousand prisoners of war working in the Eastern Command area, living in eleven different camps. The biggest of them, each with accommodation for 750, were at Barton Field, Ely, Royston Camp, Trumpington, Botesdale, Redgrave Hall (near Diss), Sawtry (Hunts) and High Garrett (near Braintree). Selected Italians were being moved out of these large camps into land army hostels, so that they could be nearer the farms at which they worked[7].

As the year progressed pressure on men, women and children increased. In August Mr Herbert Morrison announced that, with immediate effect, women between the ages of twenty and forty-five would be equally liable with men for compulsory fire prevention duties. Those who worked in offices would be liable for up to forty-eight hours' duty each month at their place of employment; other single women could be posted to any residential area within their local authority area where there was a shortage of firewatchers. Married women would only be liable to serve in the neighbourhood of their homes, and there was exemption for expectant mothers, mothers of children under fourteen, and women who worked for fifty-five hours or more a week at business premises. Mr Morrison added that all women would be exempt from duties between noon and 6 pm on Saturdays, so that they could do their shopping.

Anyone who failed to turn up for work was liable to prosecution — in July a Ramsey man on building work was sent to prison for twenty-eight days for absenteeism. In that same month the Cambridge and Norwich education

committees decided that their school teachers should have only two weeks' holiday "absolutely free from school". The schools were kept open all the time for voluntary attendance, to keep children occupied and to enable meals to be served to them.

In September the government ordered a complete overhaul of the registers to check that no men aged forty-one to fifty (who were above the age so far called up to the forces) and no women aged eighteen to forty-five had slipped through their fingers, and to ensure that every man and woman was doing a job to which they had been directed or which had been approved by Ministry officials.

At the end of September a national campaign was launched to persuade married women to volunteer for service in the auxiliary forces. The advertisements which appeared in the press were worded with great care and restraint because, as the Lobby Correspondent of the Press Association wrote:

> The government feel they must walk warily, as compulsion applied to the wives of servicemen is apt to cause some anxiety. Men abroad do not like to feel that their wives at home may be forced to do anything against their inclinations.

This was certainly true. Mrs Sarah Williams' diary contains this entry:

> Rona had a letter from her sweetheart in Africa, who tells her that lots of his friends when they hear that their girls have joined the forces promptly write to give them up.

The revolution which was taking place in the working and living habits of every man and woman could not fail to have social consequences, and part of the disquiet

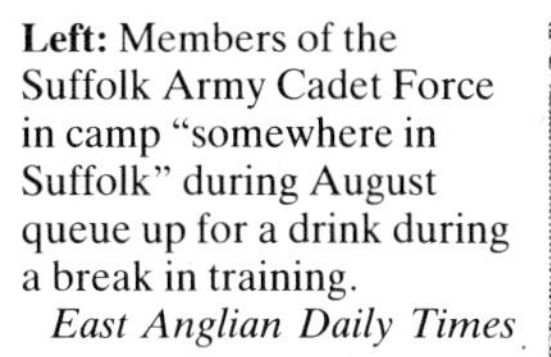

Left: Members of the Suffolk Army Cadet Force in camp "somewhere in Suffolk" during August queue up for a drink during a break in training.
East Anglian Daily Times

Right: These women were employed by the London and North Eastern Railway in painting railway bridges, essential maintenance work which could not be neglected in wartime.
East Anglian Daily Times

of absent husbands may be explained by the contents of a Mass Observation report on Chelmsford:

> Cases of married women having a glamorous life are of daily occurrence. Fidelity of many married women is on the decline and examples here and there get into the papers, where the affair assumes a complicated form. There are, however, cases which are settled within a small part of the community, or are hushed up in the interest of those involved[8].

The same report elaborates:

> Attitude towards sex: There is less restraint and more freedom. Outlook on life is also changing subconsciously, as the effect of religion is less marked
> Talk: More talk about sex by men, and most probably by girls too, because girls are working by the side of men. Naturally, men talk about various girls and their behaviour. Men whistle more and more as the girls move about the workshops.

At the end of the year Ipswich ran a special campaign for a fortnight to recruit more women. Married women who were already doing a full-time job as well as running a home were given leave so that they could call at every house in the town. They were looking for 1,500 women prepared either to work in one of the town's war factories or to take over less essential work from younger women, who could then be transferred to the war industries. The demand for yet more labour remained insatiable.

As a footnote to this story of a continuous, urgent search for men and women, we may note in passing an interesting problem which faced Ipswich Town Council during 1942. It was in need of an Assistant Medical Officer for the borough, and there were no applicants for the post who were not aliens. Interviews took place and references were taken up. The council's Public Health Committee recommended a man who had produced excellent testimonials, and whose medical education had included three years at Edinburgh University. He had fled to Britain in 1936 from the Continent, where he had been persecuted because he had Jewish blood, and now he was stateless.

But his name was Konrad Hirsch and, yes, he had been born in Germany. The debate in the Council Chamber was long and heated. The duties included those of assistant schools medical officer, and one councillor declared that Ipswich parents were in a state of great indignation about the proposal to appoint this man. Another declaimed: "Do you think the people of Coventry or Norwich would consider appointing a German medical officer?" This sort of emotional confusion, which prevented some people identifying friends and enemies, was common enough all over Britain at this time. A majority of Ipswich councillors kept their heads, and Dr Hirsch was appointed.

CHAPTER SEVEN

Saving and Sharing

BY 1942 the British people were grimly accustomed to a siege economy. The island was beleaguered, its essential supplies at constant hazard. Survival depended upon the best possible use of what was available, by conservation, recycling and fair and efficient distribution.

Shipping was the problem. So many vessels had been lost — and were still being lost — and the service demands upon the fleet that remained were increasing so much that the government's Shipping Committee foresaw a gap of 8.4 million tons between anticipated imports of food and raw materials and imports actually required to meet anticipated consumption in the eighteen-month period beginning on 1st January. How was this gap to be closed? In the first quarter of 1942 they did not expect to be able to ship in more than 5.75 million tons of non-tanker goods, compared with almost seven million tons in the worst quarter of 1941(1). This suggested that Britain's stocks of wheat would fall below the danger level by the end of February, and even lower in the two following months.

To reduce the immediate danger it was decided to increase the milling ratio, raising the wheat extraction rate to 85 per cent, so that the public had to get used to a coarser, darker bread than before. At the same time, it was resolved that the ploughing-up campaign would be intensified on the farms, to bring 300,000 to 400,000 additional acres into cultivation of wheat for the 1942–43 harvest.

Even with these two measures, it seemed unavoidable that stocks would be run down by six million tons, to the danger level, and somehow or other the desired level of imports had to be cut by 2.5 million tons. It was recognized that the risks were tremendous. If the situation got out of hand, it could dislocate military operations or war industry, or it could reduce food rations below the amounts thought essential to maintain health and strength.

Every possible idea was explored: bread rationing (finally rejected in August, 1942), a further increase in the milling ratio to 90 or even 95 per cent, a halving of beer supplies in order to dilute bread with barley, compulsory slaughter of livestock (to save feeding stuffs), reduction of fertilizer imports(2).

There was a long period of anxiety. The government sought firm undertakings that the United States would provide more ships and supplies to see Britain through. Shipping losses continued to be serious throughout 1942, but in the end it turned out that Britain's import needs had been overestimated, so that there was no desperate crisis of the kind that had been feared. At the end of the year Britain's 46,000,000 people had had at least an adequate diet(3).

As the year passed, however, it became necessary to tighten up the rationing system, with the aim of ensuring fair distribution of the limited supplies available. The extension of the war to the Far East cut off some supplies and from 26th January whole rice, sago, tapioca, imported dried beans, lentils, various kinds of peas, and all dried fruits were rationed for the first time. They were added to the range of foodstuffs "on points"; ration books contained coupons of specified points value and customers could choose from the very limited range of foodstuffs available the things on which to spend their points. For the four weeks 9th February to 8th March each person was given twenty points. A pound of dried fruits would have used up eight of those points; a pound of rice two points.

At the beginning of the year the vitamin D in margarine was doubled. "National" flour of 85 per cent extraction and the "national" loaf were introduced in March. In July chocolates and sweets were rationed for the first time and the ration of tea previously given to under-fives was cancelled, but the cheese ration was doubled to half a pound a week.

The supply of those things which were officially rationed was maintained in adequate quantity for everyone to have their fair share. Many things that were unrationed were difficult to obtain. After Mrs Sarah Williams had been shopping in Sheringham on 13th April she noted in her diary:

> There is less and less to buy in the town. This afternoon we couldn't get any bread in the place, which seems really the limit. My husband brought me some soap for a present, which was lovely . . .[4]

There were occasional shafts of sunlight. With a seasonal improvement in milk supplies, the ration for adults was increased from 29th March from two-and-a-half to three pints a week. At about the same time the Ministry of Food issued this announcement in Cambridge:

> Fresh supplies of oranges will be available in the shops in Cambridge and district, including Newmarket, Ely, St Ives and part of Huntingdon, as from Monday next, April 6th, and will be reserved for a period of five days for issue at the rate of 1lb per head to children in possession of the green ration book . . . After the five days, any surplus may be sold to other customers, but retailers are asked to give priority to children, schools, hospitals and invalids.

Throughout East Anglia, oranges were allocated to each area in turn about once a month and the above distribution formula was standard; for the first five days they were reserved for children under two and after that, if there were any left, it was a free-for-all. When, in September, an exceptionally heavy cargo arrived in the country the Food Ministry allocated two pounds to each child under five, and one pound each for the five- to eighteen-year-olds.

In May Lord Woolton announced a new Meals Restriction Order for restaurants. From 15th June it became an offence to serve a meal exceeding three courses or costing more than five shillings. Only one of the two subsidiary courses might contain any portion of fish, meat or poultry, and that portion must not exceed a quarter of the whole. Provincial restaurants were forced to close between 11 pm and 5 am. If beer was served with a meal, the price must not exceed one shilling for a half-pint of draught or 1s 6d for a bottle of beer. Where there was a service charge, it could not exceed ten per cent of the total bill.

The non-profit, government-sponsored "British Restaurants" were increasingly used for hot midday meals. Norwich had opened its first such restaurant at the Bull Close School in the summer of 1941, and at the turn of the year it opened two more — at the former Heigham Street School and in a former furniture store in

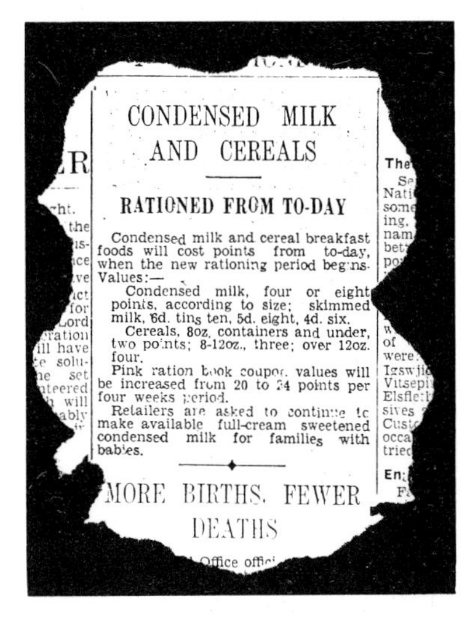

CONDENSED MILK AND CEREALS

RATIONED FROM TO-DAY

Condensed milk and cereal breakfast foods will cost points from to-day, when the new rationing period begins. Values:—

Condensed milk, four or eight points, according to size; skimmed milk, 6d. tins ten, 5d. eight, 4d. six.

Cereals, 8oz. containers and under, two points; 8-12oz., three; over 12oz. four.

Pink ration book coupon values will be increased from 20 to 24 points per four weeks period.

Retailers are asked to continue to make available full-cream sweetened condensed milk for families with babies.

MORE BIRTHS, FEWER DEATHS

Rationing may have made life more difficult for the housewife, faced with the task of producing appetizing meals for the family, but it seems not to have had any dire effects on the nation's health, to judge from these headlines. *East Anglian Daily Times*

Duke Street — with a fourth, in King Street, later. Roast beef, potatoes and cabbage, plus a choice of rice pudding or trifle, sold for ninepence. Soup and tea each cost an extra twopence. Thousands of people ate in these simple restaurants every day. When one was opened in the old *Angel Hotel* in Great Yarmouth in March, big enough to cater for three to four hundred people a day, the Eastern Area Divisional Food Officer, Colonel O. M. Lanyon, preached their egalitarian virtues. "It is quite true that the rich can afford to go to the Savoy", he said, "but they won't get any more to eat and I doubt if they will get any better quality food than you can get at the British Restaurant."

Beccles was particularly proud of its new British Restaurant; another Ministry of Food officer declared it to be "possibly the best specimen of a British Restaurant of its size in East Anglia". Local councillors clearly knew it was going to be good — the civic party attending the opening made up a third of the 150 people who ate there during the first day! Colchester already had three British Restaurants, in Ind Coope's Brewery in East Hill, at the old British School in Magdalen Street, and at Lexden Council School.

Cambridge lagged behind most other large towns, but when it opened its first British Restaurant it set a rare standard, taking over what had been one of the most exclusive clubs in the town, the oak-panelled Pitt Club in Jesus Lane. From 12th March hundreds filed each lunchtime beneath the bust of the younger Pitt and sat down to a two-course cooked meal, for which they paid a shilling. Soon afterwards, other British Restaurants were opened in St John's Hall, Blinco Grove, in St Andrew's Church Hall, Chesterton, and in the Romsey Labour Club. The Pitt Club was soon serving more than 3,600 dinners a week, and the three others well over 2,500 dinners a week between them. Lord Woolton, the Food Minister, looked in at the Pitt Club one day towards the end of the year, beaming his approval.

Alongside provision of British Restaurants in the towns, a "Pies Scheme" was introduced in most rural areas delivering hot meat pies at lunchtime to workers on the land. Something of the sort had been begun by the WVS during 1941, but now rural district councils were asked to arrange for the manufacture of pies and other suitable snacks and their distribution to workers on the job. The Thingoe RDC, one of the first to get its "rural feeding scheme" into operation, employed a

THIS WEEK'S

FOOD FACTS

Spring Fever

Out-of-doors the buds are bursting and the birds are singing, but maybe you and the family don't feel so gay. Are you listless and a little out of sorts? Spring Fever is the trouble, but you'll get over it if you pay special attention to your diet for the next few weeks. Don't give your family heavy, starchy meals just now. Plan dishes of blood-cleansing vegetables, raw and cooked, containing Vitamin C, a valuable tonic. Here are some recipes you might like to greet the spring with:

POTATO AND WATERCRESS SOUP

Time: Preparation 10 mins. Cooking 30 mins. *Ingredients:* 1 lb. potatoes, 2 bunches watercress, 1 pint vegetable stock, 1 pint 'household' milk, pepper, salt, 1 teaspoonful margarine. *Quantity:* 4 helpings. *Method:* Wash and peel potatoes and chop in small pieces. Cook potatoes in stock till soft, mash against side of pan with wooden spoon, add margarine, milk mixture and seasoning. Reheat and just before serving add chopped watercress.

TURNIP TOP SALAD

Time: 15 mins. *Ingredients:* 4 oz. turnip tops, 4 oz. white cabbage heart, 2 oz. beetroot, 2 oz. carrot. Watercress for garnishing. Salad dressing. *Quantity:* 4 helpings. *Method:* Grate or shred all the vegetables separately and arrange attractively on a large dish. Sprinkle with salad dressing and decorate with watercress. Make the salad dressing by adding vinegar, a little mustard, pepper and salt to a white-sauce.

SCALLOPED VEGETABLES WITH BACON

Time: Preparation 10 mins. Cooking 30 mins. *Ingredients:* ¼ cabbage, 3 or 4 carrots, 1 leek, 4 potatoes or any other vegetable, 2 tablespoonfuls national flour or 1 tablespoonful fine oatmeal, 2 or 3 slices of bacon, browned breadcrumbs. *Quantity:* 4 helpings. *Method:* Cook vegetables in a pint of water in a closely covered pan. Make thin white sauce with margarine, flour and vegetable water. Arrange vegetables in a fireproof dish, pour sauce over, lay bacon on top, sprinkle with breadcrumbs and crisp under grill.

Making milk . . .

To make a pint of 'household' milk put a pint of lukewarm water in a quart jug, measure 4 level tablespoonfuls of the powder and sprinkle it — a little at a time — on top of the water, while beating briskly with an egg whisk, fork or wooden spoon. It takes a little time and patience, but it is worth it. 'Household' milk mixture makes excellent white coffee and can be used in place of fresh milk in tea. Try it next time you are short and the uninvited guest drops in.

Save Our Soap

Measure *soap flakes* and *soap powder* with a spoon. Don't pour it recklessly from the packet.

Stack the dirty dishes on the draining board after each meal and only wash up once a day. This saves both *soap* and *fuel*.

It's a good plan to stick the last sliver of soap on to the new cake. Always keep the soap dry, stand it on a soap-mat or on a strainer. Wet the hands and then handle the soap. Never put the soap in the water. Don't hold the soap under a running tap. For washing very dirty hands mix 2 tablespoonfuls of soap jelly (made from ends of soap and boiling water), 2 tablespoonfuls finely powdered pumice and a small piece of whitening. Add three or four tablespoonfuls of water and boil. Use as necessary.

MF

THE MINISTRY OF FOOD, LONDON, W.1 FOOD FACTS No. 91

"Are you listless and a little out of sorts? Spring Fever is the trouble, but you'll get over it if you pay special attention to your diet. . . ." The Ministry of Food kept up a constant stream of advice through the newspapers, aiming to help housewives make the best of their families' rations.

East Anglian Daily Times

full-time catering superintendent, used two reconditioned ex-War Department vehicles, and enrolled the WVS and Women's Institutes to distribute 10,000 meat pies a week; they were sold at fourpence each. At about the same time Melford RDC announced that it was distributing 3,000 meat pies twice a week to twenty-two parishes in its area.

Provision of meals for children in school was expanded. In East Suffolk, for example, the number of meals served daily increased from 4,300 in July to 6,800 in the autumn, and the number of school canteens from thirty-six to eighty-six.

The main responsibility for feeding the nation, however, continued to rest on its housewives. The Ministry of Food advertised "Food Facts" week by week in all the local newspapers, and usually included suggested recipes. In mid-April the advertisement read:

> SPRING FEVER — Maybe you and the family don't feel so gay?
> Are you listless and a little out of sorts?
> Spring Fever is the trouble, but you'll get over it if you pay special attention to your diet for the next few weeks.

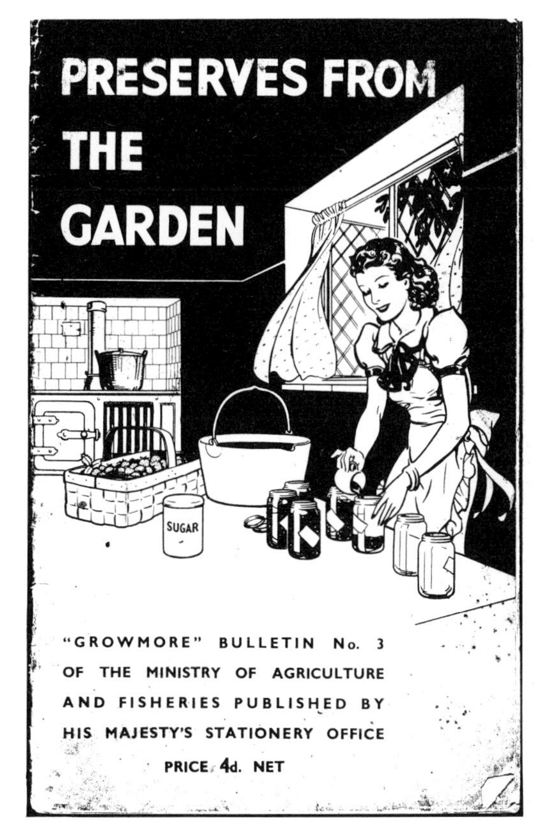

Making the best use of available food supplies included preserving fruit and vegetables both from the garden and from the hedgerow. This book issued by the Ministry of Agriculture and Fisheries gave much advice on the making of jams and pickles and the canning and bottling of all kinds of fruit and vegetables. *Mrs M. Leeson*

The recipes which followed were for potato and watercress soup, turnip-top salad, and scalloped vegetables with bacon. They showed realism, if not inspiration. Mrs Sarah Williams' diary noted a less helpful publication at about this time:

> I found today a cookery book — *The Doctor's Cookery Book* — which was supposed to be a cookery book for poorer families. Actually, the specimen recipes read like luxury nowadays — fancy having sausages and mashed potatoes *and* eggs on onions all in one day!

From 24th June a new delicacy was added to the British diet. Large round tins filled with a yellow powder appeared in the shops; these were the first consignments from the United States, Canada, Australia and the Argentine of "dried egg". Lord Woolton explained that it was made by "a new process devised in consultation between the Department of Scientific and Industrial Research and American scientists and food packers". Every two months each individual was to get a tin of it, equivalent to twelve eggs. "This is not an egg substitute", the Minister went on, "it is egg minus water and shell." After a few weeks he reported that they were "going very well . . . I hear on all hands they are very popular".

In June, too, the Ministry of Food announced that it would make an additional pound of sugar per head available for jam-making, the fruit crop having been particularly good.

Later there came another "concession". Food shops had been selling "broken biscuits" — what would normally have been the manufacturers' "rejects" were eagerly snapped up; now the Ministry told retailers they might also sell any biscuits that were broken "in the ordinary course of trade".

"Utility" was a label which became familiar to the wartime shopper in 1942—and advertisers did their best to indicate that "utility" was not synonymous with drab.
East Anglian Daily Times

Sometimes it seemed that the food problems were not evenly shared. In Bury St Edmunds, towards the end of the year, Miss Winifred Last reported:

> Twice I went in a grubby eating-house here and each time they gave me meat, a lot of Yorkshire pudding, and five different vegetables, all of it beautifully cooked . . .[5]

At the same time, a letter in the Cambridge newspaper complained of acute shortages there: no sweets, very little chocolate, few biscuits. "Is it true that supplies for this town are based on the population of 1938?" the correspondent asked.

As the year moved to a close, the Ministry of Food had one last card to play. It offered free cod liver oil and vitamin orange juice from the United States to young children and expectant mothers. Everywhere the mothers were soon queuing up for it — in Norwich, from the start, seven hundred mothers collected supplies regularly from the City Hall and 1,300 others from various welfare centres in the city.

As Christmas approached the Ministry produced the slogan "Frugal, but Festive" and announced:

> It will take more than Hitler to stop the British housewife from setting a festive table at Christmas time. Stuffed flank of beef may take the place of turkey, and a little cold tea may be used to darken the complexion of Christmas cake or pudding, but we can still contrive a spread which will delight the children and warm the hearts of the grown-ups.

The other rationing system that affected everyone was that for clothing and footwear. It had been first introduced in June, 1941, when everyone had been given sixty-six coupons to "spend" during the year ahead (a man had to surrender thirteen coupons for a jacket, a woman eleven for a dress). At mid-March 1942, the government announced a twenty-five per cent reduction in this ration: sixty coupons would now have to last for fourteen months. Even before this announcement Mrs Sarah Williams was confiding to her diary:

> Discussion in the office reveals the fact that most of us are in a sad state as regards underwear, all of us having spent our coupons on outer garments.

A letter to the editor of the *Cambridge Daily News*, signed "Clotheless", complained that things she had sent to her laundry six weeks before had not been returned. "Soon I shall be following Lady Godiva's example, substituting a bicycle for a horse," she wrote.

"Make do and mend" was one of the slogans of the time. Old clothes, pressed and brushed, could be worn as uniforms of pride. Patching was patriotic, darning a duty. A Cambridge firm of cleaners advertised:

> Let us give new life to your old shirts and pyjamas through our Repair and Renovating Service. No coupons required. New collar attached to shirt, 3s. New neck band, 1s 11d. New double cuffs, 2s 6d. Cuffs, double, turned and repaired, 2s 6d. New front, 4s 3d. Buttons, 1d each. Pyjamas — send in for repair at keenest price, or let us give you an estimate.

A firm in Ipswich advertised in June:

> CORSET REPAIRS. A new wartime service: repairs and renovations to corsets . . . invaluable to ladies whose corsets are in need of attention.

And Mrs Sarah Williams again:

> Finding that my black cardigan had worn out and having no coupons left, I investigated the remnants of my grandmother's wardrobe (she died three years ago) and found three cardigans which I could wear. I wouldn't have worn them before the war, but greeted them as great treasures today.

The circumstances of the time led to some changes in women's dress. They were excused the wearing of hats both in courtrooms and in church. And many of them took to wearing trousers, although this could cause controversy. Mrs Sarah Williams noted in January:

> Miss C, from the Sheringham office, came in today in trousers and Mr H was asked whether he would mind if we did. He immediately went in off the deep end and said we shouldn't ever be allowed to enter the office if we wore trousers, which is sheer prejudice, as official permission has been given for women Civil Servants to wear trousers, even in Whitehall. He became furious about the whole subject and I told him we should soon have to walk in and say "Heil H", which made him more furious.

Soap was rationed from 9th February: one coupon per person per week, and one coupon secured *either* three ounces of toilet soap *or* four ounces of hard

Crowded trains and unreliable timetables were not enough to put many travellers off, and the Railway Executive Committee sought through such cartoons to make would-be travellers think again about their plans. *East Anglian Daily Times*

household soap *or* six ounces of soap powder. Towels went on the ration later in the year. Tyres for motor vehicles were rationed from 4th April — a direct result of the loss of sources of supply in the Far East. The government announced rationing of

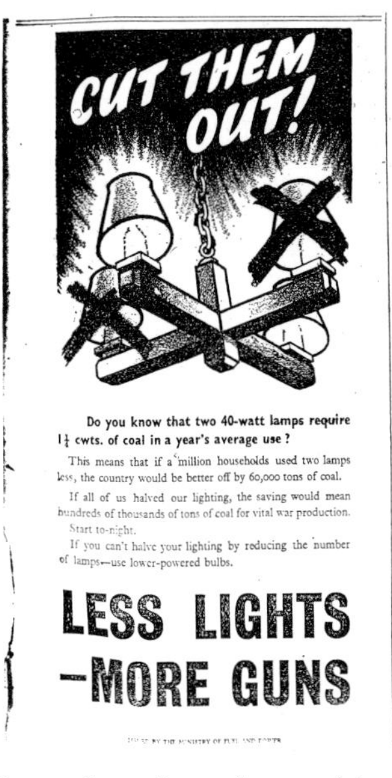

Fuel was to have been rationed, but the government changed its mind and depended on advertisements such as this to persuade people to use less. *East Anglian Daily Times*

coal, coke, gas, electricity and paraffin to start on 1st June, but then changed its mind and decided instead upon control and organization of the coal industry under a new Minister of Fuel, Light and Power, increased production, a vigorous economy campaign, and restrictions on deliveries.

The basic petrol ration was withdrawn on 30th June, and from that date the Eastern Counties Omnibus Company withdrew all its long-distance services between London and East Anglia, and declared it unlikely that they could be resumed until after the end of the war. A few months later there was drastic curtailment of bus services throughout the region. The last "outward journeys" of the day, from town centres or other termini, left not later than 9 pm, so that the vehicles were back at their home bases or garages not later than 9.45 pm. Authorized leave services for the forces were granted an extra half-hour. Restrictions were placed on taxi drivers, permitting them to travel only five miles from the boundary of the borough in which they operated, while in the case of private hire cars the limit was ten miles from the garage.

Newsprint rationing had reduced all newspapers to a fraction of their pre-war size. The *Eastern Daily Press* at the beginning of 1942 published four-page issues from Monday to Friday, with six pages on Saturdays; but by May the six-page issues had been abandoned. The *Cambridge Daily News*, which had the smaller "tabloid" page size, managed eight pages every day.

Salvage of all kinds was gathered for recycling. Here two Holbrook women are engaged in baling waste paper, an activity which was considered to be an essential part of the war effort. Those who burnt waste paper or cardboard were liable to prosecution. *Mrs M. Leeson*

Other types of paper were not officially rationed and, as a teacher in Norwich, Mrs Sarah Williams was appalled at some of the consequences of the shortage of paper for school use. She wrote in her diary on 19th June:

> We are allowed no more exercise books to the end of term because there is such a shortage of stationery. It's difficult to teach English if you can't set any written work because of lack of paper, but at any rate we shan't have such long examination papers to mark.

Two weeks later she added:

> Next year we are to be allowed four exercise books per child per year — for all subjects. Mr T, who looks after the stationery, announces that he has ordered some slates.

And later again:

> *6th July*: Mr W, the art master, says he has no paper nor pencils nor brushes. Next term he will have to use newspaper.
> *7th July*: We hear this evening that 61 million leaflets have been dropped over Germany . . .

Apart from rationing available supplies of raw materials, the government did its utmost to encourage the salvage of everything which could be recycled. Most metal railings and gates had already been swept away wholesale to provide raw material for the armaments factories, and more were being seized daily. In the Eastern Region as a whole over 7,000 tons of metal had been recovered in this way by June, 1942, equivalent to the weight of 440 tanks.

During the summer of 1942 there was a big campaign for salvage of every kind, metal, rubber, rags, paper and bones. There was actually a "Salvage Exhibition" on Christ's Pieces at Cambridge, and a big public demonstration, with speeches. As subject-matter for oratory, salvage is rather circumscribed; that, no doubt, was why some of the speeches wandered off over wider and unrelated fields. The chairman of the county council, for example, declaimed: "This county has nothing to be proud of in the war. We are sadly lagging in salvage, and we have only just been beaten by Oxford in the number of conscientious objectors we have. The latter is beyond our control, but not the former. We can put it right." The public did its best to restore his sense of pride by providing him, by the end of a fortnight's campaigning, with 456 tons of metal, rubber, rags, paper and bones, which was nearly half as much again as had been hoped for!

This salvage drive stirred up controversy of a different kind in the university city. One of the bright ideas was that the public should be asked to bring out all the books they no longer wanted and lay them along the kerbs of the pavements to make a "mile of books". One of the sites chosen was Great St Mary's. On 19th September the *Cambridge Daily News* published this letter from a young academic who was making a name as a poet and broadcaster:

> In the noose of books cast at present round Great St Mary's are many which would be welcomed by day nurseries, by members of the Forces at home and abroad, and by readers everywhere. Cannot these be put to their proper use before they are condemned to swell the salvage total? Or is all reading to be reduced to pulp? Well then, there's the University Library to be salvaged yet, Yours etc. ROBERT GITTINGS

The irony was lost on another reader, who chided Mr Gittings because he was not giving suitable priority to the needs of the men at the guns and declared that the University Library might, indeed, make a contribution. An official explanation was hurriedly produced that all the books put out as salvage would be examined and would be directed where they would be best appreciated. In Norwich, too, there was concern that valuable books might be destroyed, and a former Lord Mayor urged that no books should be given for salvage until the City Librarian had been consulted.

Later, in October, the Ministry of Supply announced that it had selected Ipswich to inaugurate a nationwide Book Salvage drive and called for 150 tons of books to be collected in a fortnight. Ipswich was chosen because its residents were said to buy more books than any other town of comparable size. From the outset it was clear that the books collected would be divided up into those that should be preserved, those that would be suitable reading matter for the Forces, and those that could be pulped. It is doubtful if such fuss had ever before been made about books. A band of the Royal Marines and another of pipes paraded the streets, trailed by four hundred schoolchildren with Union Jacks. At an evening ball at the Public Hall, the Mayor crowned a "Book Queen", Miss Kay Sheppard. The organizers set out to collect an average of eight books from each household, and they managed ten — a total of 294,587 volumes.

Ipswich announced at the outset of its general salvage campaign: "More than £5,000 a year is being recovered from the dustbins of Ipswich, but the yield can be very much greater". Its town council made one of the most spectacular of all contributions to salvage: a nine-feet high statue of a seated Queen Victoria, with four lions around her, it had stood since its unveiling in 1904 in front of Christchurch Mansion. Although it had been cast from about two tons of bronze, its value was estimated at only £50.

The Ministry of Information supplied films with titles such as *Salvage with a Smile* and *Raw material is War material*. These were shown in church halls and admission was granted in return for "one pound or more of waste paper". This formula was a great success. Two hundred and fifty people turned up at Thorpe Hamlet Parish Hall for the first of these film shows, carrying between them half a ton of waste paper. Altogether Norwich collected 375 tons.

Besides rationing and salvage, there was a third element in the government's management of the nation's resources. This was savings. The real purpose was to take money out of circulation, to discourage people from spending any spare cash they had, thus reducing the demand for goods. Mrs Sarah Williams noted in her diary on 9th May:

> I bought a new pair of shoes. One buys so much in case one shouldn't have a chance in a little while. And I don't mind spending my money. Air raids always make me feel — what's the use of saving? I may be killed and might as well enjoy it while I'm alive.

That was exactly the sort of attitude the government wanted to counter, and it was an attitude that was widespread. The propaganda for National Savings was unceasing, and much ingenuity was put into the campaign. No holds were barred. One advertisement showed a tearful child, with the caption "It's her Daddy they're taking away . . ." — a reminder of the Nazi treatment of those who opposed them in the occupied countries. The publicity greatly over-simplified matters by suggesting that extra tanks, extra planes, and extra warships would be built if people saved appropriate sums of money for the purpose.

The first major money-raising effort of 1942 was a series of "Warship Weeks" throughout the country. These were organized with some style and ceremony — by this time a great deal of experience had been accumulated. Bands played, officers of the three services appeared, processions were organized, models of warships and machines were exhibited.

Norwich announced it would raise £1,000,000, the cost of a cruiser, and the

Admiralty sanctioned the idea that the city should "adopt" HMS *Norfolk*. The Chancellor of the Exchequer, Sir Kingsley Wood, came down to open the campaign and suggested the city ought to be able to manage twice as much. The organising committee did its best; its advertising campaign summoned up "the spirit of Nelson". The total, in the end, was £1,392,649, which was just about £11 a head of the city's population. The Warship Week, here and in many other towns, took on the aspect of a popular entertainment. HMS *Norfolk's* carpenter made a six-foot model of the ship and sent it to the Lord Mayor of Norwich as a gift. One of the ship's company who was also a local lad, Able Seaman J. W. Wiltsher, was sent as an ambassador, and he showed films of the vessel and life at sea in many local halls. Later in the year Vice Admiral A. J. L. Murray visited Norwich to present a replica of the badge of HMS *Norfolk* to the Lord Mayor, Mr J. H. Barnes.

Ipswich also set a £1,000,000 target, "the cost of a complete destroyer, to be called HMS *Orwell*", but succeeded in collecting only £846,000. Possibly this result was affected by the attitude of the town's controversial Member of Parliament, Mr

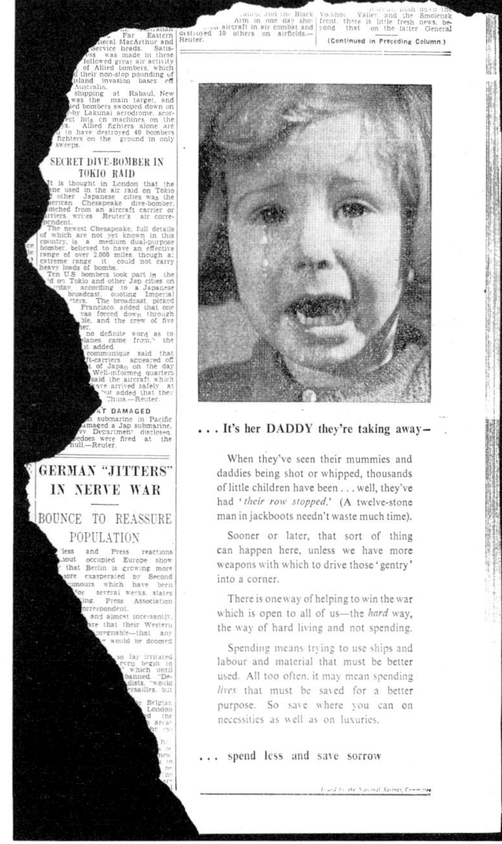

An ingenious advertisement issued by the National Savings Committee which used the vernacular to put its message across. "When they've seen their mummies and daddies being shot or whipped, thousands of little children have been . . . well, they've had 'their row stopped'. (A twelve-stone man in jackboots needn't waste much time)."
East Anglian Daily Times

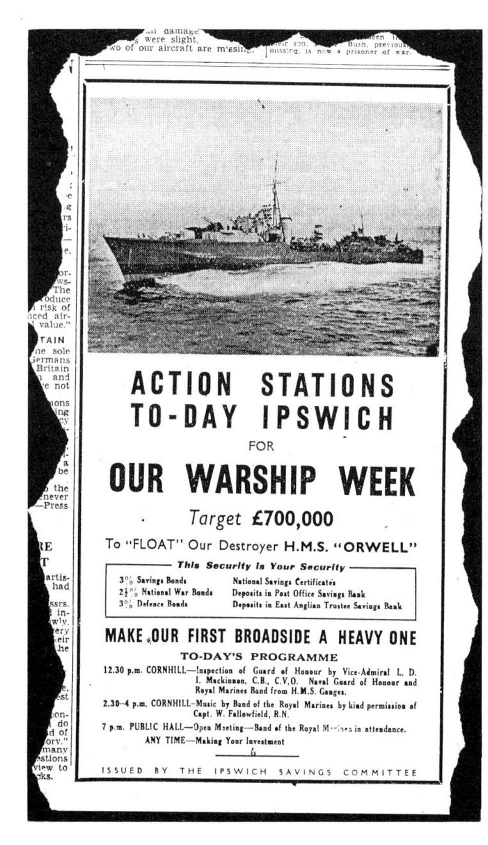
ACTION STATIONS TO-DAY IPSWICH

FOR

OUR WARSHIP WEEK

Target £700,000

To "FLOAT" Our Destroyer H.M.S. "ORWELL"

This Security is Your Security

3% Savings Bonds	National Savings Certificates
2½% National War Bonds	Deposits in Post Office Savings Bank
3% Defence Bonds	Deposits in East Anglian Trustee Savings Bank

MAKE OUR FIRST BROADSIDE A HEAVY ONE

TO-DAY'S PROGRAMME

12.30 p.m. CORNHILL—Inspection of Guard of Honour by Vice-Admiral L. D. I. Mackinnon, C.B., C.V.O. Naval Guard of Honour and Royal Marines Band from H.M.S. Ganges.

2.30–4 p.m. CORNHILL—Music by Band of the Royal Marines by kind permission of Capt. W. Fallowfield, R.N.

7 p.m. PUBLIC HALL—Open Meeting—Band of the Royal Marines in attendance.

ANY TIME—Making Your Investment

ISSUED BY THE IPSWICH SAVINGS COMMITTEE

Left: The Royal Marines band from HMS *Ganges*, a Royal Navy training establishment at Shotley, figured prominently in the programme of the Ipswich Warship Week. Failure to reach the target did not prevent HMS *Orwell* being completed—she served with the Royal Navy until 1965. *East Anglian Daily Times*

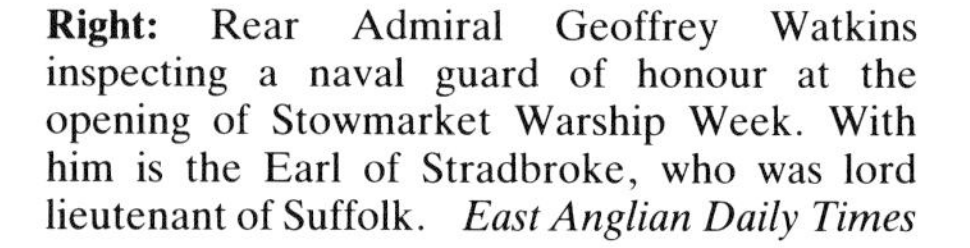

Right: Rear Admiral Geoffrey Watkins inspecting a naval guard of honour at the opening of Stowmarket Warship Week. With him is the Earl of Stradbroke, who was lord lieutenant of Suffolk. *East Anglian Daily Times*

Richard Stokes. After the campaign, he told an Ipswich audience: "I have taken no part in the Warship Week in Ipswich, because I think it is a swindle. I don't think it makes the slightest difference to the length of the war; not the slightest difference to the number of war weapons you will have; not the slightest difference to anything conceivable, whether you subscribe or not." His point was that small people were investing their savings and that the money would find its way into big financial organisations which would gain three per cent on that money indefinitely.

The failure of Ipswich to raise the cash certainly did not prevent the building of HMS *Orwell*, which was launched by John I. Thornycroft and Co. Ltd at Southampton on 2nd April, 1942. She served with the Royal Navy until 1965.

The Bishop of St Edmundsbury and Ipswich took him to task for suggesting that Warship Week organisers had been involved in a "swindle", but Mr Stokes was unrepentant. He had not imputed false motives to the organisers, he declared, but had been bemoaning the general ignorance of financial matters. The Warship Weeks produced no extra weapons, he repeated. "They merely help to prevent inflation by dispossessing the people of the immediate use of their money. If the

government wants the money, they should take it. It is a ridiculous waste of time and effort to continue these Weeks, which are insulting to the intelligence of the people."

Elsewhere, however, the Warship Weeks were a great success. Cambridge collected £825,000, and Huntingdon £609,864. Bury St Edmunds hit its target of £425,000, the cost of a submarine. Chelmsford aimed for £240,000, and raised £750,000. Colchester's target was £250,000, and its collection totalled £435,000. Saffron Walden aimed for £120,000, and collected £250,000. Newmarket set its target at £100,000, ended the week with less than £72,000 in the bank, but then went on to collect nearly £200,000.

Smaller towns set themselves more modest targets. Great Yarmouth and district, Dereham and the Mitford and Launditch rural district, and the Diss, Harleston and Depwade rural district were three among many which aimed at £250,000 — Yarmouth actually raised nearly £300,000. Woodbridge combined with the Deben rural district and set £210,000 as their joint target "to provide the hull of a destroyer". Braintree went for £150,000. King's Lynn, Newmarket and the

Blofield and Flegg rural district were among many others which each set a target of £120,000, usually with the slogan "to pay for a corvette". Thetford raised £50,000. Haverhill's more modest objective was £25,000, "the price of a hull for a motor torpedo boat". The target for the whole of Suffolk was £2,750,000.

Apart from these spectacular campaigns, the routine collection of National Savings street by street and house by house went on unceasingly. By June there were over 15,000 Savings Groups in the Eastern Region, and dozens of new ones were being formed every week. The secretary of the Cambridge Savings Committee, Mr R. P. Thorne, reported that the "small man's savings" in the town averaged £34,000 a week over the first nine weeks of 1942.

One money-catching appeal followed hard on the heels of another. In the first few weeks of the year Aid to Russia captured the attention. The Norfolk and Norwich War Charities sent a cheque for £3,000 in January to Mrs Churchill's Red Cross Aid to Russia Fund, as a first instalment. Anglo-Soviet Friendship Committees, which had sprung up in most towns, made their own collections and organized social events, and raised thousands.

Clare RDC organized a "Commando Week" and raised £50,000. There was the familiar fancy dress parade and pipe band. During the summer there was a series of "Prisoner of War Fund Weeks", when Suffolk raised £27,372, and another series of War Charities Weeks, when Norfolk raised a total of £36,000. A Red Cross and St John Penny-a-Week Fund ("a penny a week from everyone in every house in every street") raised £3,377 in its first year in Cambridge, and the money paid for food parcels, tobacco, books, games and musical instruments sent to prisoners of war.

At mid-1942 the Chancellor of the Exchequer, Sir Kingsley Wood, told the Commons that expenditure on the war was running at £12,000,000 a day, and that Parliament had voted a total of £10,050 million since its outbreak. These figures, in the financial terms of the day, were breathtaking. It was, the Chancellor said, "by far the costliest war in history", adding "but this does not dismay us". And everywhere the people dipped more deeply into their pockets.

CHAPTER EIGHT

Behaviour under Stress

ALTHOUGH normal life was almost completely disrupted, and despite food rationing and overwork, the health of the people remained remarkably good. In fact, the chairman of the Cambridge Public Health Committee declared in July, 1942, that it was improving rather than otherwise, notwithstanding the stresses and strains of war and the influx of population into the area. No serious epidemics were reported. There were occasional suicides, but they did not appear to be more numerous than in pre-war years.

There was a strange case at Bungay when a sixteen-year-old youth stole a Sten sub-machine gun and ammunition and announced that he intended to open fire on people leaving a local cinema. Fortunately he changed his mind at the last moment. He was arrested and sent to a home: it was an isolated incident.

The overwhelming majority of people remained level headed as well as physically fit. There remained many stabilizing factors in their lives, not the least of which was the sense of identity with the community at large in the face of danger. There was also a determination to make every effort to continue with normal leisure interests in off-duty hours.

Sport was one of the activities most affected. The normal pattern of football was badly disrupted, so many of the players having been taken into the forces. Norwich City continued to field a team, and it began the year by beating Northampton 4–1 at Carrow Road before a crowd of 3,549, an auspicious start which was followed by a run of successes. In April nearly 12,000 turned out to cheer the team in a quarter-finals match of the League War Cup competition, but Cup hopes vanished soon after when the team travelled to Grimsby and a 2–0 defeat.

When a new season was due to open, after the summer, the Norwich club announced that there could be no competitive football because of travel restrictions. The directors said they hoped to provide some attractive football, nonetheless, and they would continue to offer training facilities for suitable lads who came forward, so that the club's future needs would be met. The first match of the new season was played against a Suffolk Royal Navy XI at Portman Road, Ipswich, and Norwich won 8–1.

Most football in the region depended upon the availability of service teams, and they provided almost all the games seen at Ipswich. On Easter Monday, for example, a Royal Navy XI played a Free French Forces team.

The "Mays" took place on the Cam as usual, the local newspaper remarking that "it seems almost incredible in these times that a total of 62 crews should be taking part"; but horse racing had been reduced to about a fifth of the pre-war activity, and now it was further limited to a few selected courses. Newmarket was one of the favoured courses, and when the flat racing season opened on 14th April the press reported an about-normal attendance. When the Two Thousand Guineas was run on 12th May (and was won by the King's horse Big Game, with Gordon Richards in the saddle), a surprising number of people managed to take time off to travel from London. The *Cambridge Daily News* reported:

> Only one train, the 8.30 am, was scheduled to leave Liverpool Street in time for Newmarket races today. It could have been filled several times over, and hundreds had to be disappointed. An hour before the train left there was a 70 yards queue in the booking hall. It had more than doubled its length by 7.55 am, when the occupants of the queue were told that the train was full and no more tickets would be issued.
>
> A "black market" in railway tickets was created. The price of a third class return ticket is 14s 8d and one man, seeing his chance, bought a quantity. In a few minutes, he had sold out at 17s 2d a ticket — a profit of half-a-crown each.
>
> At Newmarket there was a continuous procession of people walking the three miles from the station to the course. RAF and military police were at the various entrances checking up Service passes.

At the 1942 Derby meeting, when the big race was won by Harry Wragg on Watling Street, civilian police questioned everyone who arrived in a car about their

2

MEETINGS, ENTERTAINMENTS

RITZ CINEMA

IPSWICH 'Phone 3353.
(Managed by A.B.C. Cinemas Ltd.)
TO-DAY Continuous from 1.00 to 10.25.
RED SKELTON and CONRAD VEIDT in
"WHISTLING IN THE DARK"
2.40. 5.40. 9.00. (A)
PATHE GAZETTE 1.05, 4.05, 7.15.
HERBERT MARSHALL and VIRGINIA BRUCE
in
"FEMALE CORRESPONDENT"
1.10. 4.10. 7.20. (U)
SUNDAY, March 8th, for One Day: Hugh Sinclair in "SAINT'S VACATION"; Lynn Bari in "FREE, BLONDE and 21."
Ritz Cafe Restaurant Open Daily from 10 a.m. to 9.30 p.m.

THE REGENT

CINEMA AND RESTAURANT
CONTINUOUS. 1.10 to 10.0 p.m.
THE ADVENTURE FILM THAT HAS EVERYTHING.
SUNDOWN
With GENE TIERNEY, BRUCE CABOT.
2.37, 5.34, 8.31. (A)
WILLIAM GARGAN, EDMUND LOWE, in
FLYING CADETS
GAUMONT—BRITISH NEWS. (U)
SUNDAY, March 8th, Continuous 4.30—9.30: Paul Muni in "HUDSON'S BAY" (U); W. C. Fields in "BANK DETECTIVE" (U).
FRIDAY NIGHT—COMMUNITY SINGING.

PUBLIC NOTICES

Community singing on the Friday night must have proved attractive to Ipswich cinema audiences—the films do not seem at all memorable.
East Anglian Daily Times

supply of petrol; the usual story was that the racegoer had been "saving his ration" for months so that he could have this big day out. Many of the crowd arrived on foot, some by pony and trap. Officers of all three services were much in evidence in the enclosures.

There was criticism from some quarters. Alderman E. G. Gooch — the same man who as president of the NUAW had criticized the employment of children in the harvest field — suggested at a Norfolk County Council meeting that those who attended dog races and horse races or who hunted were behaving like Nero, who fiddled while Rome burned. The Commons was told that the Jockey Club had lost three-quarters of the land it customarily used for horse racing and training, 1,668 acres having been requisitioned or "earmarked for military purposes" and a further 196 acres ploughed and cultivated. The Club was left with 495 acres. Of 7,990 acres of grassland on stud farms in the Newmarket area, 2,910 had been ploughed up and much of the remainder was used for grazing dairy herds.

The racing fraternity found things ever more difficult as the year progressed. When the St Leger meeting took place at Newmarket on 12th September civil and service police were at every entrance checking papers.

The cinema was the most popular form of relaxation, and many people went two and three times a week. "Whenever a notable picture arrives in the town, it gets mention in every quarter," a Mass Observation correspondent in Chelmsford reported(1). The four cinemas in that town had seating for over 3,600 people, and they were usually full. In Bury St Edmunds another Mass Observation reporter noted that "the three cinemas do a roaring trade"(2). The usual admission prices were 1s 10d, 1s 2d, one shilling, and ninepence.

Cinema programmes included organ recitals, as well as newsreel coverage of the war, which carried a heavy propagandist element. Audiences seemed quite happy to escape from the direct experience of war by seeking vicarious thrills watching war films! Among the most popular were *One of our Aircraft is Missing*, which was shown simultaneously by two Norwich cinemas, Noel Coward's *In Which we Serve*, and *Convoy*, with Clive Brook and John Clements. Hollywood was still sending a steady supply of films across the Atlantic, many with a war theme. Critical standards were low, but occasionally cinema audiences were given a special treat. East Anglian cinemas showed *Citizen Kane*, which established the reputation of Orson Welles, *How Green was my Valley*, and *Gone with the Wind*, starring Clark Gable, Leslie Howard, Olivia de Havilland and Vivien Leigh, a film which ran for three hours and forty minutes, and which had a four-week season at the Regal in Cambridge.

One of the Hollywood productions was *International Squadron*, the story of which was summarized thus in the local press:

> Another girl-chasing and cocksure American pilot who joins the RAF and finally makes good — but not before he has indirectly caused the death of two of his fellow members of the International Squadron.

The actor who played this role, and who was credited with "a good performance", was one Ronald Reagan.

The *Cambridge Daily News* reported that on the first night this film was shown in the town "one young lad — he couldn't have been more than seven or eight — created a great deal of amusement for the people near him by turning round to his father at the end of the film and exclaiming in a voice full of indignation and almost despair: 'He's got it all wrong'." The critic added: "This is certainly one case where the average youngster of Britain today could teach Hollywood a thing or two about RAF detail . . . [There are] very glaring technical mistakes . . . The air thrills are there, but certainly not the RAF atmosphere . . ."

By the summer some of the stage entertainment at cinemas was provided by serving men and women. The Rex Cinema in Cambridge during July advertised the film *Sabotage* along with "Sergeant Parish, RAF, at the organ, Miss Rita Legett, violinist, and AC Rene Clinch, WAAF, vocalist".

There was a renaissance of the arts at this time. During the early months of the year Cambridge audiences were offered frequent performances by the London Philharmonic Orchestra, conducted by Basil Cameron, and others by the BBC Symphony Orchestra, conducted by Clarence Raybould, and by the town's own Philharmonic Society. The programmes usually included an item of contemporary significance: as examples, a first performance of Khachaturian's *Violin Concerto* at one, Vaughan Williams' *Choral Songs to be sung in time of war* at another. At the Arts Theatre, the Sadlers Wells Ballet introduced Robert Helpmann's new ballet *Comus*, and had quickly to arrange an additional matinee to accommodate the audiences. Sadlers Wells Opera Company came a month later to present *La Traviata* and *The Magic Flute*.

University May Week brought another musical treat in Cambridge. Several thousand people gathered on the Backs on a perfect June evening to hear a choir of twenty, seated in moored punts, singing sixteenth-century madrigals. As the last light faded from the sky the punts were released from their moorings and floated away into the darkness, with the music of John Wilbye's *Draw on, sweet night* drifting over the water.

Later in the year Donald Wolfit brought his company to the Arts Theatre to present a week of Shakespeare's plays: *King Lear*, *Twelfth Night*, and *A Midsummer Night's Dream*. Louis Kentner opened a "1942/3 Series of Pianoforte Recitals" at the Arts in November. On 8th November "the largest audience the Cambridge Municipal Orchestra had ever had enthusiastically greeted its first concert of the season in the Guildhall". Also in November the RAF Symphony Orchestra gave a concert in the Corn Exchange, Clifford Curzon gave a concert at the Music School, and the Sadlers Wells Opera Company began a fortnight's Mozart Festival at the Arts.

Norwich did not enjoy so rich a menu, but it was not neglected. Early in the year the London Philharmonic Orchestra visited the city in full strength to give an afternoon concert at the Theatre Royal. The Sadlers Wells Opera came, and was followed immediately by the Old Vic Company with Chekov's *The Cherry Orchard*. Soon afterwards the D'Oyly Carte Opera opened a season with *The*

Gondoliers. At the Maddermarket Theatre the Norwich Players presented an adaptation of Euripides' *Helen* and, despite rationing and other difficulties, a reviewer made a special point of the fact that "the costumes are almost up to pre-war Maddermarket standards". In the same week as Euripides, there was ballet at the Theatre Royal — a return of the Anglo-Polish Ballet Company, which had been well received a year earlier.

In the autumn the London Philharmonic Orchestra returned to give two concerts in the Cathedral, one a special performance for over a thousand schoolchildren. At the other, every seat was occupied for a programme of Mendelssohn, Delius and Elgar. The Norwich Philharmonic Orchestra, though it announced it was having a constant struggle to survive and appealed for greater civic support, gave a successful concert in the Theatre Royal. At the Norwich YMCA, a large audience which included many soldiers heard Benjamin Britten, the twenty-nine-year-old local lad from Lowestoft who was being described as "one of England's outstanding young composers", gave a piano recital, with the tenor Peter Pears.

A new organ in Norwich Cathedral was heard for the first time at the beginning of the year, when Dr Thalben-Ball, the organist of the Temple Church, gave a recital and pronounced it "magnificent", adding that Norwich was extremely fortunate to have obtained such an instrument in wartime. Other distinguished organists came in later weeks to give recitals.

In Ipswich in mid-April the Choral Society gave a performance of Gounod's *Faust* in a crowded Public Hall, but there were only sixty voices in the choir, and fewer than a third of them were male. "From the same rostrum, Mr W. H. Dixon has conducted a chorus and orchestra of 350 in brighter days," the local paper observed sadly. In the autumn Benjamin Britten performed at a concert in St Mary-le-Tower Church; Dame Myra Hess gave a recital of music by Beethoven, Brahms, Bach and Chopin to an audience overflowing at the Public Hall; the London Philharmonic Orchestra gave a special performance for local schoolchildren, Ipswich council having accepted their offer to play for a fee of £150; Solomon gave a piano recital at the Public Hall; the Bournemouth Philharmonic Orchestra gave afternoon and evening performances of works by Beethoven and Tchaikovsky; and the Anglo-Polish Ballet performed for a week at the Hippodrome, which was celebrating the first anniversary of its resumption of live shows after eleven years as a cinema.

Gramophone records were still on sale in the shops. The Cambridge music store, Millers, advertised February's top-selling titles: Liszt's *Hungarian Rhapsody No 2*, Purcell's *Trumpet Voluntary*, and Massenet's *Meditation*.

It is doubtful if there was ever a time in our history when so many books were read as during this period of the war. Men and women in the forces during their off-duty hours, men and women in the Civil Defence services, when there were no raids, the more elderly, who did not like to venture out in the blackout, all demanded reading matter. Shortage of newsprint had reduced the size of the newspapers. Books became a prime source of entertainment and, perhaps more surprisingly, of information and instruction. The Women's Voluntary Services were largely responsible for getting them into circulation. Crime stories and spy thrillers, which had been most popular in the early part of the war, had by 1942 been supplanted by "westerns"; could this have been a by-product of the appearance of the Americans in Britain? Certainly there was a voracious appetite for travel books about Russia. Biographies were widely read, and a WVS team which took a library van once a fortnight to every camp and airfield in Cambridgeshire reported in October a rising demand for books dealing with current affairs.

Cambridge staged a month-long exhibition of Henry Moore sculptures, John Piper oils and watercolours, and Graham Sutherland landscapes at the Technical School. Eric Newton delivered a course of ten Cambridge University Extension Lectures on "Art in the World Today".

Many organizations contrived to remain in existence and to hold meetings. The Cambridge Antiquarian Society announced a lecture on the Bayeux Tapestry, the Cambridge Church Missionary Society a gathering to watch a film about missionary work in Nigeria, and the Cambridge Philatelic Society, which still had eighty members, reported "monthly meetings with a good wartime average attendance".

There was plenty of popular entertainment, too, including many concerts and social events arranged specially for those in the services; for example, Cambridge Borough Entertainments Committee organized a "Grand Troop Concert" in the Guildhall.

When the summer months arrived, the Regional Commissioner asked councils to provide all the entertainment possible to encourage people to stay at home. In Norwich a seventeen-year-old blonde shorthand typist, Jean Mudie, was chosen "Miss Norwich" by a Theatre Royal audience and she presided over the "holidays at home" programme in the city, making her own special contribution to the fun by getting married during the proceedings to an airman about to be posted overseas.

In Cambridge bands played on Christ's Pieces every Sunday evening, variety entertainments were presented once a week, and "open-air promenade dancing" took place every evening, except Sundays, between 18th May and 29th August. August Bank Holiday was celebrated with a Grand Gala on the town football ground, with military bands and the London Scottish pipers and dancers; physical training displays by soldiers, airmen and girls of the ATS; trick motor-cycling; dancing; and competitions. The crowds turned out in thousands. The reporter of the *Cambridge Daily News* thought the entertainment was "as varied as could be found between Hampstead Heath and Honolulu".

In Ipswich during July and August there was some form of public entertainment every day in Christchurch Park, including music, dancing, sports, tournaments and swimming galas. In Great Yarmouth seven thousand attended a

Headed by a drum and fife band, troops of the Royal Berkshire Regiment march across the Green at Long Melford on 10th June. *Imperial War Museum*

summer fete in the Wellesley Recreation Ground, with the proceeds going to the local hospital. And in most villages the customary fetes and flower shows continued through the summer of 1942, despite all distractions.

Some people travelled, despite the appeals not to do so. On August Bank Holiday, Lowestoft railway station was very lively, crowds emerging from every train. A railway official declared: "They've all got a reason for coming . . . to visit their homes, their parents, or their sick relatives, or they have to look after their property. All within the regulations, apparently. And they've all got their identity cards. There'd be trouble if they hadn't, of course."

The weather was kind. Early in June the sun shone fifteen hours a day, and the temperature sometimes reached the eighties, and there was more hot, dry weather in August, the temperature over 90 degrees at Cromer on a couple of days. People said it was the hottest August since 1933, and the sunshine cheered them up considerably.

Those whose homes were near the sea were sometimes able to get to a beach or a promenade, although they were denied the pleasures of peacetime. Mrs Sarah Williams occasionally took her young son to the seafront at Sheringham. She noted:

> *7th June:* We went to the prom., which is open, but looking very different from the beach in peace-time. Barbed wire, soldiers, ATS, airmen, WAAF, no bathing tents and a general atmosphere of untidiness and dirt.
> *15th August:* The weather has, at last, become lovely — really summer-like. We went down to the beach for the whole afternoon. A Walrus plane landed on the sea. Hurricanes swooped about. Minesweepers came in and went out, complete with barrage balloons. It was all very interesting.

With so many parents in the forces or working in the factories, it was not thought sensible to give the normal school holidays in August. In response to the Board of Education's request, Ipswich Education Committee, for example, closed the schools only for the Bank Holiday week, reopening them as "Holiday Schools" from 10th to 28th August. Teachers, on a voluntary rota, supervised physical training and games, dramatic work, dancing, rambles and cycle rides, handwork, concerts, gardening, sketching, drawing and painting, reading, visits, debates, first aid, and knitting for the forces. Ten to fifteen per cent of the children turned up. Meals and milk were served, as during term.

These efforts to keep people occupied and amused in off-duty hours must have helped sustain morale for much of the time, but they could not prevent despondency when things were perceived to be unsatisfactory in the conduct of the war. Churchill made another visit to America during the summer, and again it coincided with a wave of criticism of his government, linked to a military setback in North Africa, with the fall of Tobruk and Rommel's forces driving towards Egypt.

A by-election occurred at this time in the Maldon constituency of Essex, and an uninspiring government candidate was opposed by a thirty-seven-year-old Fleet Street columnist, Mr Tom Driberg, who stood as an Independent. He sailed into Parliament with a majority of nearly six thousand. It was the fourth by-election defeat for the government in as many months. At Westminster a group of MPs tabled the first-ever motion of no confidence in the government (the January debate had been made an issue of confidence by the Prime Minister, not by his critics). Two East Anglian MPs were among the signatories — Mr Richard Stokes and Mr Edgar Granville. While the two-day debate was taking place, Rommel thrust to within 100 miles of Alexandria. Churchill again refused to put any gloss on events. He admitted the loss of 50,000 men in the battle, most of them taken prisoner, and of large quantities of stores. When the battle had begun, he related, the Allies had had armed superiority, with three hundred tanks in action. By

A Supermarine Walrus of the RAF air sea rescue service is manoeuvred into position to pick up an airman from his dinghy. Operating from Ellough, near Beccles, and other airfields, these amphibious aircraft saved many ditched aircrew from the bleak waters of the North Sea. *East Anglian Daily Times*

nightfall, only seventy of them remained. The Commons voted its continued confidence in him, by 475 to 25.

Mrs Sarah Williams' diary noted on 21st June, after the German radio had reported the Allied loss of Tobruk:

> It was a lovely day, but one saw long faces everywhere. My aunt said "Whatever Hitler says he'll do, he does. I shouldn't be a bit surprised we collapse." I notice that our news at 6 is largely a translation of the German Special Announcement. Mrs H says she wonders whether some of our generals are in the pay of the Germans . . . Miss A refuses to buy her savings stamp today to buy equipment to be given to the Germans again.

Three days later the diary adds:

> There were many references today to the fall of the government. Some wondered whether Churchill would remain, while his diehard friends went . . . Mrs P from next door wants to know where the King and Queen are. She thinks that they are probably in Canada — or somewhere — but that, at any rate, they have left England.

And the following day, June 25th, Mrs Williams sums up:

> I should think Churchill's stock has never been so low.

Serious problems arose for the government in India at about the same time after the Congress Party had rejected British proposals and passed a "Quit India" resolution. Men of the 2nd Battalion, Royal Norfolks were unfortunate enough to find themselves involved. After strenuous training in the Cotswolds in the early months of the year, the battalion had sailed from the Clyde on a very overcrowded ship, the ss *Orbita*, in the largest troop convoy which had left the UK to that date. Training continued on board. "All ranks had to shoot with light machine-guns at small barrels towed astern, which came up or disappeared as the seas hit them. While shooting, men were 'distracted' by being kicked, rolled on, having buckets of water thrown over them, bugles blown in their ears, and so on. It was drastic training . . ."[(3)] All this, and much tough training later in India, was designed to prepare them for jungle warfare against the Japanese. But they found themselves in August in Ahmedabad occupying Congress House, the headquarters of Gandhi's party, and making flag marches through the mill district of the city, where Congress had most of its support.

Whatever the problems, there was not much open anti-war talk, and little evidence of defeatism. Anyone who openly talked in a way likely to cause "alarm and despondency" could be prosecuted — and a few were. A forty-six-year-old Yarmouth ex-serviceman who expressed an opinion that the war would be over within a few months, and that Germany would win, was sent to prison for three months, and a twenty-six-year-old Norwich labourer who told a girl factory worker that the British would be better off under German rule, and that German soldiers were better than British, was given a two-month sentence. Serious debate was not inhibited, however, as was shown when the Cambridge branch of the Workers' Educational Association discussed the proposition "that war should be rejected as a right method of settling international disputes". This occasion had a strange quality of the ivory tower about it, the speakers talking philosophically about the nature and psychology of *homo sapiens*, about ideas of national sovereignty and international relations. And, at the end of the debate, the proposition was accepted by 60 votes to 14.

There was a great deal of anti-German sentiment, without due distinction made between Nazis and their victims; but it seems surprising that there was not more. There was certainly no mass hysteria about the enemy. We have already noted that Ipswich Town Council appointed a German-born Jew to a senior post despite some public hostility. In Cambridge there was a German Lutheran refugee congregation which held regular joint evensong services with the members of Holy Trinity Church. The German Pastor F. Hildebrandt had before the war been an assistant to Pastor Niemöller, who had been held in a Nazi concentration camp since 1937 and had become a symbol of resistance to fascism. To mark the fifth anniversary of Niemöller's arrest the Archbishop of Canterbury, Dr William Temple, visited Cambridge to conduct a service jointly with Pastor Hildebrandt in Christ's College Chapel. The service was in both English and German.

The many Italians who had been drafted on to East Anglian farms showed the natural effervescence of the Italian character, and surprised the native East Anglians with their voluble speech and their tendency to break into laughter and song. Not everyone was favourably impressed, however. A correspondent signing himself "Ex-Serviceman" wrote to the *Cambridge Daily News*:

> Is it seemly that Italian prisoners-of-war should be allowed to lounge along the roads, blocking up the footpaths, while they appraise the looks, etc, of any British girls that may unfortunately have to walk past?

One of the farmers who had employed them responded that the Italians had "done much to make our harvest a success", and another correspondent wrote:

> I am a present serving man home on leave . . . I think the sooner that sort of attitude is wiped out as being a relic of the last war and half the cause of this one, then the sooner we shall win the present spot of bother and start a decent life again.

The original complainant's letter seems to have been noted by the authorities, however, for soon he was writing again to report that:

> There has been a very considerable improvement in the way that the prisoners-of-war now march through our villages. Instead of some fifty or more prisoners lounging along and blocking up the footpaths like so many "down-and-out" hoboes, utterly lacking in any sense of self-respect . . . some 150 prisoners-of-war, in three batches, with two guards to each batch of fifty men, came marching along the road — not on the footpaths — in columns of four, while the guards walked in the regulation positions . . . The prisoners were all laughing and talking, and seemed to be as happy and content as the circumstances would allow . . .

The Italians, however, may have had the last laugh. They began to sing more frequently and more loudly and it was noted that whenever a lorry-load of them was driven through Cambridge they sang "at the top of their voices in a provoking manner". Among the various refugee organizations in the town there was a "Free Italy Movement" and its president provided the explanation of this behaviour. The prisoners were singing well-known fascist songs! Why did the British permit "such shocking behaviour among the prisoners we treat so well? Do our authorities or do they not realize that *Giovinezza* or similar songs are seditious songs, which are an insult to this country, to our war against Fascism, and even to the best Italian traditions?"

The people of East Anglia, in the mass, maintained a remarkable sense of responsibility and a tolerant good humour. But some standards slipped. There was a good deal of vandalism, and some of it was serious. A columnist of the *Cambridge Daily News* in January condemned "a series of particularly mean acts of damage" to public telephone kiosks. Cambridge Civil Defence Committee was told soon afterwards that "every possible thing removable had been taken from existing shelters. Wires had been cut, tools, bulbs and fittings removed. Even parts of the ceiling had been taken in one case. So disgraceful were the conditions in even the children's shelters that they might not be safe." A few days later the town's senior National Fire Service officer reported that the safety wire mesh over static water storage tanks had been cut and damaged, and in one case almost entirely removed.

Undergraduates appear to have held themselves under restraint during these extraordinary times, but a few black sheep appeared in court. Three were fined two pounds each in June for "a foolish prank" — they had bent the post at a bus stop until it was level with the pavement.

Drunkenness was not a serious problem, perhaps in part because beer was sometimes in short supply. The Norwich Chief Constable told the annual licensing meeting during February that the city was achieving a new level of sobriety. The number of drunks had fallen to half the previous year's total, despite the number of troops stationed locally and a large floating population. The experience was the

Cambridge University despatch riders photographed in New Court at St John's College in June. Of this force of thirty or forty undergraduates, a section of five was on duty each night. They were described as the "eyes and ears" of the Regional Commissioner, Sir Will Spens, and they proved their worth during the Baedeker raids on Norwich. *Cambridge Daily News*

same elsewhere; Newmarket, for example, reported only one convicted drunk in a year.

Sexual behaviour had become very much more relaxed. Miss Winifred Last described in her diary the situation in Bury St Edmunds:

> The town is simply packed with people, natives and outsiders . . . At night, soldiers loiter on the town pavements watching for girls, and the girls here think it is just lovely. I suppose they had very dull lives before the war and any strange man gives them a thrill. Parents complain they have no control over the girls and the Moral Welfare House cannot step in at their request until *after* the girls are pregnant . . .[4]

The courts were kept busy with petitions for divorce, and bigamy was widespread, and getting more common. In the early weeks of the year Mr Justice Singleton dealt with cases, and commented critically, when he presided over the Suffolk Assizes in Bury St Edmunds, the Norfolk Assizes in Norwich, and the Essex Assizes at Chelmsford. At Norwich he sent a forty-one-year-old mother of ten children to prison for six months for bigamy, and the soldier she had "married" to prison for six months for aiding and abetting her. At Chelmsford, after dealing with several bigamy cases, he said the great increase presented

> a difficult problem for the Judges. They realize, and are often reminded, that an able-bodied man is of more use in the Navy or Army than he is in prison, and yet they have to remember that if some offences are passed over, that fact in itself may encourage other people to think lightly of the crime and lead to further increases in it.

A remarkable case of a less serious kind but one which was indicative of the reduced sense of responsibility in some quarters came before the court at Bottisham. A twenty-two-year-old private in the Royal Fusiliers and a nineteen-year-old ATS girl were summoned for making a false statement on a marriage register at Quy Church. Evacuees living in Bottisham planned a double wedding: a brother and sister from each of two families formed the intended pairs for marriage. At the hour of the ceremony, however, one of the bridegrooms, who was coming from his Army unit on leave, had not arrived. Amid the consternation, someone suggested that his best man (who was also his brother) might stand in for him at the wedding ceremony, and "hand over" the bride afterwards when the groom arrived. This plan was adopted, the stand-in led the bride to the altar, and afterwards signed his brother's name in the register. The clergy, who had never seen any of the parties before, had no reason to suspect that anything was amiss.

The true bridegroom, however, did not put in an appearance, nor was any message received. The bride's mother spent a sleepless night and then went to the priest and told him the whole story. By the time the case came to court it had been established that the intending bridegroom had been posted overseas at short notice. From distant parts a letter had arrived saying how much he looked forward to getting married when he returned to England. And no-one had broken the news to him that his bride had married his brother! If, indeed, she had. At the time of the hearing, no legal authority had been found who was prepared to pronounce on the validity of the marriage. The couple were each fined £5.

There was a great deal of petty thieving. When four youths appeared before the Cambridge Bench accused of stealing radio components, the chairman declared: "The amount of thieving that is going on is really getting to be a national concern," and when a "gang" of five teenage lads and two girls aged fifteen and twenty-four appeared at Norwich Quarter Sessions the prosecuting counsel said they had caused tremendous trouble to the police by "roaming round Norwich breaking into premises and collaring anything they can lay their hands on".

The most common offence was theft of cycles and cycle accessories, particularly in those towns close to service camps. The Chief Constable of Cambridgeshire reported that "there is no doubt that Army and Air Force personnel are largely responsible" and he appealed to officers to do something to help servicemen trying to get back to their units when they had missed a last bus. In Norwich the Deputy Chief Constable told the magistrates that 126 cycles had been stolen in the city in the first fifteen weeks of the year, and he commented that "it hits the working man very hard in these times of transport difficulties, when he has to rely on his cycle". When fines of ten shillings or one pound failed to deter offenders, Benches took a much tougher attitude. Cambridge magistrates sent a twenty-year-old RAF man who stole a cycle from Cambridge railway station to prison for three months, and doubled this sentence in the case of a former naval and merchant seaman who stole two cycles. In Norwich a twenty-five-year-old mother of two children, wife of a serving soldier, appeared at Quarter Sessions charged with stealing seven cycles and selling them, and the Recorder sent her to prison for six months.

The trouble did not end with bicycles. Perambulators began to be taken. A Norwich mother left her three-year-old child in a pram just inside the door at Woolworth's while she made some quick purchases. Pram and child disappeared. The youngster was later found in an air raid shelter. Norwich Police put out a statement: "Recently numerous perambulator thefts have been caused because of the difficulty of obtaining new 'prams' and the increased value of second-hand ones. The Norwich Police are keeping a special watch for perambulator thieves."

The courts only dealt with a fraction of the problems. A diary entry by a clerk working in Bury St Edmunds read:

> A lot of kleptomania about and things keep vanishing from the Shirehall. Lost my best fountain pen last week — shouldn't have left it on my desk, I suppose. The Solicitor lost his gloves today.

Some of the thefts were made to supplement rationed goods. A Norwich engine driver went to prison for three months for stealing food, clothing and cigarettes in transit at Thorpe railway station. "The losses suffered by the railway companies at the present time are disastrously heavy," the prosecuting solicitor declared. In Cambridgeshire, two railwaymen, each with twenty-three years' service, with no previous convictions and stated to have "excellent characters", were sent to prison for a month for stealing a case of herrings in tomato sauce from a wagon; elsewhere a man was sent to six months' hard labour for stealing twenty-four gallons of petrol from an RAF aerodrome, and a coalman was fined £5 for taking three sacks of coal and selling them privately.

It was not only "the little man" who tried to evade the strict rationing regulations. A case at Huntingdon attracted much attention. Several garage proprietors were charged with supplying a total of 16,686 gallons of petrol outside the rationing system, and a large number of their customers with being in unlawful possession of the petrol. The latter included a Knight of the Shire, the chairman of the Lea Conservancy Board, a former Mayor of Huntingdon, a few of the country gentry, "a soldier of distinction, adjutant of his regiment", several police constables, a schoolteacher and a hotel proprietor. A remarkable feature of the case was that nobody had made any profit out of the transactions. But the judge told the garage proprietors and salesmen that they had "engaged in a long series of transactions dealing with enormous quantities of petrol, in a complete and open defiance of all regulations" and he sentenced seven of them to prison terms varying from two years to three months. All those who received petrol were heavily fined — the total of the fines exceeded £5,600.

Men serving in the forces sometimes came before the civil courts. Two young privates of the Royal Norfolk Regiment were sent to prison for six months at Norwich for housebreaking, and three others to Borstal for three years for attempting to break into a shop after going absent from their units without leave. There were regular cases of service and government property being appropriated or traded. At Newmarket two soldiers in the Pioneer Corps who sold 2 lb of butter and two tins of corned beef belonging to the Army, and a Gazeley civilian who bought them, were each fined £1, and an RAF corporal was fined £2 for stealing fourteen RAF blankets and a civilian £1 for receiving a pair of RAF boots; at Suffolk Assizes a private was sentenced to three years' penal servitude and a

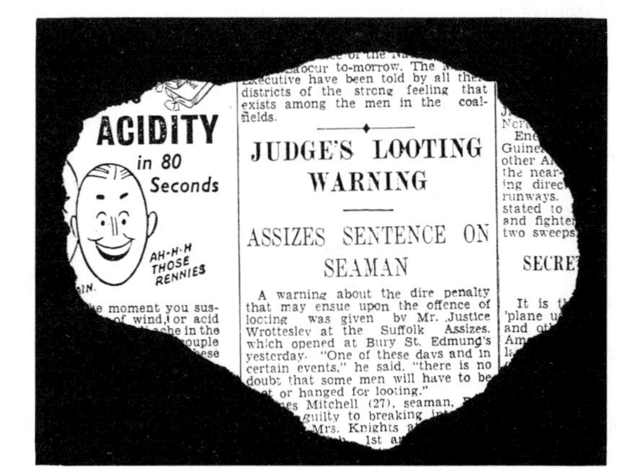

ACIDITY in 80 Seconds

AH-H-H THOSE RENNIES

... occur to-morrow. The ... Executive have been told by all the districts of the strong feeling that exists among the men in the coalfields.

JUDGE'S LOOTING WARNING

ASSIZES SENTENCE ON SEAMAN

A warning about the dire penalty that may ensue upon the offence of looting was given by Mr. Justice Wrottesley at the Suffolk Assizes, which opened at Bury St. Edmund's yesterday. "One of these days and in certain events," he said, "there is no doubt that some men will have to be ... or hanged for looting."

... Mitchell (27), seaman, ... guilty to breaking ... Mrs. Knights ... 1st ...

"Some men will have to be shot or hanged for looting," said the judge at Suffolk Assizes when sentencing a seaman who had stolen from a bombed house at Lowestoft.

East Anglian Daily Times

corporal to eighteen months' imprisonment for stealing corrugated iron, wire netting and plywood valued at £250, and a sergeant-major to four years' penal servitude and a sergeant to three years' penal servitude for aiding and abetting.

There were a few cases in which officers were accused. A colonel serving in the RASC at Colchester was dismissed the service because he "permitted soldiers to be engaged on domestic duties, permitted the supply of rations to an Essex country house, and permitted repairs to be done to his private car", and a captain was cashiered for permitting his private car to be repaired by soldiers and civilians in War Department time and permitting three soldiers to be employed on full-time domestic service.

Most people regarded looting as the worst of crimes, their attitude having been set by horrific childhood accounts of the "looting and pillaging" of invading armies — always foreigners. It was behaviour of which, it was tacitly understood, the

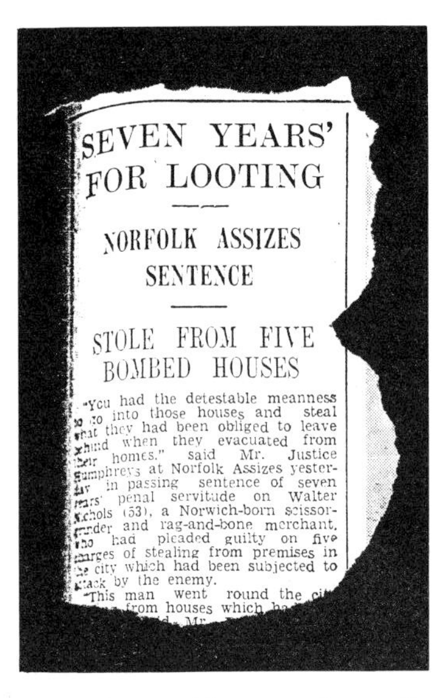

SEVEN YEARS' FOR LOOTING

NORFOLK ASSIZES SENTENCE

STOLE FROM FIVE BOMBED HOUSES

"You had the detestable meanness to go into those houses and steal what they had been obliged to leave behind when they evacuated from their homes," said Mr. Justice Humphreys at Norfolk Assizes yesterday in passing sentence of seven years' penal servitude on Walter Nichols (53), a Norwich-born scissor-grinder and rag-and-bone merchant, who had pleaded guilty on five charges of stealing from premises in the city which had been subjected to attack by the enemy.

"This man went round the ci... from houses which ha...

"You had the detestable meanness to go into those houses and steal what they had been obliged to leave behind when they evacuated from their homes," the judge told a man convicted at Norfolk Assizes of looting bombed houses in Norwich.

East Anglian Daily Times

English would never be guilty. But in Norwich in May a labourer employed on salvage work after one of the raids on the city pleaded guilty to taking a gold watch, two gold chains and a petrol lighter from a public house that had been bombed; he was sent to prison for six months.

When a group of youngsters was brought before the juvenile court in Lowestoft in May the emotive word "looting" was avoided on the charge sheet and they were accused of robbery. But the Mayor of Lowestoft, Major S. W. Humphery, who presided over the court, would have none of that. "It appears that there is a gang of these youngsters going about looting from bombed houses," he said. "It is a very serious thing and the magistrates feel that it is time a stop was put to it. So we are going to do a thing we have never done before since juvenile courts were instituted in Lowestoft. We are going to order four strokes of the birch for six of the boys." These six, aged nine to twelve, were duly birched — but looting did not stop. Four months later, two Cromer girls, aged ten and eleven, were found guilty of looting local shops of watch straps, darning silk and penholders. They were placed on probation for two years.

It was recognized, reluctantly, that some Englishmen — and women and children — were capable of looting the belongings of their unfortunate neighbours who had had their homes destroyed by bombs. Charge sheets now called it looting, and the courts took a severe view of every case. It was a strange and sad feature of most of them that the looters took things which were comparatively useless. A soldier who had been drafted into Norwich to assist the NFS during raids helped himself to a few odd items from a bombed office to the value of £2 2s, and went to prison for three months. A local seventy-year-old pensioner took a curtain and a lady's vest, and went to prison for a month. At Cromer, a soldier took "a crumb brush, two pairs of shoes, a wallet, shoelaces and a torch" while he was helping with rescue work after a raid; he was sent to prison for three months. The most severe sentence was that imposed at the Norfolk Assizes in October on a Norwich scissors grinder who had stolen goods worth £45 10s from five different bombed houses; he was sentenced to seven years' penal servitude.

Many kinds of behaviour that would have been permissible in peacetime were now likely to land offenders in court. People were regularly fined, usually five shillings, for entering the restricted coastal area without permits. In Norwich in March a large store, Jarrolds, were summoned for selling a map of the area; but before the case was brought they had consulted the Ordnance Survey Department about selling such maps and had been told that they were unlikely to prove of great value to an enemy "as it was probable any invading force would be well supplied with maps". After that evidence had been given, the case was dismissed.

A Cambridge man who rented an allotment from the borough council was taken to court because he removed a piece of turf just over a metre square. In the same town a twenty-one-year-old aircraft riveter was sent to one month's hard labour for absenteeism from his job "without reasonable excuse", and a West Runton cowman was fined £5 for missing a Home Guard parade. In Norwich, two unmarried local women, twenty-three and thirty, were sent to prison for a month for refusing to take hospital jobs when ordered to do so; they were the first women in East Anglia prosecuted under the National Service Act. A well-known Cambridge costumier was fined £100, with the alternative of four months' imprisonment, for selling ladies' clothes without taking coupons. A nurse at a hospital near Chelmsford was fined 10s for attempting to obtain rationed articles from outside the United Kingdom. She had written a letter to her sister in Eire and asked another nurse, who was going to Ireland on holiday, to post it to Dublin. "I have no coupons left and am desperate for undies," she wrote. The nurse messenger was stopped at Holyhead and the letter found.

Despite this endless procession through the courts, and despite the pressures upon everyone, most people kept their problems to themselves, kept their heads above water, and kept out of trouble. For countless women, it was the separation from their husbands which weighed most heavily. Mrs Sarah Williams' diary is full of pining for her soldier husband, and on 5th June she noted a conversation with a colleague with a similar problem:

> I went to school with Mrs G, whose husband has just gone abroad. She says she feels quite empty inside and can't settle to anything at all. She can manage a day at school, but at home she wanders restlessly from room to room and feels lost. She feels so dreadful because she wouldn't know if he were ill and needed her. But she has been married only a month — it is worse when you have lived with your husband for years and your whole life is torn apart. Mrs L, whose husband is a parson, says she feels ashamed sometimes that he is still with her when so many have been parted from their husbands.

It was worst of all for those wives who had no idea where their husbands were, or even if they were still alive. These were the men who had been sent to the Far East just before the fall of Singapore. When a meeting of relatives was held in the Diocesan Hall in Ipswich in July, hundreds of wives and mothers turned up and were queuing long before the meeting was due to start. Many carried tiny babies who had not been seen by their fathers. Some had to be directed to an overflow meeting in the nearby Church of St Mary-le-Tower. The women were told they were unlikely to receive any official news before September, but that indications were that the men had been taken to one of the best permanent camps in the Far East, and that their food situation was good.

September came, and the Cambridgeshire Troops Comfort Fund announced that there were still no lists of prisoners of war held by the Japanese. The following month many families were distressed by the return of parcels they had posted nearly a year before to men reported missing after the fall of Singapore, but the authorities insisted that no special significance should be attached to this development; it did not indicate that the men were no longer alive.

When a service was held at St Andrew-the-Great in Cambridge in November for the relatives and friends of prisoners of war, Professor R. D. Whitehorn, Principal of Westminster College, gave an address in which he reminded them that they were sharing their ordeal with countless wives, mothers and sweethearts throughout the world. The report of the service in the local newspaper read:

> He beseeched them to think of the prisoners of war in our hands, and those who were anxious for them. There was a vast multitude of whole races of people who had suffered the same things as they themselves had, and somehow, after the war, the fellowship of suffering and sacrifice might bring peace to the world.

Eventually, towards the end of November, the first official lists prepared by the Japanese reached Britain, together with 1,900 postcards from men taken prisoner at Singapore, apparently smuggled out in some way, which indicated that they were fit and well treated. But the first list of local names was so short as to be

East Anglia's newspapers daily reported news of men "missing at Singapore" or "missing in Malaya". But real news of the men's fate did not come through for a long time.
Eastern Evening News

Pte. J. S. Fountain, Army Catering Corps (attached Royal Norfolk Regiment), missing in Malaya. His wife is living at 104, George Pope-rd., Norwich.

Pte. J. W. Springall, Royal Norfolks, missing at Singapore. His wife lives at Ash Close, Swaffham, and his parents at 275, Gertrude-rd., Norwich.

Telegraphist R. A. Hayhoe, R.N., reported missing, presumed killed. His home is at 3, Stevenson-rd., Norwich.

Pte. S. H. Syder, Royal Norfolks, missing in Malaya. His wife lives at 1, Wood's Yard, Short-st., and his parents at 128, Motum-rd. Norwich

bitterly disappointing, and only one East Anglian regiment, the Suffolks, was mentioned. Families were told that further lists were expected to arrive at monthly intervals. Their long, anguished wait went on.

The Citizens' Advice Bureaux — there were sixty-two of them in the Eastern Region, staffed entirely by volunteers — did invaluable work. They accepted messages from the families of serving men and women for onward transmission through the Red Cross Postal Message Scheme. The general public flocked to them to get advice on all manner of problems: war damage to their homes, rationing difficulties, hire purchase, pensions and allowance queries.

The determined effort to sustain morale during this difficult year was epitomized by the Cambridge shopkeeper who advertised in his local newspaper under the slogan: "Let us Laugh". The face of Mr William A. Coad, who kept one of the town's leading household goods stores, looked out from his autumn advertisements, grinning. The text related that he had been to Birmingham looking for towels, because there had been none in Cambridge for some time. He hadn't found any . . . but the message was still "Let us Laugh". As winter came, even Mr Coad was finding life a little too tough. His advertisement slogan had changed to "SOS"; he looked distinctly discouraged in his photograph, and the message was: "This is a signal of distress. I've got piles of stock . . . but I want more help."

And so did a lot of other folk!

CHAPTER NINE

A Bountiful Harvest

FARMERS in East Anglia knew that the New Year would involve them in immense effort; but they believed, with every justification, that their achievements in 1941 had been so remarkable that little more could be expected in the year ahead.

The revolution in agriculture which began in 1939 had gained powerful momentum. Over three-quarters of the Norfolk farmlands had been brought under the plough — well over 750,000 acres. In the Victorian heyday of Norfolk arable farming, back in the eighteen-seventies and eighteen-eighties, the proportion of arable had not been higher than that, if one made allowance for the land that had been taken for non-agricultural development in the intervening years. Great expanses of grassland had been ploughed, including much parkland. In Ipswich thirty-two acres of Chantry Park was scheduled to be planted with oats and five acres with market garden crops, and seventeen and a half acres of Bourne Park with potatoes. Sheep had disappeared from several thousand acres of parklands and these were producing some of the best crops in the county. The alluvial grasslands between King's Lynn and Great Yarmouth had been surveyed and as much as possible cultivated, to produce large crops of potatoes. On the long-established farmlands in other parts of East Anglia some farmers had increased their production by 200 and even 300 per cent. Machines were being introduced more widely, but labour shortages made life difficult.

Despite these achievements, East Anglian farmers faced 1942 in a dissatisfied and anxious mood. As regards their income, they asserted, the 1941 harvest had been one of the worst for years. When Mr James Alston was re-elected chairman of the Norfolk farmers in January, he was very critical of "politicians and bankers" who had suggested that farmers were doing well, on the evidence that their overdrafts had been reduced. The explanation, he said, was that farmers were getting many of their requisites on loan from the government, and that they had had to reduce by millions their bullocks, sheep, pigs and poultry, so turning stock into cash. Another speaker at the NFU annual meeting declared it had been wrong to force so much stock off the land at the beginning of the war; he wanted the sheep population brought back to the level of 1870, a breeding ewe to every five acres on every farm not carrying cows, and a breeding sow to every acre.

Work on most farms was running behind schedule as the year began. The sugar beet crop was of great importance to the East Anglian farm economy — Norfolk grew a quarter of the national total, and East Anglia as a whole about one third.

Most of this crop had been lifted, but there was still a lot in clamps, because shortage of lorries, petrol and labour had delayed delivery to the factories. Bad weather had compounded the problems, and it was mid-February before the last dumps were cleared. At the Ipswich factory lorries were sometimes delayed all day, waiting to be unloaded.

The weather held up farming operations. Muck carting, hedging and ditching were all in arrears. Arctic conditions had gradually taken a grip on the countryside. After a few isolated snowfalls, the last ten days of January saw 20 inches of snow deposited on Norfolk farms, and it turned out to be the third coldest month of the century.

February was even worse. Records were set as bitter north-easterlies blew in from the frozen continent. Snow lay deep for thirty-five continuous days. The mean temperature remained below zero throughout two months. There was more snow and more icy wind early in March, but on the 9th the temperature rose above 50 degrees F for the first time in three months. By that time most farmers were about a month behind with their spring seeding. Not until 25th March, at last, was there some pale sunshine, so that work could go forward normally again. By this time, the fields were unusually bare. The winter wheat had done badly. The old adage that by March there should be enough growth to "cover a hare" was disproved. On the light land farmers began to drill oats in mid-March, and kept at it all month.

– it's better!

ENTIRELY BRITISH MADE • AGENTS EVERYWHERE

CANNELL & SONS
LODDON - NORWICH

750 FARMERS HAVE THEIR OWN FOOD PLANTS

They are producing from straw, chaff and cavings a valuable food for their stock.

The inclusion of straw pulp in the feed saves part of the ration of hay, concentrates or roots, and solves many of the worries caused by shortage of feedingstuffs.

There is convincing evidence from all parts of the country that cattle thrive on straw pulp, which is easily, quickly and cheaply produced. Order the plant now, whilst materials are available.

Full information from your County War Agricultural Executive Committee.

STRAW PULP

will help save the food situation

RECTOR AGED 7
RE-ELECTED

Waste not, want not, was a message that the government was keen to get over to everybody, including East Anglian farmers. *East Anglian Daily Times*

And they grumbled. Firstly, there was fierce controversy about the schedule of farm prices for the year ahead. Trade union organization of farmworkers was proceeding rapidly — the National Union of Agricultural Workers had recruited well over two thousand new members in Norfolk alone during the previous year. This new strength, reflecting the key role in the Churchill government of Britain's most influential trade union leader, Mr Ernest Bevin, enabled the farm workers' representatives to set a firmer tone in wage negotiations, and the national minimum wage for farm workers had been increased to £3 a week from 1st January.

The farmers believed they had a pledge from the government that farm prices would be increased sufficiently to cover the extra wage costs. When, by the third week of January, there was no sign of a decision from Whitehall they were apprehensive that the bargain would not be kept. When the Suffolk branch of the National Farmers' Union met at Ipswich on 20th January it was reported that the NFU negotiators were talking to the government in terms of 85s 6d a quarter for the coming wheat crop. The Suffolk chairman insisted that 100s a quarter was necessary to grow wheat profitably in the county. The meeting recorded "grave dissatisfaction" with the way the negotiations were being conducted.

The new price schedule was announced on 20th February and was greeted in the Eastern Counties as "most discouraging". It would give farmers £5 an acre less than they had been hoping for, said the Norfolk NFU secretary. Another farmers' representative spoke of "catastrophe". The Suffolk NFU Executive called for concerted action, with other counties, without specifying what might be done. The President of the NFU, Mr C. Neville, made a trip to Ipswich to confront 250 Suffolk farmers; and eventually he persuaded them that the government had met its pledges to the farmers. They bombarded him with questions and called for a revision of some of the prices agreed, particularly that for wheat. The temper of the Suffolk branch of the NFU was not improved when, at a meeting at this juncture, it learned that the Minister of Agriculture, Mr R. S. Hudson, had accused them of juggling the figures — citing maximum costs and minimum yields in pressing their claims: "the costs appeared to have been inflated by assuming an unnecessarily heavy rate of manuring and a far too high estimated cost of dung; also the horse labour costs were exaggerated."

This was like a red rag to a bull because, quite apart from the farmers' complaints about farm prices, there was a fundamental clash between their view on how East Anglian farms should be managed and the recommendations of the government's agricultural advisers. In Norwich and Chelmsford leading farmers met once a week in "round table" to discuss the problems of the industry. Most of their problems, as they saw it, were created in Whitehall. "Lavengro", the agricultural columnist of the *East Anglian Daily Times*, was a faithful retailer of their complaints and in January, 1942, he wrote of "the important part they play behind the scenes in formulating schemes for the betterment of agriculture, and, what is of greater moment, of demonstrating the likely evil results of changes in

Women who had joined the Timber Corps of the Women's Land Army take a break from work during their four-week course at a training centre in Suffolk. The first training centre of its kind in Britain, this one was able to accommodate 120 girls on each course. *East Anglian Daily Times*

farming methods emanating from those who know 'so little about so much'." He went on:

> Such men, despite years of severe depression, have kept their heads above water because they know that stock production, whether it be beef, mutton, or pork, spells fertility and with cereals must go hand in hand. Whether it be distasteful or not to those holding contrary views, and have offered advice accordingly, the members of such a "Farmers' Brains Trust" would not hesitate to enforce their unalterable view that successful arable farming must not be divorced from stock-keeping.

A little later, "Lavengro" reported that "Farmers have held meetings of late up and down the country, not because they are disgruntled, but because, as men who know their job, they realize a mistaken agricultural policy is operating against maximum food production . . ." The nub of the matter was that the East Anglian farmers were wedded to traditional mixed farming; the new agricultural scientists argued that by using fertilisers the land could produce bigger arable crops.

The agents of Whitehall were the County War Agricultural Committees. Farmers were given directions as to what they should grow; if they failed to produce according to plan, they were liable to prosecution and, after due warning, to have their land taken away from them and placed under the control of the appropriate County Agricultural Executive Committee. So not only did the county committees transmit the Ministry's orders, and supervise their implementation, but they farmed themselves, and purported to set an example of the way things should be done.

By the beginning of 1942 the West Suffolk War Agricultural Executive Committee was farming 12,000 acres. The Essex committee, in contrast, held only 1,400 acres. Among the land the East Suffolk committee had in hand were 700 to 800 acres of heathland in the southern half of the coastal area, where it was growing rye and oats. The road from Ipswich to Felixstowe, an observer wrote, "affords pleasing proof of what has been possible in the way of cropping bracken and gorse-covered land." Levington Heath was planted with rye early in January. In the Fen country, between Thetford and Downham Market, 1,500 acres near Feltwell had been so successfully cultivated by the War Agricultural Executive Committee that they had been able to hand it over to a private enterprise farming company. Now the committee was moving its men and equipment into neighbouring Methwold Fen to start a reclamation scheme of comparable magnitude.

Their methods were watched with interest, with some suspicion, and not always with goodwill. Some of the land they had in hand had been requisitioned from farmers whose efforts had been judged to be inefficient. If there were points to be scored, the traditionalists did not miss a chance. Thus, when sheep were brought in to manure some particularly poor soil and straw was spread, one newspaper commentator wrote:

> It is recognized in the management of such land that, contrary to the ideas prevailing among a certain section of agricultural advisers, it will never do to pour artificials on light land, since they will not stop there if there is nothing to bind the soil together.

The government was insistently demanding more wheat. The Minister of Agriculture, Mr Hudson, told the nation's farmers in March that their next harvest might well be a critical factor in the future history of the British Isles and the world; they must be prepared "to fight to the last ditch". The War Agricultural Committees issued directions that at least fifteen per cent of arable acreage must be planted with wheat. They instructed every occupier of land to apply, before 15th May, one hundredweight of sulphate of ammonia to each acre of land sown with wheat, rye (to be harvested as grain), barley and oats. And they warned that they might be unable after the summer to issue coupons for farmers to purchase feeding stuffs for animals. It was up to the farmers to find sufficient food for their stock to be self-supporting through the coming winter.

As the government called for more wheat, the brewers were scrambling for the remaining stocks of barley from the 1941 harvest, which had been poor, so that prices had been pushed up. Some farmers, as a result of this experience, wanted to grow more barley and less wheat.

Farmers were disconcerted to find that their case was not everywhere accepted at face value. A particularly sharp criticism was made by the MP for South West Norfolk, Mr Somerset de Chair, who was home on sick leave after having been wounded while serving in the Army in the Middle East. At a Dereham meeting in March, Mr de Chair bluntly asserted that some farmers were putting their personal interests before the national interest. There were some in the Fens, he said, whose annual income had reached £1,500, five times what it had been before the war, and yet they were boasting that they paid no income tax. Other farmers were getting "fantastic prices" for malting barley. Were these farmers putting their country first? Broadening out his attack, Mr de Chair spoke of a village lad getting £6 15s a week, after paying tax, for driving a lorry between a sandpit and an airfield, while other young men were fighting for a shilling or two a day. Perhaps, he concluded, it was time the government conscripted everyone. These were emotive words, particularly coming from a thirty-year-old serving lieutenant hobbling on crutches after being blown up while on active service.

The arguments about prices and methods were often bitter, but eventually the farmers came to accept that they could do nothing more to advance their case, for their thoughts and energies were fully engaged on work for the new harvest. By the beginning of April most farmers and their workers were on the job for sixty hours a week, drilling corn as fast as they could, but breaking off now and again to get some sugar beet in. By the end of the month things were beginning to look better. An *East Anglian Daily Times* correspondent wrote:

> April has been a really good month. Arrears, which at one time appeared insurmountable, have now been almost wiped off. The young corn is showing a strong growth in the ridges, the result of a good seed bed . . . The first welcome notes of the barley bird, cuckoo and nightingale were heard last weekend, bringing the summer so much nearer . . .

By early May a bigger acreage of potatoes had been planted than ever before. In June the cutters were at work on the grasses and clover. A newspaper correspondent reported that recent growth had been "amazing". But still the farmers were not happy. They argued that the absence of sheep on the light lands was having adverse results, and that this land was not in good heart. And they foresaw dire problems in harvesting the corn, because it would probably overlap with the lifting of potatoes and sugar beet; they asked for immediate assurances that more labour would be available.

The April Budget added to their problems; it brought changes which made many more farmers liable to pay income tax, which meant additional form-filling. Further, in association with the farm workers' new £3 minimum wage, the changes meant that many labourers had to pay income tax for the first time in their lives, and this made some of them disinclined to work overtime.

Despite their professed anxieties about shortage of labour, the farmers failed to make use of that help on offer from the Women's Land Army. After East Suffolk WLA girls had marched in procession through Ipswich streets in April, the chairman of their county committee, Lady Cranworth, told them that they had had a rough road to tread. "A crowd of splendid girls" had been ready to work on the farms from the beginning of the war, she said, but there had been no demand for them. Only a few far-seeing farmers had taken some and trained them during 1941. She thought things were beginning to change, as conservatively-minded farmers had at last realized they must look to the WLA for the help they desperately sought.

A first Women's Land Army hostel in Norfolk was opened at Holkham Park on 29th June with accommodation for thirty-two girls. A training centre, the first of its kind in the country, was opened in Suffolk where 120 girls at a time took a

Looking very unfeminine in their breeches, woollen stockings and heavy overcoats, members of the Women's Land Army muster for a march through Ipswich in April. *East Anglian Daily Times*

four-week course before joining a WLA Timber Corps. By October there were two large hostels for the WLA in West Suffolk, but resistance to the employment of Land Girls was broken down only slowly. The number employed in East Suffolk rose from two hundred in January to five hundred by June. Although in West Suffolk the numbers increased from 223 girls in October, 1941, to 620 a year later, more than a third of them worked for the agricultural committee, and a further 140 in the Timber Corps, leaving only 268 in private employ. As the year ended, an average of only three land girls per village in Suffolk were being employed, and new appeals were being made to the many farmers who were still resisting the coming of women to the land.

A demonstration of WLA skills at Park Farm, Shimpling, "to show what women can do on the land, and that farmers . . . need have no hesitation in accepting their services" only brought more clearly into the open male bias against the women. Press reports conveyed a sense of wonder that women *could* do this sort of work. When a Cockfield girl was seen hoeing a twenty-three acre field of sugar beet with a tractor, the farm foreman was quoted as saying: "She can steer a drill across a field as well as anyone." When a former dietician was seen driving one of the most powerful of caterpillar tractors, it was emphasized that she spurned help to start it, and was keen to maintain it herself.

Even at this stage, the cry in some farming quarters was for schoolchildren rather than land girls. "Lavengro" in May waxed indignant:

> Up and down the country an embargo on children going on to farms at seed-time and harvest is being exercised by rural and town education authorities. Is it not time their activities in this direction were curbed?. . . Is this the time, on an under-staffed farm, to prevent the employment in the most critical period of the farming year of boys who are due to leave school three months hence? Here is a striking example of bureaucratic stupidity in the greatest crisis in our history.

In fact many schoolboys helped, willingly, with the harvest.

East Anglian farmers as a body were unenthusiastic about the new agricultural machinery coming from the factories, and about the new farming practices that came with them, and many of them were still deeply attached to the working horse. When the Suffolk Horse Society held its two-day show and sale at Ipswich the number of horses was quite inadequate to meet the demand. One hundred and twenty were sold at an average price of £120. A report on the Woodbridge Horse Society event on Easter Monday stated: "Wartime rations have not in any way affected the stamina of our county breed, which all agree were brought out in a fit working condition, and perhaps was the best collection ever seen at Woodbridge." Many farmers had kept gigs and traps from pre-war days and, now that cars were swept from the roads, they brought them out and harnessed up their ponies. Notwithstanding the continued enthusiasm for horses, there was a desperate shortage of blacksmiths, because of call-up and death, and farmers declared it "practically impossible" to get their horses shod.

Lady Roland Burke presenting a cup to Sir Charles Bunbury, owner of the champion Suffolk stallion, at the Woodbridge Horse Show on Easter Monday. *East Anglian Daily Times*

The amount of livestock on East Anglian farms was in rapid decline but the local markets still functioned, albeit with reduced activity. At Cambridge Cattle Market on 23rd March, for example, there were 209 beasts, 251 sheep, 259 pigs, and 105 calves. In the same week, Haverhill Sale Yard had received 72 fat pigs, 43 fat sheep, ten fat cattle and two veal calves, but the changed circumstances of the market were shown by the report that "all were allocated to Ministry slaughter-house in accordance with instructions".

The sheep sales failed to meet popular demand. At the opening lamb sale of the season at Diss on 2nd July the entry of 9,570 was 1,200 up on the previous year. The auctioneer said that 84,100 sheep had been fattened in Norfolk during the year. A week later more than 1,800 lambs and ewes were sold at Bury St Edmunds and 1,500 lambs and 500 breeding ewes at Haverhill. Later, 2,000 were sold at Stowmarket and 1,750 at Braintree. Attendances everywhere were good, and trade brisk. In spite of the shortage of feeding stuffs, the quality had rarely been equalled. Some of the old Suffolk flockmasters had withdrawn, but newcomers had moved in and were producing pedigree black-faced of very high standard.

"Sheep were never so badly wanted on the land as today," remarked "Lavengro", and now officialdom agreed with him. The East Suffolk War Agricultural Committee advertised a supply of "agisted sheep" — hill sheep available for winter folding on light lands with sugar beet tops and other root crops. The committee supplied the sheep, but retained their ownership; the farmer provided attendance and gear and received from the committee an agreed price per score per week.

The Ministry of Agriculture did its utmost to stimulate interest in machinery and to educate farmers in its use and maintenance, for there was little skill of this kind available on most farms. It arranged a number of exhibitions in the Eastern Counties. Ploughing demonstrations led to earnest debate about the relative merits of two- and three-furrow tractor ploughs. A robot planter which handled kale, cabbage, sprouts and potatoes was a principal centre of attention. Thatching and thatch-making by machinery was demonstrated — the old breed of thatchers was dying out and a great deal of stacked corn could not be thatched in the traditional way. A "chamber of horrors" demonstrated how the use of incorrect oil or the failure to adjust nuts could cause damage to tractor parts which could not easily be replaced. It was headline news when in August "the largest combine harvester in Britain" was at work in Norfolk, cutting, threshing and sacking five acres an hour. It looked primitive. The machines were advancing, but even at the end of 1942 "Lavengro" was defiant: "In very wet seasons", he wrote, "the use of the tractor must of necessity be strictly limited. That being so, horses are indispensable . . ."

Before harvesting began, the WAEC invited farmers to make evening visits to those farms which were setting high standards and producing record crops. The idea was to stimulate a little friendly competition and to get purposeful discussion going. Education by example was the official policy, and the farms under direct control of the agricultural committees provided opportunities. At the end of June the Minister of Agriculture attended a demonstration on a farm at Kelsale, near Saxmundham, which the East Suffolk committee had taken over in February, 1940, when its arable land was foul and its pasture derelict. Now 267 acres were bearing fine crops of wheat, barley, beans, oats and mixtures.

The government had requisitioned a total of thirty-six square miles of land in East Anglia by this time. One of the most remarkable achievements of the whole war was the reclamation of vast areas of Fenland, and such progress had been made that those in charge were keen to show off their success. King George VI and Queen Elizabeth were the first visitors, in mid-June, and soon afterwards parties of Members of Parliament and of agricultural scientists followed. These tours began at

King George VI and Queen Elizabeth inspecting land girls when they visited a Fenland reclamation scheme in June. *Cambridge Daily News*

Swaffham Prior House, which had become a WAEC hostel for sixty-five girls of the Women's Land Army. Reporting the visits, the *Cambridge Daily News* wrote:

> The whole 5,000 acres at Swaffham Prior Fen and Adventurer's Fen, Burwell, is nothing more nor less than a battlefield where men and women, armed with the latest weapons of agriculture, are carrying out relentless warfare against rushes, scrub, bog oaks and flooding.

Of these 5,000 acres, more than half had been derelict in 1939, and the remainder produced only moderate crops. Most of the land lay sixteen feet below high tide level at King's Lynn. The peat "droves" which provided the only access to the fens were impassable for six or seven months of every year. Mosquitoes bred among the eight-foot rushes and scrub. Just below the surface lay massive bog oaks, remains of trees which had peaked 4,000 years before, some of them as much as eighty-four feet long and three to five feet in diameter.

Before the outbreak of war, the River Great Ouse Catchment Board had been contemplating a vast new drainage scheme for this area, and a further 5,000 acres adjoining it. It installed a powerful new pumping station, drew out 180 tons of water every minute, and eventually brought the land to the point at which clearance and cultivation could be started. New concrete roads were built across the reclaimed land, nearly twenty miles of them, until every field was within reasonable distance of a hard surface. The War Agricultural Committee then took over.

Special "stump jumper" ploughs were dragged over the land to locate the bog oaks. These were uncovered, split by explosives, and dragged out by caterpillar tractors. Sometimes units of the Royal Engineers had to be called in to lend assistance. Disc harrows afterwards cut up the roots of the rushes, which were carried off and burned. Ditches were hand dug through the heavy clay and high banks were constructed to contain some of the lodes, the channels once used by the Fenland barges carrying cargo to isolated communities. By the time the King and Queen came in the summer of 1942 the reclaimed land had been fertilized and was growing good crops of potatoes, sugar beet, wheat and barley.

The royal visitors were taken on a long tour over the new concrete roads, shown the "bog oak cemetery" of trees that had been removed, embarked on a barge at Cock-up Bridge on Burwell Lode and taken for a short cruise, drifting high

Land girls and other workers cheering as the King and Queen passed by during their tour of reclaimed land in the Fens. *Cambridge Daily News*

above land which only a year before had been wild, but most of which now carried crops. Proudly showing off this remarkable transformation were the Minister of Agriculture, Mr R. S. Hudson, and the chairman of the Cambridgeshire WAEC, Mr W. C. Jackson. The cost of the reclamation was quoted at £10 to £20 per acre.

Sometimes the county committees found that friendly persuasion did not produce results, so if they issued instructions to farmers which were persistently ignored they prosecuted. The Saffron Walden bench in July, for example, imposed a fine of £50 on a St Aylotts farmer who had planted ten acres with barley after he had been told to grow sugar beet. He had farmed the land for fifty years, and his father before him, and he declared it was too heavy and sticky for sugar beet. He

Troops, aided by schoolboys, gathering the harvest in one of the East Anglian "battle school" areas in August. In the background is an early combine harvester towed by a caterpillar tractor, machinery almost unknown on East Anglian farms before the war. *Imperial War Museum*

lacked machinery and had only one man and two boys to help with his 280 acres; he had never been in conflict with any sort of authority before. But farmers around him had obeyed the instruction, and his failure to do so was considered a serious offence; the fine, therefore, was severe.

By August it was clear that the 1942 harvest was going to be a good one everywhere. Cereals production was the best for some years and there was so much sugar beet that it was difficult to gather it all. There were renewed complaints about the shortage of labour. The Norfolk NFU declared that some farmworkers were refusing to do overtime for their regular employers if it led to their paying income tax, but were going off to work for other, smaller, farmers who were not liable to make tax returns.

There was a special urgency about harvesting because German planes were dropping incendiary bombs in the crops, trying to set them on fire. Yet the work went on steadily. The Army made available troops and, if necessary, military transport. The new combine harvesters proved their worth. Farmers arranged double shifts and ploughed by night — new regulations sent to all police authorities permitted tractors to be fitted with lights fore and aft, and allowed tractor drivers to use torches.

The Press Association's agricultural correspondent reported at the end of August that "the greatest harvest of all time" was being cut or stacked. Even if yields proved to be average, he wrote, the harvest of grain and potatoes would be up by two-thirds on pre-war years. Three weeks into September, the East Anglian harvest had been safely gathered. All reports agreed it had been bountiful, and that it was in better condition than usual.

When all had been gathered in, a new cycle of farm production began immediately. In London, the Minister of Agriculture's mind was already on the 1943 harvest. That was now "the vital one". He wanted an additional one million acres of grassland ploughed, with 600,000 more acres of wheat. He told the Commons that " if certain arrangements we are discussing now mature, farmers will be expected to work by night as well as by day." The figures were staggering. When he heard them, Mr J. F. Wright, Norfolk NFU secretary, remarked: "I fear the difficulties are not altogether appreciated by those concerned with the direction of policy." It would, he said, be a tremendous task simply to maintain maximum production on existing acreage. Additional acreage would not necessarily mean additional food.

East Suffolk farmers learned that they would be expected to plough 4,000 acres more, West Suffolk an additional 3,500 acres. Occupiers of land were called upon to make returns of their proposed cropping for 1942–43, and directions were served where thought necessary. In West Suffolk, for example, farmers with fifty or more acres were required to plant not less than twenty-five per cent of their arable land with wheat for harvesting in 1943.

New farm prices had been announced in June. There was to be a £3 per acre

Left: "The largest combine harvester in Britain" at work on a farm in Norfolk, where it was cutting, threshing and sacking five acres of rye in an hour.
Eastern Evening News

Right: Threshing in the old manner with a steam engine on an evacuated farm in one of the battle school areas. Soldiers and army vehicles were employed, the work being organized by the War Agricultural Committee.
East Anglian Daily Times

"acreage payment" on all land cropped for wheat in the autumn. The basic price for the 1943 crop was to be 65s 3d per quarter. This meant that farmers who grew an average crop of four quarters per acre would get a total basic return of 80s 3d per quarter, which was eight shillings more than they had received for the 1942 harvest. The maximum price of barley, however, was reduced by 30s a quarter, and a Suffolk spokesman immediately declared that a farmer with fifty acres under barley and fifty acres under wheat would be over £4 a week worse off than in 1942. Nevertheless, the NFU Suffolk branch promised an all-out effort to produce more. Norfolk, which produced a fifth of Britain's barley, was also upset at the reduction in its price. The Norfolk NFU secretary assessed the growers' loss at £6 an acre or, with 200,000 acres of barley in the county, £1,200,000 a year of income.

While this argument proceeded, the work on the farms went forward. Immediately after harvest, the ploughing up of stubble began. Then there was a race to drill rye for grain by the end of September, and then to plant wheat by the end of October. There was also the lifting of sugar beet (deliveries to the factories began during the first week in October) and potatoes, some red clover seed to gather, and, of course, muck carting. Wet weather delayed the sugar beet badly. That, in turn, set back the drilling of wheat, much of which was scheduled to go on the same land. The winter wheat needed to be in by mid-December, and many farmers decided that they would have to switch to a greater proportion of spring-sown wheat, although they argued that that was a greater gamble.

The Fakenham branch of the NFU was plaintive in late November that acute

shortage of labour meant that "corn crops cannot be threshed, vegetable crops are being spoiled, and sugar beet are in grave danger of being frozen . . . arrears of work in preparation for 1943 crops are fast accumulating". When the Norfolk NFU Executive met just before Christmas it recorded its view that, with the labour likely to be available, it would be impracticable to increase the acreage under cultivation. It resolved, therefore, to ask the Agricultural Central Wages Board to increase minimum working hours from fifty to fifty-four a week from March, 1943, although it conceded that it was already difficult to get some men to work fifty hours when, by doing so, they became liable for the first time in their lives to pay income tax.

Wage levels were now back on the agenda. During the 1942 harvest, farm workers were paid £3 a week for males of twenty-one and over for a fifty-hour week, and £2 3s a week for females of twenty-one and over. Casuals and part-time workers were paid 11¼d an hour. In November the Cambridgeshire and Ely Agricultural Wages Committee resolved that the national minimum wage should continue to be £3 a week, but with an increase for overtime working. The Agricultural Workers' Union pressed a claim that women workers should get 48s for a forty-four-hour week; the farmers argued for 43s, and eventually a compromise was agreed at 44s. A week later the Ministry of Agriculture announced that the government had taken the whole matter out of the hands of the county committees; thereafter the Central Wages Board would fix the wages and hours of all workers on the land.

The year ended with confirmation that 1942 had produced a record harvest, in bulk and in value. Despite everything, the Women's Land Army had played an important part in gathering it, and the assistance of a mass of part-time helpers had been important: Army and RAF personnel, many individual volunteers, Boy Scouts and schoolchildren. Many farmers had employed children who did not possess the "labour cards" which education committees had been issuing. In West Suffolk alone the equivalent of 15,000 school attendances were lost in the five months to September, and a further 15,000 in October because of potato-lifting.

Another activity by schoolchildren was seen to be wholly beneficial. The Ministry of Supply had set up a Country Herb Committee to organize the collection of medicinal herbs and the Board of Education asked schools throughout the Eastern Region to help collect buckthorn, red poppy petals, elder flowers, comfrey, coltsfoot, horseradish, hyssop, hemlock, henbane, foxglove, dandelions and stinging nettles, all used in the manufacture of drugs. The National Federation of Women's Institutes was also involved in collecting, drying and despatching the herbs by rail to chemical works. Rose hips made syrup for young babies, "conkers" produced tannic acid for creams and lotions for the treatment of burns.

Towards the end of 1942, two important East Anglian agricultural estates changed hands. The executors of the late Mr C. F. Ryder sold the 12,280-acre Great Thurlow Hall Estate to Mr J. G. Hannay, who "bought for investment". The estate included, apart from Great Thurlow Hall, sixty-seven farms and small-holdings, 254 houses and cottages, over 1,000 acres of woodlands, and the greater part of the villages of Great Thurlow, Little Thurlow, Great Wratting and Withersfield, with an estimated rent roll of £13,196 a year. The purchase price was not disclosed. Soon afterwards, the Brightwell estate between Ipswich and Felixstowe was sold by auction at Ipswich; twenty-four farms and smallholdings, woodlands, gravel pits and development sites, over 5,000 acres in all. Levington Hall, famous for its association with Margaret Catchpole, the Suffolk girl whose escapades resulted in her being transported to Australia for life, was sold with 40 acres for £3,500*.

The Ministry of Information did its best in 1942 to create a wider and better understanding of the importance of British farming in the mind of the general public. Its efforts included a forty-minute film *The Harvest Will Come*, which was shot entirely in Suffolk and which told the story of forty years of British agriculture. The Ministry worked hard, too, to persuade individuals to grow more food, so that the farmers' efforts were supplemented by tens of thousands of enthusiastic gardeners. When an "Allotments Brains Trust" was arranged at Cambridge Guildhall in November, with Freddie Grisewood, a well-known BBC figure, as questionmaster, there was an audience of over eight hundred. They plied the experts with inquiries about wireworm, earthing up of potatoes and whether onions should be planted in the same bed every year. The Mayor of Ipswich, Alderman

*Her story was told in fictional form by Richard Cobbold in his book *History of Margaret Catchpole a Suffolk Girl*.

John Slater, left, in the film *The Harvest Will Come*, which was shot almost entirely at Badley and in the Needham Market area of Suffolk. The film was an attempt to increase public awareness of the importance of agriculture. *East Anglian Film Archive*

R. F. Jackson, set a fine example; two visitors to his home in Beechcroft Road in August were so impressed that they wrote to the local paper:

> Among all sorts of plants are potatoes, onions, leeks, lettuces, beet, etc, and marrows are being grown on top of the air raid shelter. What struck us most was that he had planted the grass verge in the front of his house with potatoes.

As 1942 came to its close, an NFU spokesman in Norwich delivered the verdict that it had been "a wonderful year for agriculture", and a leading article in the *Eastern Daily Press* pointed the way ahead:

> After a year of the biggest British harvest in living memory, [the farmers] have been told that for 1943 another million acres must be under the plough . . . It means that, with a much smaller labour force, British agriculture is being asked — or rather told — to increase output so that, instead of 66 per cent of our food supplies being home-grown, we shall have to have 75 per cent — or tighten our belts . . .

CHAPTER TEN

Getting to Know the Yanks

THE FIRST contingents of American forces arrived in Ulster in January, 1942, but the first US Army Air Force units did not reach East Anglia until June. Their arrival was not reported in the press, as their movements were subject to censorship on grounds of military security. People saw American airmen walking the streets of many of the towns and visiting the pubs in many of the villages before they read anything about their presence. Information might be said to have seeped out.

A process of conditioning of the local population began during the summer months. "Glad to see you, Americans!" proclaimed a *Cambridge Daily News* headline on 1st August. The story bore the hallmarks of a Ministry of Information handout:

> Already the American uniform is becoming a familiar sight in our streets. The men now among us are the vanguard of a vast army coming to aid in the restoration of liberty to the enslaved lands. To these American boys Britain is a foreign land. Many of our customs and habits will be very strange. There are differences in national temperament that may lead to misunderstanding. In dealing with our other Allies, we instinctively make allowances for such differences. Just because we start with a feeling of kinship and because we share the same language, we are apt to be less understanding when we meet an American. There is a deep welcome in our hearts for these friends and Allies and there will be a widespread readiness to do all we can to make them feel at home. As comrades now in winning the war and as comrades in building a better world tomorrow, we offer them a friendly greeting and a warm welcome.

In Washington the US War Department was preaching a similar message. Every GI bound for Britain was handed a booklet full of good advice: don't brag or bluster; don't make fun of accents; don't criticize the beer, the food, or the cigarettes — or Royalty; don't draw attention to differences in pay; don't intrude. This booklet declared:

> You won't be able to tell the British much about "taking it". They are not particularly interested in taking it any more. They are far more interested in getting together in solid friendship with us, so that we can all start dishing it out to Hitler.
>
> You will naturally be interested in getting to know your opposite number, the British soldier, the "Tommy" you have heard and read about. You can understand that two actions on your part will slow up the friendship — swiping his girl and not appreciating what his army has been up against. Yes, and rubbing it in that you are better paid than he is.
>
> The British don't know how to make a good cup of coffee. You don't know how to make a good cup of tea. It's an even swap. The British welcome you as friends and allies,

> but remember that crossing the ocean doesn't automatically make you an hero. There are housewives in aprons, and youngsters in knee-pants in Britain who have lived through more high explosives in air-raids than many soldiers saw in first-class barrages in the last war . . .

Despite all these efforts, problems arose. Some were due to the clash of cultures, but some to simple misunderstanding. For example, some British servicemen, who had been overimpressed by the design of American uniforms, discovered that they had been saluting men of a rank similar to, or lower than, their own! The local newspapers published a "guide to American uniforms — some insignia hints". It began: "Both officers and men of the US Army wear well-cut uniforms very similar in appearance . . . How then are we to tell them apart?"

One East Anglian observer's analysis went deeper:

> First impressions were positive, and we were inclined to be patronizing; they were cheerful, chatty, not over-disciplined — which, we thought morosely, would be a bad thing. Fancy going to fight a war, and treating your officers as "buddies"(1).

A publicity picture of an American airman wearing an old-style US Army hat and a British airman by the ball turret of a B-17 Fortress bomber. The American is said to be "explaining the ball turret guns to an RAF colleague". *East Anglian Daily Times*

Belts of 0.5-inch ammunition snake across the foreground of this photograph of a waist gunner in a B-17 Fortress stationed "somewhere in England". These and the B-24 Liberators of the 8th US Army Air Force soon became familiar in East Anglian skies.
East Anglian Daily Times

It was not the uniforms, nor the measure of egalitarianism, that provided the main contrast between the British and American serving men, but, as had been foreseen, the pay. The British private received a basic two shillings a day, US privates five times as much. A US captain got three times the pay of his UK equivalent. It might not have been purely coincidental that as the new Allies began to flood into Britain the pay of British servicemen was improved. An increase in Forces pay was announced in the Commons in September; the lowest rate was increased to 21s a week; the allowance for a first child went up from 8s 6d a week to 9s 6d, for a second child from 6s 6d to 8s 6d, and for the third and subsequent children from 6s to 7s 6d each.

It was not until September that the East Anglian newspapers discussed plainly the presence of the Americans in the region. A paragraph in the *East Anglian Daily Times* stated:

> American soldiers in Britain will worship side by side with British churchgoers, instead of attending services in a camp, hall or mess building. This arrangement has been made between US Army chaplains and local clergymen, it was announced yesterday. Church members are inviting American soldiers to church teas, suppers and outings, and to their homes.

The Ipswich Hippodrome celebrated the first anniversary of its reopening with a show called "Yankee Clipper". A British Railways advertisement depicted American servicemen, with the slogan "*Their* Journey is necessary". There was a photograph of US Army Air Corps bomber crews "completing their training at airfields which American authorities have taken over from the RAF." A little later there was another photograph showing "American Flying Fortresses, in operation daily from airfields in this country", and then a report on 8th September stating:

> Flying Fortresses, battleships of the air, armed with thirteen machine-guns, most of heavy calibre, have had a remarkable record. They have carried out about a dozen day raids, and Sunday was the first time that any had been lost. Two did not return.

The next day there was another picture of the Americans and their planes; and then, on 12th September — more than two months after they had arrived in the Eastern Counties — the *East Anglian Daily Times* published the first clear and definite indication that all this American activity was, indeed, taking place in its circulation area. It was given in a letter from an East Bergholt reader, who wrote of the friendly treatment of RAF men in Canada and the USA, contrasted it with British attitudes to the GIs, and then complained: "Surely we can smile, or say a word of cheer to them as we pass, even if we cannot entertain large numbers, owing to rationing."

At last the spell — or rather the censorship — was broken. Other readers joined in. A Claydon lady who had lived many years in Canada sought to correct any impression that the Americans were trying to be "fresh" when they spoke first. She related:

> Last week I was in a teashop in an Essex town. A very young American soldier came in, nodded to a bus-driver who was sitting with two girls, and breezily said "Howdy". To my amazement, none of them answered, and the two girls burst out laughing. I shall never forget that boy's face . . . None of our boys who go to America or Canada would be put through such a thing.

Mrs Sarah Williams was holidaying at home in Sheringham when the first US servicemen appeared in East Anglia. Not until she returned to her school duties in Norwich does her diary contain a reference to the American presence. On 22nd September she wrote:

> I notice in the streets of Norwich that the American soldiers are left strictly to themselves. I feel very sorry for them, but people in Norwich say that ever since they have been there they have been unpopular. They look most unhappy, but perhaps this is because they are cold.

An editorial in the *Eastern Daily Press* on 28th September still avoided stating plainly that the Americans were in Norwich. It read, in part:

> In many parts of England the presence of American soldiers in the streets of our towns and cities has now become a familiar thing . . . In the brief off-duty hours when they roam our streets, quite evidently full of curiosity and interest about the places and the people here in England, one gets an impression, which we could hope is not well-founded, that the degree of friendly contact between them and ourselves has not developed as fully as we all wish to see it . . . So far as this area is concerned, the spirit of everyone in East Anglia is one of the heartiest welcome.

Perhaps this editorial had some effect. At any rate, Mrs Williams' diary soon had a different tale to tell:

> *5th October*: I see the Americans in Norwich are managing to find themselves girls. There weren't so many lonely soldiers about.
> *6th October*: Our boys have a new game: American soldier spotting. On the bus they count to see who can see the most.

A reader wrote to the *Eastern Daily Press*:

> Many of us have approached Americans in Norwich and offered them our homes as their homes whilst they are over here, but so far we have had no success. Most of them seem to be looking for something a little more "peppy" than home life during their first few weeks in this country. Moreover, it seems to have been drilled into them very thoroughly that we are a proud people living on the border-line of poverty and starvation, with the result that we can do nothing for them without raiding the baby's money-box or, worse still, his ration card! If you can help us to clear away these misapprehensions and assist us to find some Americans who would appreciate an armchair by the fire, a cup of coffee, a smoke and a talk, we are waiting to open our homes and our hearts to them.

A "Norfolk Dumpling" as he signed himself, followed this up with a story that he had shown two Americans around Norwich and in the evening "they were just too tickled at playing darts for the first time".

By this time the Americans had staged a baseball match at Carrow Road in

Radio star Bebe Daniels photographed with American soldiers during a visit to their East Anglian camp.
East Anglian Daily Times

Norwich between the Wildcats and the Cheyenne Broncs, and in Woodbridge two American engineering units were arranging an exhibition baseball game, with a broadcast explanation of the proceedings, as part of an effort to raise money for the Prisoners of War Fund. Once these public events were being advertised, most of the secrecy was at an end.

But still one important fact did not break through into print: that some of the US Servicemen were *black*. Again, it was publication of a letter from a reader which made the disclosure. The Vicar of Haughley, the Rev. W. Grainge White, wrote in the *East Anglian Daily Times* on 23rd September:

> I should like it to be known that Mrs White and I will welcome visits from Negro or coloured troops, to whom Haughley is accessible. The Vicarage rest room — so long as we can afford to keep it open — will be for their use. It has comfortable furniture, writing-table, and free materials, papers and books, a wireless, and a good piano.
> As I was born in Guiana and attended the Grammar School, mixing with boys of different races, and as I travelled to the Guiana diamond fields and worked there with a Negro friend, and Negro and coloured men, visitors may feel assured that our welcome will in no way be tainted with condescension.

This initiative by an individual reader was cathartic. The following day the *East Anglian Daily Times* published a photograph of "US paratroops in Britain, drawn mostly from the southern states". Though the caption did not say so, they were clearly black; equally clearly, they — or others like them — were based close at hand. Soon there was another photograph, of the popular radio star Bebe Daniels "visiting coloured American soldiers in their isolated camp to sing".

Thus, oh so gently, was the news about the American presence released to the public. And by this time the East Anglian skies were busy with American planes; the air bases reverberated with the roar of engines being tested; the liberty trucks arrived nightly in the main towns of the region loaded with men seeking amusement; the white-helmeted US military police paced the streets and were immediately christened "Snowdrops".

Nobody was told, of course, just how many Americans there were. The *Cambridge Daily News* gave its readers a clue about the scale of the American influx by quoting from a United States broadcast:

> American Army Air Force units now operate from their own aerodromes in Britain, and more are coming into use, the units furnishing their own ground crews. Air Corps pilots are arriving here in increasing numbers. An American broadcast, transmitted through the BBC during the weekend, stated that the US Air Force would operate from 150 aerodromes in Britain, with a total ground personnel of 400,000.*

Once the American presence was openly acknowledged, all sorts of activity became possible. The Rotary Clubs in Cambridge, Colchester, and other towns invited American guests to each of their weekly lunches. Reporters went into the streets to interview the visitors. The *Cambridge Daily News* published some of their

*Eventually, at the peak, there were 122 US air bases situated in East Anglia.

impressions. What did they think of English beer? "It took some getting used to, but from now on I'm sticking to it," responded one GI. And what of Cambridge? "A nice little burg," said a lad from Illinois. King's College? "Mighty wonderful." But when the reporter encountered two young men from New York and asked them what most impressed them about Cambridge, they evidently surprised him. The bookshops, they said, and the availability of works by Dickens, Joyce, Huxley, Eliot and Samuel Butler. "They know their literature, art and stage inside out," the reporter concluded, adding wryly: "We British have got to watch out if we are not going to be caught out of our depth when discussing literature and the English arts with some of our American Allies."

Relations steadily became closer and more friendly. When the four squadrons of the Air Training Corps which comprised the Norwich wing paraded in October before the Lord Mayor and the Sheriff, a colonel of the US Army Air Force was invited to review them. There was a cookery demonstration in the city, specially arranged to help the catering trade and voluntary organizations to meet American tastes. A messing officer of the US forces explained the mysteries of a hamburger, and recipes were provided for items called "pumpkin cream", "Johnny cake" and "chocolate pin wheels".

Most of the Cambridge colleges established direct links with the visiting Americans and extended them their hospitality. The United States Ambassador, Mr John G. Winant, visited the town on 27th October, expecting to address a small group of student members of the University Society for International Affairs, but they had thrown the meeting open and a thousand students packed the Guildhall and gave him a wild ovation. Professor G. M. Trevelyan, who was Master of Trinity, presided.

Seven days later a great stimulus was given to Anglo-American relations by a flying visit to Cambridge by Mrs Eleanor Roosevelt, wife of the US President. She arrived by car from London at mid-morning and, in typical November weather, made a hectic round of calls: first at Queen's College, where she was welcomed by the Mayor of the town and the Vice-Chancellor of the university; then to the WVS headquarters in the town and a WVS hostel, then on to an American Red Cross leave hostel taking shape in the Bull Hotel, and then to a centre where WVS members had made over four thousand camouflage nets for guns and lorries during the previous year. She also inspected a Red Cross flying squad and a WVS Queen's Messengers Food Convoy, as well as the communal feeding kitchen which prepared meals for seven villages five days a week. She chatted with the cooks and watched the vans leave. One rather unusual delivery vehicle caught her eye: a tradesman's tricycle which had once sold ice cream in Detroit and which an American lady had donated to Britain's war effort. Wherever she went in Cambridge, the President's lady was greeted by a sea of miniature Stars and Stripes which had been thoughtfully distributed in advance by the WVS.

Mrs Roosevelt was then driven to Arrington, near Royston, where she

Mrs Roosevelt in the first court of Queen's College, Cambridge, during her visit to Cambridgeshire. In the middle of the group, in civilian clothes, is Sir Will Spens, the Regional Commissioner.
Cambridge Daily News

watched a meal being cooked on an open-air "blitz" cooking fire. A rather splendid lunch, by the standards of the time, had been arranged for her at a nearby country hotel, and a good company of "top brass" had assembled to sit down with her. But Mrs Roosevelt brushed it all aside. She wanted to try the results of the open-air cooking: soup, stew with roast potatoes and Brussels sprouts, apple pie, and coffee. A corner of the village hall was hurriedly cleared, a few folding tables were set up, and as many of the party as could find chairs made a show of enjoying the ordinary, everyday fare of the English working class. Many of the distinguished company had to eat, as best they could, standing.

Mrs Roosevelt afterwards left in good spirits to return to London, the local children lining the rails of the village school and cheering.

By this time, not surprisingly, a number of problems had arisen. The American servicemen had a way with the girls, whom they approached in a happy, relaxed manner which left most of the uniformed British lads speechless and often resentful. They came, too, loaded with offerings: nylon stockings, chocolates, flowers. They had money to spend in dance halls and restaurants. They held parties and dances at their camps, and the girls who went to them in the special buses provided marvelled at things that could be produced from the PX stores, and fancied they were having a glimpse of Hollywood glamour.

So was it surprising that, by October, a conference on juvenile delinquency was being told that some young girls were "throwing themselves" at American, Canadian and other overseas troops? "The men need as much protection from these girls as the girls from the men," declared one speaker. The *Cambridge Daily News* front-paged the item, but did not indicate if it had any specifically local application. In the same issue, however, it reported that a twenty-three-year-old

Royal Engineers of the Canadian Army were among those engaged on the construction of airfields from which the bomber offensive would soon be launched against Germany. In this picture they are laying the concrete runways. *East Anglian Daily Times*

girl living in Cambridge, who was German by birth and was therefore required as an alien to stay indoors between the hours of 10.30 pm and 6 am, had been fined 40s at the local magistrates' court because she stayed out late "to explain something of this country to two American soldiers".

There was a great spontaneity in the way in which relations developed, but the British government and officialdom in general had, of course, done much planning before the Americans arrived. For example, a new law was drafted — and passed through all its stages in Parliament during August — to cover offences by US Servicemen in Britain. The "USA (Visiting Forces) Bill" removed from the jurisdiction of United Kingdom courts all criminal offences committed by the Americans while they were serving in Britain; such cases were to be dealt with by American court-martial procedure. One of the first such cases in East Anglia came at the end of December when a US private was court-martialled for driving an army car at a "reckless and dangerous speed" in Newmarket Road in Cambridge. He was found guilty of the "involuntary manslaughter" of a four-year-old boy and sentenced to six months' hard labour and loss of forty dollars a month of his pay for the same period.

But the main advance preparation was the provision of bases into which the American forces could move when they arrived here. The construction of the East Anglian airfields had almost as dramatic an effect on the local population as did the arrival of the Americans who used them. The older RAF bases in East Anglia were being converted from grass to concrete runways to make them suitable for the new heavy bombers, and now, alongside that work, a massive programme of new aerodrome construction had become necessary. In June formal government approval was given for work to begin immediately on new bomber bases at Wormingford and Boxted in Essex, at Sudbury in Suffolk, and at Old Buckenham and Little Snoring in Norfolk. Target date for completion of these aerodromes was 16th December.

Most of the new bases were needed specifically for the USAAF, once it had been agreed that Britain was to be the base from which American forces would join in the assault on Germany. In July authorization was given for twenty-two more bomber bases, all to be completed by the following February. Sixteen of them were designated from the outset as US bases: Great Saling, Great Dunmow, Stansted Mountfitchet, Chipping Ongar, Birch, Boreham and Matching in Essex, Nuthampstead in Hertfordshire, Glatton in Huntingdonshire, Winfarthing in Norfolk, and Beccles, Debach, Butley, Hepworth, Eye and Raydon in Suffolk. The others were at Ely and Mepal in Cambridgeshire, Gosfield and Hadstock in Essex, North Pickenham in Norfolk, and Lavenham in Suffolk. In August two more bomber bases in Norfolk, at Deopham Green and Rackheath, and one in Suffolk at Tuddenham were added to the programme[2].

It was impossible to overstress the urgency of construction, impossible to throw too much into the effort. The Air Ministry spent at the rate of £6.5 million a month on new aerodromes during 1942. Immense quantities of material and large numbers of men and women were brought into the region. Labour was recruited in Wales, Scotland and even in neutral Ireland. The workforce was built up from 31,237 in February to a peak of 52,868 by May. The men were accommodated in special camps and taken by lorry to the sites. Locally-recruited women proved they could perform even the heaviest duties. Mrs Sarah Williams noted in her diary on 7th March:

> My cousin working at a nearby aerodrome arrived this evening to tell of women working as bricklayers and labourers and of the high praise the foreman has for them. He said that when the men don't turn up because of the weather, the women were all there.

Lorries and tippers were mobilized far and wide; a call went out for two thousand of them to work in just one five-mile coastal belt between Cromer and the Thames(3). Large tracts of farmland were commandeered for the new air bases — nearly 100,000 acres in Norfolk alone.

Considerable disturbance was caused to agriculture, and sometimes strong feelings were roused. The NFU complained to the government in October that in one area of East Anglia gangs had been cutting down hedges, clearing ditches and draining runways for two years and had then suddenly abandoned the site and served notice on six farmers that they must surrender 400 acres of highly cultivated land situated only a stone's throw away. The Minister replied blandly that the original site "no longer suited its original purpose".

By the end of 1942 new airfields were operational in all the Eastern Counties and the others which had been authorized were well on the way to completion. The example of Ridgewell, in Essex, illustrates the scale of construction. There were five hundred separate buildings, about thirty miles of drains of various kinds, and a sewerage plant to handle a population of 2,500. This involved 1,170,000 manhours' work and used a million cubic yards of concrete.

The standard pattern for the new bases was a main runway of about 2,000 yards by 50 yards wide, with two shorter subsidiary runways and enough dispersal area to accommodate two bomber squadrons. Hangars were huge buildings, usually 240 feet long and 115 feet wide, sufficient to house the largest planes; from 1942 most bases had two such hangars, used mainly for major servicing. Most of the new airfields were scheduled to cost £800,000; frequently the cost turned out to be more than a million pounds. Normal construction time was about seven months, and about 1,000 men were employed on each site at the height of the work(4).

The British were responsible for this construction work, the RAF controlling the work of civilian contractors, but soon US engineer battalions, with more sophisticated equipment, were sent in to assist. Some of the first American servicemen to appear in East Anglia were men of the US Army Engineer Battalions who arrived, with heavy symbolism, on American Independence Day, 4th July, 1942. On that day units turned up in Essex to start work on four new

An early photograph of a Consolidated B-24 Liberator bomber "at a US Army Air Corps station in England." *East Anglian Daily Times*

airfields, at Great Saling, Great Dunmow, Earls Colne and Stansted*. One US unit which appeared unexpectedly during the night at Gosfield Hall, in Essex, which was being used as a troop billet, met a challenge from the private on guard duty with the declaration "We've come to build an airfield".

An Essex observer later recalled:

> The labour gangs in uniform, which were the first US troops to reach the Colchester district, were not their country's best ambassadors. The difference in their pay and our Forces' was the first bone of contention, enabling them, as they did not hesitate to do, to buy up the last bottles of whisky at £5 each, and the easy conquests to be made of English girls compared to the etiquette of the States had the inevitable results(5).

The first USAAF planes and crews arrived before the new airbases were completed, so some existing airfields were designated for American use. Alconbury was vacated by Bomber Command during August and taken over by the Americans, and the first B-24 Liberators to be based in Britain arrived almost immediately. These planes constantly flew low around the neighbourhood, watched by one youthful enthusiast who afterwards recorded that: "The Americans were raring to go into action, and when one talked to them, one sensed that they did not understand that it could be a dangerous activity . . ."(6) The first US heavy bomber base in Norfolk was established at about the same time at Shipdham, but the first arrivals there, the 319th Bomb Group (Medium), used it only as a staging point on their way to North Africa. In October the 44th Bomb Group arrived with

*Great Saling was known from April, 1943, as Andrews Field. These four air bases became operational between April and July, 1943.

B-24Ds, and when they had settled in they went into action against targets in France, on 7th November.

During September and October the Americans flew into and took over RAF bases at Attlebridge, Bassingbourn, Hardwick, Hethel, Honington, Horham, Horsham St Faith and Wattisham. Advance ground staff arrived in mid-December at Rattlesden and Rougham, but planes did not reach these bases until several months later. In some cases the Americans' first task was to build concrete runways, as at Attlebridge and Wattisham. At Bassingbourn, on the other hand, they took over virtually new facilities of such a standard that this base was christened "The Country Club". By the end of 1942 work was well in hand on bases at Butley in Suffolk and Wendling in Norfolk, and the base at East Wretham was completed and awaited American occupation*.

Despite the concentration on meeting the needs of Britain's new allies, the RAF still managed to acquire some new airfields for its own use: Chedburgh, where a squadron of Stirlings moved in during October; Downham Market, with more Stirlings; Great Sampford, a fighter station; Ridgewell; and Sculthorpe.

By the end of 1942 there were 510 operational airfields in Britain, with 106 under construction, and 51 more projected[7].

Most people knew little — and were not supposed to know anything — of what was happening at these air bases. Security was very strict, but not strict enough to prevent groups of youngsters who were eagerly looking forward to joining the RAF from reconnoitring in their own ways, identifying planes and trying to monitor bombing operations. And the word got around.

Americans had been fighting as Britain's allies long before Pearl Harbour; volunteers had crossed the Atlantic of their own free will in sufficient numbers to form three Spitfire squadrons, the so-called Eagle Squadrons. With the USA fully engaged in hostilities, these fighter pilots were officially transferred to the USAAF, becoming the 4th Fighter Group at Debden in September, 1942.

Well before the arrival of the first USAAF planes, American crews went into action. The first combat operation from Britain for men of the 8th USAAF was on 29th June, 1942, when American crews flew a group of RAF Douglas Boston light bombers from Swanton Morley in a joint RAF–USAAF low-level attack on four enemy airfields in the Low Countries. One of the American flyers had two cousins serving in the Luftwaffe. US crews continued to fly Bostons in raids during July and then on 17th August there was the first all-American raid mounted from the UK, when twelve 8th Air Force aircraft bombed marshalling yards at Rouen in daylight. For the rest of the year the US 8th Air Force held to a policy of daytime raids on targets in France and the Low Countries; no American plane crossed the German frontier. This policy, and the fact that the planned build-up of the USAAF in the UK fell behind schedule, disappointed the British[8].

*There were no planes at Rattlesden and Rougham until well into 1943. Butley air base was known as Bentwaters from January, 1943.

As far as off-duty activities were concerned, British officialdom worked hard to develop the closest possible friendly relations with the Americans. Notwithstanding the initial secrecy about their presence, the Eastern Regional Commissioner, Sir Will Spens, acting in association with the Ministry of Information, set up a series of committees, ten in all, to cater for "a very large number of American soldiers" who, it was anticipated, would wish to visit the towns in the region when they had leave or who, it was suggested, might be "passing through".

The Cambridge committee, under the chairmanship of the Mayor, first met on 7th August. It accepted an offer by the English-Speaking Union to provide an information bureau in Cambridge for the American visitors, and this was opened on 1st October at Matthews Cafe in Trinity Street. The Ministry of Information

Armourers and other members of the ground crew beside a Boeing B-17 Fortress of the US Army Air Force at an East Anglian base. *Imperial War Museum*

appointed a full-time organizer, and the public at large was invited to supply her with offers of hospitality and information about suitable entertainments and sporting events. Committees of this kind co-operated with the American Red Cross and others to assist in providing day and night hostels, staffed by the American Red Cross, with a good deal of assistance from English voluntary organizations. In Norwich a committee set up as a result of consultations between the Lord Mayor and representatives of the American Red Cross and the Army quickly found a suitable building and began to convert it for use as a residential hostel, club and information bureau, and there were soon several small clubs elsewhere in Norfolk.

In Suffolk, however, matters did not proceed so smoothly. Despite the letters

Left: Displaying old-style US markings, a Boeing B-17E which "may soon be striking at the heart of Germany in the mass raids which are promised" by the RAF and the US Army Air Force. *East Anglian Daily Times*

Right: A B-17 Fortress being bombed up in readiness for a daylight raid, one of the first to be launched from the Americans' East Anglian bases. *East Anglian Daily Times*

published in the *East Anglian Daily Times*, weeks passed and there was no move from local civic or other official quarters. A photograph then showed the King visiting three 8th US Army Air Force bases, and another reader's letter was printed drawing attention to "our neglect of the stranger in our midst". Mr A. E. Bentley, of Ipswich, followed this up with a blunt inquiry: "Might I ask the Mayor to state what has been done, or what is likely to be done? The matter is surely of the most urgent importance?"

Unfortunately the Mayor was ill, and this was probably the cause of the delay; he died soon afterwards. After a decent interval, Mr Bentley returned to the attack, offering to organize a public meeting himself if the civic authorities had nothing in hand. Only then, on 5th December, was an appeal issued from the town halls at Ipswich and Bury St Edmunds asking for volunteers to entertain Americans to a meal over the Christmas period. "We understand that those Americans who receive invitations will be in a position to contribute a certain amount of food," the signatories said.

These official efforts to act as good hosts were supplemented by the activities of entrepreneurs who were quick to see opportunities to provide a service. Liberty trucks from the various bases brought young Americans with money to spend into the nearby towns, and they became the best customers of many dance halls, cinemas, pubs and restaurants. In Norwich, for example, a thousand dancers could crowd the floor at one time in the Samson and Hercules Ballroom on Tombland. It had always been a popular services rendezvous, particularly with the RAF during

The Samson and Hercules House in Norwich was a popular resort of both British and American servicemen in their off-duty hours.

the Battle of Britain period. By the end of 1942 it had been virtually taken over by the Americans. Its owner at the time, Norwich businessman Mr Edward (Teddy) Bush, provided them on three nights a week with the sort of music and entertainment that reminded them of home. He could afford to recall from a successful career in the London entertainment world a local musician, Gerry Hoey, and his band.

Thanksgiving Day and Christmas were occasions for major Anglo-American festivities. In Norwich Miss G. V. Barnard, at the request of the American Red Cross, organized a Thanksgiving Day dance at the Stuart Hall. The Bishop of Norwich and the Town Clerk, with their wives, joined two hundred American officers and men, and a corresponding number of British service girls were invited. At several American bases local schoolchildren joined the celebrations.

In Cambridge the first American hostel, in the Bull Hotel, had not been quite completed, but that did not prevent US servicemen taking it over for the Christmas period and throwing a party for a large number of the town's children. An appeal for volunteers to staff the dining room and the snack bar had a good response, and the party gave youngsters who had experienced three years of wartime austerity a glimpse of pleasures they had all but forgotten. Balloons cascaded down from the ceiling to raise their excitement, and there was a non-stop flow of fresh orange juice and ice cream.

In Norwich as Christmas approached four hundred British homes offered hospitality to the Americans, arrangements being made by the Lord Mayor's committee. One hundred and sixty men and ten officers of the US forces stationed in Norfolk were able to accept; the other invitations were taken up by British servicemen and women. There was generous return hospitality. The officers at one base in Norfolk asked that sixty of "the most deserving children in Norwich" should be chosen to be their guests on Boxing Day. These children were given lunch in the officers' mess, saw a variety entertainment and a film, then collected bags of "candies" from Father Christmas beside a Christmas tree, and finally were loaded into lorries and returned to Norwich to see the pantomime *Dick Whittington* at the Theatre Royal. At another base five hundred young guests watched Father Christmas waving from the cabin of a plane circling overhead. When he had landed, men in uniform and the children sang carols together before Father Christmas distributed sweets.

Apart from these local initiatives, the British War Relief Society of the United States sent two thousand gifts to Norwich City Hall, and members of the American Junior Red Cross sent more. The place was piled high with boxes of candies, boxes of toys and games, brush and comb sets, cases of pens and pencils. Much of it was distributed through the schools.

Delighted and sometimes dazzled, beguiled and sometimes bewildered, cautious but nonetheless captivated, the East Anglians learned to live with their new neighbours.

CHAPTER ELEVEN

Wound up for Action

THE NATIONAL temper was steadily wound up for action. There was scarcely a week without several big military parades in the Eastern Region, in which thousands marched. At Cambridge fourteen-year-old Girl Cadets and First World War Old Contemptibles paraded together, with bands playing, at a drumhead service on Parker's Piece. At Ely 1,200 young Cadets from all over Cambridgeshire gathered for the biggest parade of its kind in the United Kingdom. These were typical of dozens of such displays throughout the Eastern Counties.

Most of Britain's fighting forces were bottled up in the United Kingdom. The Navy was fully extended, the RAF was developing its bombing attack and the Army was engaged in North Africa, but most of the fighting was being done by the Russians in Europe and by the Americans and Commonwealth forces in the Far

An Army Cadet Force band taking part in a parade at Ely when 1,200 young cadets from all parts of Cambridgeshire were mustered. *Cambridge Daily News*

East. It was important to demonstrate that much preparation was being done in the homeland for the decisive campaigns in Europe which alone could defeat Hitler's armies. There was, as we have already noted, public impatience to see more action, and the native Communists were echoing Moscow's appeals for the opening of a Second Front in Europe.

The mobilization of men and women and materials was carried to the limit. Reinforcements arrived from the Commonwealth countries, particularly Canada, and the forces of the USA were steadily built up in the United Kingdom. As 1942 progressed the re-equipment of the forces with modern weapons achieved dramatic momentum. Foot-slogging became a thing of the past as all divisions were mechanised. Aeroplanes, tanks, troop carriers, trucks and lorries poured from Britain's factories and streamed across the Atlantic from the USA, until the flow of equipment matched the supply of troops. Training appropriate to the kind of war which lay ahead then became possible.

On 8th March, 1942, the Chief of the General Staff circulated a paper which stated:

> The Commander in Chief considers that one of the most urgent needs in training at the present moment is realistic battle practice for all arms in co-operation, using live ammunition. He considers that for this purpose each Corps should have available a field firing area in which Brigade Groups could be exercised with all weapons, except the anti-tank gun, without unrealistic restrictions. As a guide, such an area should be about six miles by six miles in extent(1).

Six weeks later this proposition was put to the Minister:

> It is essential that formations should be given areas in which to use their weapons in the most lifelike battle conditions. Ammunition for this purpose is still insufficient, but some can be made available. Suitable areas of land, however, are still lacking.

By this time a "Training Areas Selection Committee" had already examined the services' requirement to requisition land for use as battle training areas, and at the committee's very first meeting the Army had pressed for such a requisition of land near Thetford.

Part of the land which was sought was already being used for tank training by the Army and for bombing practice by the RAF. In June, 1941, some farmers in the Thetford area had been told to expect to see troops moving through their woods and tanks exercising over their fields. "Those were days of uncertainty for us; we never knew if tanks would suddenly descend on the farm and go over the crops," one of them recalled later(2).

Now the government authorized the requisition of seven areas in various parts of Britain, two of them in East Anglia. One consisted of 18,000 acres around Thetford, the other 9,000 acres of arable land, heathland and salt marshes forming the hinterland behind Orford Ness. These requisitions involved the expulsion from their homes of about 750 inhabitants in the Thetford area, where the villages of

West Tofts, Stanford, Langford and Tottington were evacuated, and about 450 in the Orford area. A woman farmer at Tottington recorded:

> We were told on June the thirteenth and requisition took place on the twentieth — seven days, and they actually thought we could all be moved in that time! Eventually we were given until the eighteenth of July; and I can only think of those five weeks as hell let loose . . . A lot of the early time we had was wasted in going round with a petition which was to be sent to the King . . .[3]

More than half of the land which was to be requisitioned here formed part of the Merton Estate, owned by the eighth Lord Walsingham. It was one of the oldest estates in Britain; Lord Walsingham was Lord of fourteen of the ancient manors in the area, and at least six of the families who were to be expelled could trace their ancestry in the local records back five hundred years. Lord Walsingham, who was fifty-eight, had retired from the regular Army in 1921 with the rank of lieutenant-colonel and at this time was commanding the 30th (Home Defence) Battalion of the Royal Norfolk Regiment, with detachments defending airfields in Norfolk, Suffolk and part of Cambridgeshire. Battalion HQ were at his home at Westmere Farm, Tottington.

News of the requisitioning hit the inhabitants, landowners, tenant farmers and workers alike, like a typhoon. The breckland was marginal and during the nineteen-thirties many of the tenant farmers had paid no rent, while a number had absconded when they could no longer pay wages. As a result, Lord Walsingham had taken in hand 4,000 acres and had run up a mortgage of £40,000. The loss of the land, without compensation at that stage, was a serious matter. The loss of homes was even worse.

On 18th June everyone affected was called to a meeting in Tottington. Farm workers came straight from the fields and were joined by the tenant farmers and the tradespeople. Some were in khaki, either soldiers home on leave or older men going on Home Guard duty. They gathered at the edge of the two-acre meadow beside the smithy worked by Joe Balls, whose home was just across the meadow at the post office, where his sister was postmistress. Their mother, who lived with them, had never travelled more than the two and a half miles to Watton in her very long life, and there were a lot of elderly folk whose experience was similar.

Lieutenant-General Sir Kenneth Anderson, General Officer C-in-C, Eastern Command, came in person to address the meeting. His message was stark: within four weeks they must be out of their homes and off their farmlands, lock, stock and baggage. He did his best to put it diplomatically, and they listened silently.

"This is the most unpleasant task of my Army career," the general began. And later he said: "There is little you will want to hear in the way of sympathy, and the last thing anyone wants to do is to turn Englishmen from their homes . . . I don't deny we are causing a lot of grief, pain and trouble, and I am deeply sorry for it, but this is one of the places where the disturbance will be least felt."

He said that plenty of people talked glibly about a Second Front, without

Their possessions piled up outside their homes, inhabitants of one of the battle school areas await evacuation in July. Some would never return. *East Anglian Daily Times*

realizing what it really meant. "Those of you on leave and many of you in the Home Guard and Civil Defence know how futile many of the defence exercises are in their stupid imaginary situations," he went on. They needed training in which they could actually use bullet, bomb and shell. He had been asked to find an area twice the size of that being taken, but there were limits to what people could be asked to do. He promised that there would be no wanton damage, that everything would be done to protect homes and churches and places of interest. He hoped he might be able to arrange a fortnight's "lull" so that they could return and harvest the grain they were growing, and another one later to get in the sugar beet; but he would not make any cheap promises, because he realized that when tanks had been over the fields, there might not be much to harvest.

When the general had finished there was, amazingly, a burst of applause. "My word", exclaimed Lord Walsingham, who was presiding over the meeting, "I am proud to belong to an area where such people live." But he added his view that the situation was a calamity, and said he could only hope that the training to take place might shorten the war.

The Deputy Regional Commissioner, Lord Cranbrook, and a War Department valuer were present to fill in the details. There was to be no compensation except the value of the standing crops, less harvesting costs. Promises were made

Men of the 1st Duke of Wellington's Regiment in training at Cromer in preparation for the invasion of Europe. On 21st April they landed on Cromer beach and attacked up the steep cliffs under live machine-gun, rifle and mortar fire. *Imperial War Museum*

that war agricultural committees would arrange alternative accommodation for farmers, that the cost of moving stock and furniture would be met, that the military would be prepared to store furniture, and that efforts would be made to rehouse workers in new areas.

Lord Walsingham sought and obtained written undertakings from the Commander, Home Forces and the Lord President of the Council, Sir John Anderson, that the land and the property on it would be handed back after the war, and he passed on these assurances to the people affected*.

All their belongings were loaded on to farm carts and lorries and moved to surrounding villages. The local authorities and the WVS were left to find them accommodation in an area where there were already many London evacuees billeted. Old cottages which had been condemned for years were hurriedly patched up, and cottagers who were already overcrowded were persuaded to take in families. There were no alternative farms for the tenant farmers.

The same pattern of events took place in the smaller battle ground area, near Orford. There was a similar meeting, addressed by a major-general, with Lord Cranbrook and the local MP, Mr W. Ross Taylor, in attendance. The officer climbed on to a sack of oats in a high-roofed barn to deliver his message, his audience gathered round in a circle. The MP said he had discussed the matter with the Under-Secretary of State for War, Lord Croft, and had written to the Prime Minister. "Mr Churchill has great sympathy with you," he declared. The rector of one of the villages affected protested vigorously at the absence of compensation to cover any increased rents that might need to be paid elsewhere. Then the meeting broke up into small groups, talking. Some button-holed the officer and officials. Gradually they all drifted away, walking or cycling to the homes they were about to lose.

Efforts were made to get the authorities to change their mind, but they were half-hearted, for in the circumstances of the time it was recognized that defence requirements had an absolute priority. Sir James Grigg, the War Minister, told MPs who made representations that every possible alternative area had been considered but rejected "for cogent reasons". After the harvest it was reported that troops, with assistance from boys from Norwich Grammar and Repton schools, had gathered the crops from about 3,300 acres.

Elsewhere in East Anglia, planning for an invasion of Europe gave a new emphasis to much of the local activity. At St Osyth, commissioned in April, 1942, as HMS *Helder*, and later at Woolverstone Hall, as well as at Harwich and Lowestoft, Combined Operations Training Bases were developed. Flotillas of landing craft were assembled. In August a "suspense station" for landing craft was

*In 1950 it was announced that the land in the Stanford Principal Training Area would be compulsorily purchased and retained by the Ministry of Defence in perpetuity. Compensation was paid to owners at the rate of £25 per acre — a valuation based on the 1938 price of land, it being argued that owners "ought not to benefit from temporary wartime inflation". Tenants were invited to claim "hardship" payments, but otherwise got no compensation.

No 2 Motor Boat Company of the RASC at West Mersea was part of "the Army's navy". Here a boarding party stands by to board the sailing barge *Nellie Parker* in the Blackwater; part of their job was to check all craft entering the "special defence zones" *Imperial War Museum*

established in the River Orwell, and eventually twenty-four tank landing craft and seventy-two small combined operations craft were assembled there. West Mersea became a training base for coxswains and crews of landing craft in small boat seamanship. Local fishermen watched in wonder as amphibious tanks "swam" up the creeks, crawled over mudflats, beaches and hards, and trundled away across country.

A new organization was formed which would be responsible for building advance airfields in the invasion zones after the assault on Europe. In July the 1st

Aerodrome Construction Group gave a two-day demonstration at Bottisham aerodrome, near Cambridge. On the first day they reconnoitred the site and planned the operation; on the second they brought in all the necessary stores and equipment and completed the laying of two 1,000-yard runways[4].

It was impossible to keep all these activities from public view, and the Postmaster-General announced that censorship might be applied from time to time to communications from areas in the neighbourhood of ports, aerodromes and other localities of operational importance.

When in June Churchill made a third visit to Washington it was generally believed he was consulting on the question of a Second Front. Speculation on these lines in the press was not discouraged by the Ministry of Information. The diplomatic correspondent of the Press Association, in an item published in most newspapers, wrote:

> There are growing hopes that so rapid has been the multiplication of Allied power and munitions of war that the free nations will be in a position to abandon their defensive role and turn to a general offensive this year.

At about this time it was publicly announced that Britain and the Soviet Union had reached an understanding about the possibility of a Second Front before the year was out, and had signed a twenty years treaty. That this accorded with public sentiment was shown by the way in which a small town like Sudbury celebrated the announcement with a rally and fete in the Belle Vue Recreation Grounds. Large crowds turned out. The town's Folk Dance Society paraded in costume from Market Hill and gave a display, and there was community singing of English and Russian songs, led by the choir of Sudbury Grammar School. Local Communists contributed a puppet show.

Later, however, in a speech to the Commons in November, Churchill said he had given the Russians a written document in June which made it quite clear that, while Britain was preparing to make a landing in 1942, she could not promise to do so. In this speech, the Prime Minister explained how the military chiefs were facing up to the challenge ahead:

> The attack which will be made in due course across the Channel or the North Sea requires an immense degree of preparation: vast numbers of special landing craft and a great army, trained division by division in amphibious warfare. All this is proceeding, but it takes time. But should the enemy become demoralized at any moment, the same careful preparations would not be needed. Risks would be run on a large scale, but this is certainly not the case at the present time. Preparations have been very greatly advanced. Enormous installations have been, and are being, brought into existence at all our suitable ports. But no one would have been justified, nor would it have been physically possible, to have made an effective invasion of the Continent during the summer and autumn months of 1942.

A great deal was happening during that summer and autumn, but only limited assistance to the Soviet Union proved possible. Convoys carried supplies to Russia's northern ports, often at great cost. One of them, Convoy PQ17, lost

Vice-Admiral Lord Mountbatten, Chief of Combined Operations, with members of a Russian military mission watching a demonstration of new equipment at Travellers Hill, near Bury St Edmunds, on 27th April. *Imperial War Museum*

twenty-four of its thirty-seven vessels. A somewhat disastrous raid on Dieppe in August in which ten thousand men of all three services took part, most of them Canadians, was said to have helped the Russians, too, because it held down German troops and resources in the west. Churchill declared that "military opinion seemed unanimous that until an operation on that scale was undertaken no responsible general would take the responsibility of planning for the main invasion", but later he conceded that "the casualties of this memorable action may seem out of proportion to the results"[(5)]. Tanks were landed and there was fierce fighting and heavy losses. Nine hundred Canadians were killed and 2,000 taken prisoners. The RAF lost ninety-five planes — its biggest loss in any single day since the war had begun.

Landing on an enemy coast and advancing through enemy territory were rehearsed in the new battle areas. In August the King spent a whole day in East

Anglia watching a simulation of a Second Front invasion, with live ammunition. Soon afterwards, the military correspondent of the *East Anglian Daily Times* provided a graphic description of the type of "hardening course" to which the troops were subjected:

> I went over this course with section commanders, torn and bleeding, soaked, dead-beat and unrecognizably muddy, fighting exhaustion with their last ounces of will-power . . . They struggled 200 yards through the mud of a ditch, negotiated a tunnel in cramped positions, with only nine inches of headroom in which to keep rifles dry, and scaled a nine-foot brick wall before dropping four yards into a slippery, mud-filled crater. From that point they went on through more water, shoulder-high, in a large pond. There were explosions everywhere. Half-pound charges went off with crashes immediately beneath the men poised precariously on wires, and depth charges sent up big clouds of mud from the bed of the pond. By this time there was not a man who was not fighting for breath, yet little more than half the distance was covered. There were rough scaffolds slung high across more trees to be negotiated. Beneath them an area of wire entanglements waited to receive any who fell, and there were, too, notices which disconcertingly suggested that live mines lurked beneath this wire. At the end of it all, officers and NCOs had to hurl themselves over a parapet, plunging through a smoke-screen into the unknown — another water-filled crater — before taking up position for pot-shots at momentary targets.

By this time anxiety about a possible German invasion of Britain, which had been a feature of the opening months of 1942, had given place to an expectation of

King George VI is cheered by the men of the 56th Division, 11th Corps, when he visited them "somewhere in East Anglia". *Imperial War Museum*

an early Allied invasion of the Continent. On 26th June it was announced that a European Theatre of Operations for the US forces had been formally established, with headquarters in London and with Major-General Dwight D. Eisenhower in command. "He is already in England," it was stated.

The air assault on enemy targets was maintained by the RAF at night and the USAAF by day, the Americans working up to "the greatest daylight raid" on 10th October, with 115 bombers, including Flying Fortresses and Liberators, and 500 fighters attacking Lille. Some of the most experienced RAF bombing crews were constituted a new Pathfinder Force, their task to fly ahead of the main formations, positively identify the target, and mark it with flares. This new force was established at RAF Wyton, near Huntingdon, and squadrons were transferred there from Alconbury and Oakington.

Road signposts which had all been removed in 1940 were re-erected in urban areas (although they were still forbidden everywhere within twenty miles of the coast). The decoy airfields, the so-called "K" and "Q" sites built to mislead Luftwaffe crews attacking Britain, were closed down, having served their purpose.

Efforts were stepped up to collect intelligence in the occupied countries which might soon be invaded. At Gaynes Hall, near St Neots, Colonel Buckmaster of the Special Operations Executive (SOE) trained secret agents who were flown into Europe. Many of them left England from an airfield at Tempsford nearby, the existence of which was known to few people, even in the RAF.*

In September, and for the rest of the year, headlines told of the Red Army's grim struggle to defeat the Germans in Stalingrad, where the German 6th Army suffered huge losses in street-to-street fighting, and was eventually encircled. A new wave of admiration of the Russians swept Britain.

The British Communist Party grew ever more clamant for the opening of a

*Amazingly, a thirteen-year-old Kimbolton schoolboy, Ian Whiteman, gained admittance there one night in the autumn of 1942, and forty years later he recalled, in a letter published in the *Cambridge Weekly News* on 5th May, 1983:

> "I was enjoying an evening with family and friends, amongst whom was an RAF officer. He invited me to accompany him on a visit to a local airfield, and with parental consent I grabbed hat and coat, excited at the prospect. We travelled in the inevitable Hillman, with masked headlights probing the darkness like pale fingers. The journey from Kimbolton was short, and we were soon at the entrance to Tempsford Airfield where, after a short halt, we were waved through by the RAF sentry. We drove towards a collection of small buildings and pulled up near to them. My companion took me towards one of them and ushered me inside with instructions to keep very quiet and unobtrusive . . . My eyes wandered over the maps on the wall, and I wondered what the significance was of the pins and markers which were stuck into various points on the maps. As I looked towards the half-open door which led to another room, and through which my companion had gone, I heard the sound of an aircraft engine starting nearby. At the same time, a man with a flying jacket over his uniform came from the other room, followed by a man and woman dressed in civilian overcoats and carrying small cases. My companion followed them and beckoned me to join him. Outside we stopped and the three others walked towards what I could see was a Lysander aircraft with engine running. They boarded the plane, the engine roared and the aircraft moved off and, after turning through 90 degrees, began its short take-off run, disappearing into the darkness with its mysterious passengers. Something told me I should not ask any questions, and I did not, but I felt as though I had been witness to something very secret. . ."

Second Front. The Market Committee of Cambridge Borough Council refused them permission to hold a public meeting on Market Hill, at the heart of the town, and wrapped up their refusal in a resolution which sought to deny the facility to all political organizations. The full council thought better of it and removed this blanket prohibition. In Ipswich, a suggestion was made, but not followed up, that Russian should be taught at evening classes, or even in the schools. In Norwich, when the Theatre Royal staged a musical extravaganza starring Tamara Desni it called it *Moscow Belle* and a local critic wrote: "Except for Miss Desni's association with Russia (she was born in Moscow) and the decor and costume of two or three of the scenes, it is not easy to see why the title *Moscow Belle* has been bestowed upon this show." He was being disingenuous; everything Russian had a popular appeal at that time. The BBC bowed to the prevailing spirit, as Mrs Sarah Williams noted in her diary:

> *7th November*: I observe with amazement that the BBC at last plays *The Internationale*.

Armistice Day, when it came, had a special quality because now it was shared with allies. In Cambridge it was noted that American servicemen who were on the Market Hill when the clock of Great St Mary's struck 11 am stood motionless for the full two minutes, as if on parade. At the war memorial in Station Road, where the civil heads laid the usual wreaths, there was a delegation of three from the Red Army. One of them, Junior Lieutenant Ludmilla Pavlichenko, laid a wreath

Ludmilla Pavlichenko, described as a "Russian woman sniper", placing a wreath at the foot of the Cambridge war memorial on Armistice Day. She was a member of a Red Army delegation to Britain at that time.
Cambridge Daily News

Left: Prime Minister Winston Churchill watches 9th Armoured Division exercises near Newmarket on 16th May from the top of a Covenanter tank.
Imperial War Museum

Right: Men of the 7th Battalion of the Queen's Own Royal West Kent Regiment transferring from a destroyer to a landing barge during a combined operations exercise at Orfordness in September. Members of all three services took part in the operation.
Imperial War Museum

bearing the inscription: "To the memory of the British soldiers, 1914–18, from three Soviet soldiers who are fighting to finish all war for ever." Ludmilla, it was reported, had "annihilated 300 Germans in the fighting at Kiev, Odessa and Sebastopol" and had been awarded the Order of Lenin. This Red Army delegation was touring universities and colleges in Britain and the USA; the main part of their message, as they delivered it to a meeting of the Cambridge Union, was this: "The Allies had to help the USSR more actively and participate in military action. The Second Front was the shortest way to victory."

By this time, however, the British and the Americans were engaged in spectacular military action. After a three-month lull, the 8th Army under General Montgomery had struck against Rommel in Egypt, and when Churchill spoke at the Lord Mayor of London's annual luncheon at the Mansion House on 10th November he was able to say: "We have victory, a remarkable and definite victory . . ." He went on to strike a cautious note: "This is not the end. It is not

even the beginning of the end. But it is, perhaps, the end of the beginning . . ." The following day, when he reviewed the war situation in the Commons, he disclosed that the British divisions which had reinforced the 8th Army had left the UK back in May and early June, and American Sherman tanks had been shipped into Suez in the early days of July.

With this victory at El Alamein the tide had turned and Churchill's reputation seemed to have been restored. And now, as Rommel was being driven from Egypt, "Operation Torch" began at the other end of the North African coast, with US and British forces landing successfully on either side of Casablanca, at Oran, and on either side of Algiers. German and Italian forces occupied Vichy France, justifying this invasion by suggesting that an allied invasion of the South of France was imminent, and there was fierce French resistance in North Africa. But Algiers surrendered to the Allies on 8th November, Oran on the 10th and Casablanca on the 11th.

There was a general state of euphoria at home, as is clear from entries in Mrs Sarah Williams' diary:

> *9th November*: We are awakened by my mother in a state of extreme excitement because of the landings in North Africa, which even thrilled me and made me feel that perhaps this war will soon be over . . . Perhaps it is a sign that shows the way that things are going . . .
> *10th November*: Was everybody happy today! Mrs M was saying she wouldn't be surprised if the war were over in a fortnight and Mrs G was delighted because she was expecting her husband home by Xmas, the war being by then all over.

On Sunday 15th November, the ban on the ringing of church bells was lifted, and victory peals rang out across the Eastern Counties — although not without some difficulties, because many ringers had been called up. In Norwich there were enough to ring only at St Giles from 9 to 10 am and at St Peter Mancroft from 10 to 11 am — and even there the eight local ringers had to be supplemented by two visiting servicemen. One or two other churches in the city tried tentative peals.

They rang again at Christmas, and by then there was more good news. The *Cambridge Daily News* Christmas Eve edition front-paged:

RUSSIANS ACCELERATE ADVANCE —
OFFENSIVE BECOMES NAZI ROUT

Field Marshal Jan Smuts provided an end-of-year prophecy: "Next year will be the great offensive year. It ought to see great blows struck which may prelude the end . . ." Victory, he declared, would come in 1944.

CHAPTER TWELVE

Eyes Turned to the Future

THERE had been very few opportunities for relaxation or contemplation in the year that was coming to an end, but Christmas provided a brief respite from the effort and the anxiety. The war news was better, but in the run-up to the holiday there was little else to put people into a celebratory mood. The blackout persisted, so that there were no bright lights in the shops. Nor were there many things to buy. William Stock, who was himself a shop assistant in Chelmsford, noted in his diary:

> In normal times, the shops would be full of Christmas fare, gifts, etc, but this year, apart from Christmas cards and calendars, there is very little of a Christmas nature. It gets worse every year(1).

Mrs Sarah Williams watched the Christmas shopping crowds in Norwich and noted on 4th December:

> I feel sorry for the mothers I have seen coming out of shops and saying "It's no good, I can't afford them"(2).

But when it came to Christmas Day most people managed to find something extra to grace the table. William Stock noted in his diary what he and his family had to eat:

> Breakfast: Egg and bacon (instead of ham);
> Dinner: Duck with vegetables, Christmas pudding;
> Tea: Trifle, iced cake, mince pies, etc;
> Supper: Cold tongue and pickle.

He noted also that items "scarce or missing" included alcoholic drinks, nuts, figs, dates and other fruit. But there were more sweets than at the previous Christmas.

The Christmas break provided a natural opportunity for folk to look back over the year that was closing. It had been tough for them all, but they tried to look on the bright side. Casualties had been fewer than during the earlier war years. Norwich and the coastal towns had suffered grievously, but taking the country as a whole only 3,100 had been killed, compared with 23,729 in 1941, and the reduction in the number injured and detained in hospital was in the same ratio.

Some leading figures in the region had gained honour and distinction. The King's Birthday Honours in June had included a knighthood for the chairman of Norfolk County Council, Mr H. E. S. Upcher, and a baronetcy for Norwich MP Geoffrey Shakespeare, and there were three Cambridge names in the list: the economist John Maynard Keynes became a baron; Professor E. D. Adrian,

Captain N. Goodman, of Ipswich, was among those honoured during 1942. He is seen outside Buckingham Palace with his wife and five daughters after receiving the MBE. *East Anglian Daily Times*

Professor of Physiology at Cambridge University, was awarded the Order of Merit; and Professor Ralph H. Fowler, Plummer Professor of Mathematical Physics and an expert on anti-aircraft devices, became a Knight Bachelor.

At Westminster Mr R. A. Butler, the MP for Saffron Walden, was establishing a reputation as an energetic President of the Board of Education; at thirty-eight he was the youngest member of the Cabinet. His father, Sir Montagu Butler, Master of Pembroke College, had been unanimously re-elected Mayor of Cambridge for a second year. Mr Henry Strauss, a Norwich MP, had been appointed Parliamentary Secretary to the Ministry of Works and Buildings.

Norwich had a new bishop, its sixty-seventh: Dr Percy Mark Herbert, who had come from Blackburn to be enthroned in the Cathedral in July, before a congregation of three thousand. He succeeded Dr Pollock, who had resigned at the age of seventy-eight after thirty-two years there.

During the year about a score of serving men from the region had been awarded decorations for courage and valour.

East Anglia had lost some of its leading personalities. Sir Jeremiah Colman, Bart, the chairman of the Norwich firm of J. and J. Colman Ltd, which his great uncle had founded in 1804, had died in January at the age of eighty-two. He left a fortune of £1,832,000, of which £983,597 was paid in estate duty. In the same month the death had occurred at the age of sixty-nine of Mr Cyril Ridgeon, owner of a Cambridge timber and building goods business which he had founded in 1913. Another well-known Cambridge businessman, Mr David Gregory Marshall, had died in July, also aged sixty-nine; he had founded a motor firm in the town in 1909 and a flying school in 1929, and had opened the aerodrome at Cambridge in 1938. In September, Lord Eltisley, of Croxton Park, near St Neots, a famous agriculturalist, had died at the age of sixty-three; he had been a member of Cambridgeshire County Council from 1904 to 1920, its chairman in 1919–20, Conservative MP for the Borough of Cambridge from 1922 to 1934, in which year he became a peer, and High Steward of Cambridge for four years up to the time of his death.

Several important buildings had been destroyed or damaged by fire during the year. At Melford Hall, the Suffolk seat of the Hyde Parker family, a big blaze in

Salvaged furniture in front of Melford Hall, part of which was badly damaged by fire in February. Shortly after the picture was taken a part of the wing on the right collapsed. *East Anglian Daily Times*

February had destroyed a large part of the north wing, including a room and its four-poster bed in which Queen Elizabeth had slept in 1578. Firemen had come from several areas and used fourteen pumps, drawing water from the moat and river, but the wing had been gutted, although the walls remained standing. The roof of the west wing was also badly damaged, and the whole building had been affected by water.

On 24th April a fire at the Sir John Leman School in Beccles had destroyed the roof and badly damaged the upper storey, but two hundred children who were in the building had been safely evacuated. And in May there had been a big fire at Burston, near Diss, when the mills, granaries and warehouses of W. F. Tuck and Son, millers and merchants, had been completely destroyed. They had been rebuilt in 1931 after a previous fire. Within half an hour of the outbreak the buildings had

Soldiers stationed in East Anglia quickly learnt country skills, and the 2nd Corps headquarters became almost entirely self supporting, growing its own vegetables and keeping pigs and turkeys. These are two of the turkeys fattened up for Christmas. *Imperial War Museum*

been a sheet of flames, and it was described as "the most devastating fire seen in the district for some years".

On the credit side, Saffron Walden had acquired a new youth hostel in August, at 1 Myddylton Place, with twenty-five beds initially and plans to expand later.

There were, perhaps surprisingly, a lot of people with plans to expand or improve. It was an interesting feature of the national psychology throughout 1942 that — despite the fact that the major effort involved in winning the war still lay ahead, and it was too early to have any clear idea of the costs that would be involved, and their long-term consequences — there was enthusiastic discussion of post-war reconstruction plans and hopes for a brighter future.

The government had given some encouragement to this thinking and planning. When Winston Churchill had become Prime Minister in May, 1940, one of the Labour leaders taken into his government was Mr Arthur Greenwood, who was appointed a Minister without Portfolio but was particularly concerned with post-war reconstruction. The widespread destruction caused by bombing in London and other big cities naturally led to much thought about the way these cities were to be reconstructed, and that involved some sort of policy for future development.

If London was thinking about its future, why not the towns of East Anglia? Most local authorities gave some attention to what they would like to see in their own areas. Probably because the bombs had already ensured that much of the town would need to be rebuilt, Lowestoft's Planning and Reconstruction Committee was one of the most active and imaginative. It presented a report early in the year envisaging maintenance of a medium-size fishing industry, expansion as a health and pleasure resort, plus more light industry. A little later it produced proposals for a tunnel under the harbour for vehicular traffic, for an "air station", for a bypass around the town and a green belt of open spaces, and for municipal offices grouped in a single civic centre near the main shopping area. The Borough Surveyor, Mr F. G. Southgate, assured Lowestoft Rotarians that planning and reconstruction had taken a hold on the public imagination, adding: "The subject has a tonic effect on a large number of people."

Not everyone shared that view. Some who were engaged in public life were impatient with efforts to look to the future. When Alderman W. J. Taylor was re-elected chairman of Cambridgeshire County Council in May be bluntly advised: "Do not count the chickens before they are hatched, and don't waste time with what is going to happen after the war."

By the summer, however, Norwich and Great Yarmouth councils had joined this planning exercise. Norwich City Council set very wide terms of reference for its committee: should the post-war city be larger or smaller? Should it have more, or fewer, industries? How could it best ensure jobs for returning servicemen? Great Yarmouth Town Council called for a twenty-year plan dealing with its development as a holiday resort, but also giving special attention to the potential for new industries. In December the local Chamber of Commerce took a hand, setting up a series of specialist sub-committees. One member thought a local aerodrome would be essential, as that was how the visitors of the future would arrive.

Cambridge, although not much damaged by bombs, was not going to be left out of an intellectual exercise of this kind. Indeed, it was a pacesetter from the start. In January the town's Rotarians gathered to hear "the eminent architect" Theodore Fyfe speak on "Design in Reconstruction". He told them that there were only three shopping streets in Cambridge worth preserving: King's Parade, Bridge Street and Trinity Street. Some were even more startled by his proposal that some post-war houses should be built, deliberately, to last only fifteen years. In July Professor Ernest Barker addressed the same audience on "Ideas and Plans for Reconstruction" and argued that the ideal size for an urban community was 50,000; he urged that Cambridge should not try to grow any bigger than it had been before the war.

Discussion and debate was not restricted to the physical reconstruction that would be necessary after the war. It ranged over every aspect of social and economic policy as well. Early in the year the Eastern Counties Liberal Federation and the Cambridgeshire Federation of Labour Parties held meetings in Cambridge at which prominent Members of Parliament led discussion of post-war problems, and the same theme was chosen for a Cambridge conference of the Town and Country Planning Association. The Norwich Chamber of Commerce at its annual meeting urged the need for more information from the government about its plans for industry after the war, and for a statement about social policy. The next day Dr Hugh Dalton, President of the Board of Trade, was in Norwich and he assured the Chamber that the government was pursuing these matters with great energy and determination. Their own local MP, Mr H. G. Strauss, was one of the ministers devoting a large part of his time to post-war problems, said Dr Dalton.

Three Cambridge doctors formed a Medical Commission and spent much of 1942 considering what sort of health service should be provided for the people after the war. In October they presented their recommendations to a meeting of the Cambridge Rotary Club, saying that they wished to test the reactions of the lay mind. The main features of their proposals were that there should be central administration of medical services, with regional units working in close collaboration; that each regional unit should cater for 500,000 people; that there should be group medical and health centres, with a central clinic in every community for diagnosis, consultation and X-ray and other examinations; that all GPs should be on the staff, paid a basic salary, plus capitation fees.

There was a great deal of debate about the future of education, as the government was expected to bring in a new Education Act when circumstances permitted. The fact that the President of the Board of Education had been the MP for Saffron Walden since 1929 and that he was closely associated with Cambridge increased interest in this subject. When he presented education estimates to the

Commons in June, Mr R. A. Butler outlined some of his thinking. He argued that the school-leaving age should be raised from fourteen to fifteen when a chance occurred; that the whole system of industrial and commercial training, including apprenticeship, should be reviewed; and that the examination system and the curriculum of secondary schools needed re-examination. He announced the setting up of four separate committees to look into these matters. The Education Secretary of the Cambridgeshire County Council, Mr Henry Morris, was appointed a member of one of them, the Youth Advisory Council.

Soon afterwards, Mr Butler visited Cambridge, and his parents, the Mayor and Mayoress, arranged to be "at home" in the Guildhall to a large number of those in the city who had a special interest in education. "Rab" told them he was not promising a new Heaven and a new earth, and he warned them that they had to "go through the fire first", but he left them with a vision of a better world, with improved educational opportunities, when the war was over.

The poet T. S. Eliot was one of those who joined in the debate. In his presidential address to a conference of the Classical Association held in Cambridge he argued strongly the case for preserving a heavy emphasis on the teaching of Greek and Latin.

Cambridge University at this period was facing increasing difficulties. When the new academic year opened in October, 1942, the Vice-Chancellor, Dr J. A. Venn, disclosed that there were sixteen vacant chairs, apart from the absence of sixteen Professors and three Readers on National Service. Of 370 University lecturers and demonstrators, only 143 remained at Cambridge.

The number of undergraduates in residence fell to 3,028, of whom 2,553 were men and 475 women, which was not much more than half the pre-war total. The total university population had fallen from 6,883 in 1938 to 4,364[(3)]. Dr Venn had one piece of good news: under Lend-Lease arrangements with the USA the Cavendish Laboratory had acquired "one of the very few electron microscopes available in this country".

The number of Freshmen who came up in 1942 was 1,508, slightly down on the previous year. Trinity and St John's topped the list, with 145 each. But the future prospect looked bleak, for the government now decreed that from October, 1943, entry to universities would be confined to scientific and technical students and others taking short courses, and to a few nominated by the services. Meanwhile, the University proceeded to create a Naval Division, analogous to its Army Senior Training Corps and Air Squadron, so that it could thereafter provide all three services with potential officers who had been trained before their call-up.

The government was tightening the call-up regulations all round. Parliament passed an Act just before Christmas which authorized the registration and medical examination of young men four months before they were eighteen, so that they could be immediately available for training when they reached that age. This registration, and the pressure put on youths from the age of sixteen to join the voluntary service organizations, caused some perturbation about the hours and conditions of employment of juveniles, and, in the words of *The Times*, "gave renewed anxiety lest the value of humane studies in both the war and the peace efforts be overlooked."

A situation had now been reached where more than two-thirds of the 33,000,000 persons of working age in Great Britain were engaged in some form of national service. All men up to the age of fifty and all women to forty-five had had to register, but a good many women between thirty-five and forty-five were still working in the distributive trades, and the government wanted to comb them out and get them into industry. Even though married and not themselves mobile, it was thought they could be transferred into factories near their homes, so releasing women who were mobile for the auxiliary services and the munitions industries.

There were some who foresaw that there would be long-term social consequences of this large-scale involvement of women in the war effort. In September, 1942, the Lobby correspondent of the Press Association wrote:

> Unnoticed by most people, a strong movement has begun which is designed to secure equality between men and women when the war ends. So far, the full force of the new campaign — in which millions of women are actively interested — has not been generally realized because it has shown itself only in a series of little rivulets of rebellion.

Soon afterwards Mrs Walter Elliott spoke to an audience of women in Cambridge Guildhall and told them: "The womenpower of the country has been mobilized as in no other country in the world . . . We have got in the women's services a body of wholly-trained women such as this country has never had in its history. If this grand achievement and adaptability can be achieved by a majority of women who left school at fourteen and a half, what might be done if our educational system was carried on to the age of fifteen or sixteen? In the future many will want to get back to their homes and to civilian life — but many will desire to give their skill to the community in general."

The debate about Britain's aspirations and future prospects was brought to a climax with the publication on 1st December of the Beveridge Report. Eighteen months earlier, the Churchill government had commissioned Sir William Beveridge, a former distinguished civil servant and one of the country's leading academics, to survey existing schemes of social insurance and workmen's compensation and to make recommendations for their co-ordination and improvement. Beveridge now proposed that all social services should be grouped together under a new Ministry of Social Security, which he thought could be created in time to operate from July, 1944. He recommended a new "all-in" insurance scheme which would guarantee everyone their basic needs in every situation. This implied the abolition of physical want, because every citizen would be guaranteed a subsistence income. Beveridge set his scheme in the context of a wider social policy which would avoid mass unemployment, establish national health and rehabilitation services, and pay allowances to dependent children.

The proposals were based on a compulsory all-in insurance scheme, with all employers and employees making a joint contribution of 7s 6d per week per employee. In return, all would be entitled to free medical and hospital treatment, pensions of £2 a week for every couple, child allowances of eight shillings a week, and a big increase in unemployment and disability benefits. The hated "means test" would disappear.

In the country at large, the Beveridge Report was enthusiastically received and it became a bestseller, but some did not hesitate to line up against its proposals. The Member of Parliament for Cambridge, Lieutenant-Commander R. L. Tufnell, declared that Britain could not hope to pay for any such scheme until she had regained the export markets she had lost because of the war, and he did not believe the scheme could solve the problem of unemployment. At a meeting of the West Suffolk County Council Lord Bristol criticized all such reports making long-term

Church parade for an armoured division at Ely Cathedral on 6th December. Taking the salute is Major M. B. Burrows, with the Dean of Ely beside him on the saluting base. *Imperial War Museum*

EAST ANGLIAN DAILY TIMES, THURSDAY, DECEMBER 31, 1942

UPHILL TOWARDS VICTORY IN 1942

OUTSTANDING EVENTS OF THIRD YEAR OF WAR

AXIS HOPES DASHED IN RUSSIA

JAPANESE FORCED ON DEFENSIVE

SECRET FACTORS OF "SECOND FRONT"

At the beginning and again at the end of the year 1942, there figured conspicuously in the news the three factors chiefly essential to victory.

for co-operation in peace. The Anglo-Russian entente was further reinforced by a visit paid to Moscow by Mr. Churchill in August, in company with President Roosevelt's representative, Mr. Harriman.

Consequently it came as a surprise to public opinion here when, only a few weeks after Mr. Churchill's visit, Premier Stalin voiced in an abrupt message to the American Press his dissatisfaction with Allied assistance, and urged the creation of a Second Front. The only logical, practical answer to such an unexpected message seemed to be an early assault on the Germans in Western Europe. For that the world seemed to be looking. So, too, was the enemy, who redoubled his defensive preparations in Norway and elsewhere in Europe. Thus, as was revealed later, was ensured the surprise of the Anglo-American descent upon North Africa.

That a front in ... the military ... Nation...

promises, declaring that their authors were "reopening old sores, knocked on the head after the last war". All he could say was that these government committees should give more consideration to the commandments "Thou shalt not steal" and "Thou shalt not covet". These sentiments earned him applause.

No wonder Mrs Sarah Williams struck a note of scepticism in the entry she made in her diary:

> *1st December*: I have just heard the Beveridge Plan and think how wonderful it sounds. I should think it unlikely that it would ever be accepted. But it would make this war almost worthwhile.

After a day's reflection her scepticism had increased:

> *2nd December*: The more I hear of the Report the less I think of it. It's only trying to bolster up something falling to pieces.

But the general public's enthusiasm for Beveridge was unmistakable. William Stock reflected the popular view in his diary entry:

> It is something to look forward to after the war, if it is achieved. It is one of the most encouraging signs so far that the world after the war will perhaps be a little happier to live in.

With a year of great trial behind them, with the certainty of an enormous challenge still to be faced, and the probability of incalculable sacrifices still to be made, the people of East Anglia grasped eagerly at a message of hope.

Notes on Sources

The leading newspapers published in East Anglia have been principal sources of information: the *Eastern Daily Press* for coverage of Norfolk, the *East Anglian Daily Times* for Suffolk, and the *Cambridge Daily News* for Cambridgeshire. As these are readily available at libraries and/or record offices in the region, detailed references have not been given when these sources have been quoted. For other material, references are given below.

The Mass Observation Archive is held at Sussex University. Throughout the war Mass Observation regularly received reports from appointed observers, and also copies of the personal diaries of a large number of individuals, some of whom lived in East Anglia. The diarists are identified in the Archive, but they were promised anonymity and their identities have been concealed in these pages by use of pseudonyms.

The standard reference books have been used for the national and international background: Sir Winston Churchill's *The Second World War* and various volumes of the official *History of the Second World War*, as detailed below.

Details of airfields, air operations and enemy air raids during 1942 have been painstakingly researched by several regional authors and acknowledgement is made of the value of Michael J. F. Bowyer's *Action Stations — Wartime Military Airfields of East Anglia, 1939–45* and *Air Raid! The Enemy Air Offensive against East Anglia, 1939–45*, and of Winston Ramsey's *Airfields of the Eighth — Then and Now.*

For information about the Army's requisition of the Thetford battle area the author is indebted to Lord Walsingham, whose father owned much of the land in 1942.

Chapter 1

(1) Mass Observation Diaries, Ref. S5205.
(2) Arthur Bryant: *The Turn of the Tide 1939–1943*, page 303. Collins, 1957.
(3) Mass Observation Diaries, Ref. D5301.
(4) Bryant, *op. cit.*, page 343.
(5) Sir Charles Webster and Noble Frankland: *The Strategic Air Offensive against Germany 1939–45*. HMSO, 1961.
(6) Winston S. Churchill: *The Second World War, Vol IV: The Hinge of Fate*, page 753, Cassell, 1951.
(7) Bryant, *op. cit.*, pages 324.

Chapter 2

(1) Report in *Cambridge Daily News*, 22.9.42.
(2) Mass Observation Town and District Survey, Box 3 — Chelmsford 1942.
(3) Bryant: *op. cit.*, page 292.

Chapter 3

(1) Public Record Office, Ref. WO 199/641.
(2) PRO Ref. WO 199/642.
(3) PRO Ref. CAB 93/1
(4) PRO Ref. WO 199/722.
(5) PRO Ref. CAB 75/14.
(6) PRO Ref. WO 199/404.

(7) PRO Ref. WO 199/722.
(8) PRO Ref. HO 207/1158.
(9) Mass Observation Diaries, Ref. D5301.
(10) Suffolk Record Office, Bury St Edmunds. Ref 676/10.
(11) PRO Ref. HO 207/1049.

Chapter 4

(1) H. G. Hitchman and P. Driver: *HMS Badger — Harwich: 5 Years in the Front Line.* Privately published, 1985.
(2) A. P. Herbert: *The Battle of the Thames — The War Story of Southend Pier*. Published by the County Borough of Southend-on-Sea, n.d.
(3) S. W. Roskill: *The War at Sea, 1939–45*. HMSO, 1954.
(4) The importance of the Clacton bomber to Brightlingsea research was revealed to the author by Captain R. C. Lewis, DSO, OBE, RB, who was in command of the flotilla and who dealt with this mine.
(5) Roskill, *op. cit.*, pages 254-256.
(6) PRO Ref. WO 199/625.
(7) Mass Observation Diaries, Ref. D5301.
(8) B. R. Hart: *Lynn Air Raids, 1939–42* (unpublished MSS).

Chapter 5

(1) Alderman Herbert E. Witard: Introduction to *Norwich — The Ordeal of 1942*, by E. C. Le Grice. Soman-Wherry Press, Norwich, n.d.
(2) Mass Observation Diaries, Ref. D5301.
(3) *Cambridge Daily News*, 2.5.42.
(4) Webster and Frankland: *op. cit.*, page 459.

Chapter 6

(1) Mass Observation Diaries, Ref. S5205.
(2) *We Also Served — The Story of the Home Guard in Cambridgeshire and the Isle of Ely, 1940–43*. Cambridgeshire and Isle of Ely Territorial Army Association, Cambridge, 1944.
(3) Ibid.
(4) Mass Observation Diaries, Ref. C5271.
(5) Mass Observation Diaries, Ref. D5301.
(6) PRO Ref. WO 199/405.
(7) PRO Ref. WO 199/405, 406 and 407.
(8) Mass Observation Town and District Survey, 1942. Box 3, File F.

Chapter 7

(1) W. K. Hancock and M. M. Gowing: *British War Economy*, pages 421–422. HMSO, 1949.
(2) Ibid. pages 424–426.
(3) Ibid. page 432.
(4) Mass Observation Diaries, Ref. D5301.
(5) Mass Observation Diaries, Ref. C5271.

Chapter 8

(1) Mass Observation Town and District Survey, 1942. Box 3, File F.
(2) Mass Observation Diaries, Ref. C5271.

(3) *History of the Royal Norfolk Regiment, 1919–1951*, published by the Royal Norfolk Regimental Association, 1953.
(4) Mass Observation Diaries, Ref. C5271.
(5) Mass Observation Diaries, Ref. D5301.

Chapter 10
(1) Jean Lancaster-Rennie: *And Over Here!* George R. Reeve Ltd, Wymondham, 1976.
(2) PRO, Ref. WORKS 46/7.
(3) PRO, Ref. HO 207/1157.
(4) PRO, Ref. WORKS 46/7.
(5) Hervey Benham: *Essex at War*, page 56. Benham, 1945.
(6) Michael Bowyer: *Action Stations*, page 47. Patrick Stephens, 1979.
(7) PRO, Ref. WORKS 46/7.
(8) Webster and Frankland, *op. cit.*, pages 311–312.

Chapter 11
(1) PRO, Ref. WO 199/808.
(2) "A Norfolk Woman" (Lucilla Reeve): *Farming on a Battleground*, page 51. The Model Press, Wymondham, n.d.
(3) Ibid. pages 76–77.
(4) PRO, Ref. W0 227/1.
(5) Winston Churchill: *The Second World War, Vol. VI, The Hinge of Fate*, pages 457–458.

Chapter 12
(1) Mass Observation Diaries, Ref. S5205.
(2) Mass Observation Diaries, Ref. D5301.
(3) *Cambridge Review*.

A Selected Bibliography

Volumes in the official *History of the Second World War*, published by HMSO:

Collier, B. *The Defence of the United Kingdom*, 1957.

Hancock, W. K. and Gowing, M. M. *British War Economy*, 1949.

O'Brien, T. H. *Civil Defence*, 1955.

Roskill, Capt. S. W. *The War at Sea, 1939–45*, 1954.

Webster, Sir C. and Frankland, N. *The Strategic Air Offensive against Germany, 1939–45*.

History of the Royal Norfolk Regiment, 1919–1951. Norfolk Regimental Association, 1953.

Banger, J. *Norwich at War*. Wensum Books, 1974.

Bowyer, M. J. F. *Action Stations — Wartime Military Airfields of East Anglia, 1939–45*. Patrick Stephens, 1979.

Box, Charles G. *Great Yarmouth—Front Line Town, 1939–45*. Great Yarmouth Town Council, n.d.

Briggs, S. *Keep Smiling Through*. Weidenfeld & Nicolson, 1975.

Bryant, A. *The Turn of the Tide, 1939–1943*. Collins, 1957.

Churchill, W. S. *The Second World War*, Vol 4, *The Hinge of Fate*. Cassell, 1951.

Collier, B. *A Short History of the Second World War*. Collins, 1967.

Lund, P. and Ludlam, H. *Trawlers Go to War*. New English Library, 1975.

Nicholson, Capt. W. N. *The Suffolk Regiment, 1928–46*. East Anglian Magazine, nd.

Jenkins, F. *Lowestoft — Port War, 1939–45*. W. S. Cowell, Ipswich, nd.

Johnson, D. E. *East Anglia at War, 1939–45*, Jarrold, 1978.

Ramsey, W. *Airfields of the Eighth — Then and Now*. Battle of Britain Prints International Ltd, 1978.

Cambridge Daily News

Eastern Daily Press

East Anglian Daily Times

Lynn Advertiser

Index

Illustrations in bold type

Principal Events in 1942

	National and International	*Regional*
January	Twenty-six nations pact signed in Washington. Bardia recaptured by Imperial forces. New Russian offensive begins. Japan invades Burma. American troops arrive in N. Ireland.	Arctic weather delays farming operations. Parish Invasion Committees warned: "heavy attack" possible in East Anglia. Worst raid on Lowestoft—69 killed. Great Yarmouth Council refused financial aid from Whitehall.
February	Norwegian puppet government set up. Pacific Council set up in London. *Scharnhorst, Gneisenau* and *Prinz Eugen* escape from Brest. Japanese occupy Singapore. Battle of Java Sea (Allies lose five cruisers, six destroyers). Combined operations raid on Bruneval (near Le Havre).	Below-zero temperatures and deep snow throughout the month. Confirmation that East Anglian regiments fought in Malaya; no reliable news. East Anglian farmers revolt at new farm prices proposals. Drive to persuade East Coast residents to leave homes voluntarily.
March	National Service Acts extended to men of 41–45. Japanese occupy Rangoon. Allied forces on Java capitulate. Combined operations raid on St Nazaire.	Fierce attack on Allied convoy off East Coast; HMS *Vortigern* sunk. Norwich MP Mr H. G. Strauss appointed to junior government post. Massive aerodrome construction programme gaining momentum.
April	Japanese bomb India for first time. US surrender of Bataan. *Dorsetshire, Cornwall* and *Hermes* sunk by Japanese aircraft in Indian Ocean. Indian Congress rejects British proposals. Laval returns to power in France.	Ban reimposed on visits to East Coast. Big parades in all towns on Empire Youth Sunday. First two "Baedeker raids" on Norwich. "Hot pies" scheme introduced—WVS and WI deliver lunches to farm workers.
May	British evacuate Mandalay. Japanese land at Corregidor. Russians launch offensive in Kharkov sector. Anglo-Soviet treaty signed. Germans attack in Libya. RAF's first thousand-bomber raid.	Norwich looters sent to prison. Regional Commissioner warns against unfounded rumours in region after raids. Norwich cathedral damaged in raid. Big crowds at Newmarket race meetings.
June	Battle of Midway: US inflicts heavy losses on Japanese Navy. US–UK Production & Resources Board and combined Food Board set up. German offensive on Kharkov front. Fall of Tobruk.	Army commandeers battle areas near Thetford and Orford. King and Queen visit Fenland reclamation. Tom Driberg defeats National Government candidate in Maldon by-election.